DANVILLE PUBLIC LIBRARY

W9-BSS-093

# A THEATERGOER'S GUIDE TO
## *Shakespeare's Themes*

# A THEATERGOER'S GUIDE TO
# *Shakespeare's Themes*

## ROBERT THOMAS FALLON

DANVILLE PUBLIC LIBRARY
DANVILLE, INDIANA

*Ivan R. Dee*

CHICAGO

A THEATERGOER'S GUIDE TO SHAKESPEARE'S THEMES. Copyright ©
2002 by Robert Thomas Fallon. All rights reserved, including the right to
reproduce this book or portions thereof in any form. For information, address:
Ivan R. Dee, Publisher, 1332 North Halsted Street, Chicago 60622.
Manufactured in the United States of America and printed on acid-free paper.

Library of Congress Cataloging-in-Publication Data:
Fallon, Robert Thomas.
    A theatergoer's guide to Shakespeare's themes / Robert Thomas Fallon.
        p. cm.
    Includes index.
    ISBN 1-56663-457-1 (alk. paper)
    1. Shakespeare, William, 1564–1616—Themes, motives.    I. Title.

PR2987 .F36 2002
822.3'3—dc21                                                    2002022253

822.33
Fal

091316

*To the Shakspere Society of Philadelphia*

# Contents

# Prologue

IN HIS ADVICE to the actors about to perform their play, *The Murder of Gonzago,* Hamlet counsels them to avoid overacting: "Suit the action to the word, the word to the action." The sentiment is a familiar one, the playwright complaining about actors butchering his lines; but Hamlet goes on to explain that "the purpose of playing" is to "to hold the mirror up to nature, to show virtue her own feature, scorn her own image, and the very age and body of the time his form and pressure."

Shakespeare defines his art in these lines. "Nature" here is human nature in all its variety, its "virtue" and its "scorn," to which we may add its capacity to love, hate, fear, laugh, mourn, and rejoice. The playwright "holds a mirror up to" all the glory and folly of the human condition so that an audience may behold it. The same may be said of any art form—of the novel, painting, poem, or sculpture, though these artists cast their net wider to represent landscapes, objects, and creatures of the natural world as well as abstractions and impressions that dwell in the mind. The playwright is limited in range because by definition the theater places living men and women on the stage before us; and no matter how they may be costumed, as cats, machines, or discarded waste in trash cans, they are unmistakably human. The natural world enters Shakespeare's lines, to be sure, but chiefly in poetic images that enrich his vision of humanity, as in Romeo's "What light in yonder window breaks? / It is the east, and Juliet is the sun!" and Lear's invocation to the tempest:

> And thou, all-shaking thunder,
> Strike flat the thick rotundity o'th'world,

Crack Nature's moulds, all germens spill at once
That make ingrateful man!

Hamlet goes on to caution clowns to "speak no more than is set down for them," that is, to restrain their natural inclination to reach for a laugh, since any uncalled-for antics on their part may cause an audience to overlook "some necessary question of the play." They may miss some thought, some idea, some theme embedded in the lines that is essential to understanding the actions and emotions—the "nature"—of the actors who are holding that mirror up for enlightenment or amusement. A theater audience expects a play to arouse familiar emotions—pity, fear, awe, joy, sorrow, or outrage. But of equal importance, they expect a play to have meaning, even a comedy that provokes harmless laughter at some all-too-common human folly. The play, in brief, must have something to say about our nature.

This essential meaning, this "necessary question," this theme is the subject of these pages. A theme, then, may be thought of as a life experience, one that history and literature tell us is endemic to the race, to be observed at any time and any place in the long chronicle of human existence. Men and women have always fallen in love, else how could the species have survived? We have fought one another since time immemorial, either in a clash of armies on the field of battle or in a sudden eruption of human pride in the drawing room or city street. We have plotted for advancement, for more wealth, power, or prestige; and we have done so for a variety of motives—out of depravity, an exaggerated estimate of our own worth, or a sense of public duty. We have endured the trials of growing up, of coming to terms with the expectations of parents and the standards of a society we must enter as adults. We have all dreamed, loved, hated, suffered humiliation, felt rejection, and been eaten by jealousy, exalted by joy, or saddened by regret.

This is the human condition—and these are the themes of Shakespeare's plays. They are identified in the language of scholarship and the theater in words or phrases such as love, warfare, ambition, coming of age, loss of innocence—or in terms of the human conflicts these experiences give rise to: love vs. duty, war vs. peace, reason vs. imagination, the individual vs. society, justice vs. mercy, reality vs. illusion, and so on. In Shakespeare's plays we witness characters wracked by these conflicts, a monarch intent upon conquest contemplating its cost in human suffering, a daughter torn between the urgings of her heart and devotion to her family's welfare, a jealous husband who grieves over lost love and at the same time rages for revenge, an old man who refuses to accept reality when confronted with the specter of aging.

A play may be compared to a piece of music. At first hearing, a symphony may strike the ear as little more than a sequence of sounds; but once a theme emerges, in the strings or horns, it begins to delight the senses. In like manner a play may at first look to be a series of unconnected speeches until the theme emerges to tie them all together. A theme is what the play is about, what it has to say, the idea that gives it reason for being; and an awareness of that idea will deepen our understanding of the events paraded before us.

A play will succeed as theater if it faithfully places before us real human beings confronted with choices and actions we recognize, in a way that mirrors our own life experiences or those of others as we perceive them. Of course, playgoers need not always be consciously aware of the ideas Shakespeare pursues in his works. Events may pass before our eyes too quickly, and in such abundance, that there is often no time to pause and note that we are observing this or that theme. The poet portrays experiences shared by all human beings, and as we watch figures on a stage convey love, or anger, or ambition, the very familiarity of the emotions will resonate on our pulse. In a good play those shared experiences move us to laughter, horror, or pity.

Yet a familiarity with these themes cannot help but enhance the pleasure we derive from a performance. Shakespeare rewards a second or a tenth look, a return to his lines time and again. His achievement is remarkable: thirty-eight plays in the course of some twenty years, three of his greatest, it is said, composed in the space of a single year—*Henry V, Julius Caesar,* and *As You Like It,* a history, a tragedy, and a comedy. We survey this achievement as we might a mountain meadow at high summer as it lies before us in its dazzling sweep of colors. That meadow becomes all the more enchanting, however, if we examine a single square foot or even square inch of its surface, when we can marvel at the intricate interplay of plants, the infinite variety of miniature blooms in that small space, and, looking more deeply, at the swarm of life in the soil beneath. Just so, Shakespeare rewards close attention to a single act, or scene, or half-dozen lines, over which we may pause briefly to savor the subtle maneuvers of statesmen weaving plots, the passion of lovers consumed by desire, the sparkling exchange of wit between agile minds, or the brooding meditation of those about to die. How could one man, we may ask, capture in words the essence of so many familiar moments in the passage of human life?

And Shakespeare can surprise us. His villains speak truth, his fools wisdom, and his heroes nonsense. The young can often see farther than their elders, and the old, despite their long experience, can be blind. It is revealing to note how many of the poet's best-remembered lines come from the mouths of improbable characters. It is the villainous Iago who says, "Reputation is an idle and most false imposition, oft got without merit, and lost without deserving." A lady's maidservant pens the line, "Some are born great, some achieve greatness, and some have greatness thrust upon them." A fool says, "Thou shouldst not have been old till thou hadst been wise."

Of course, Shakespeare's plays are largely about kings, queens, dukes, and generals, figures that few of us have encountered, or are likely to, in our lifetime. Their fate affects the lives of thousands, the destiny of nations, and the sweep of history. But his characters are also fathers, mothers, sons, daughters, and lovers; and these plays bring such lofty figures within the scope of our own lives, as they grieve and laugh and scheme and rage as we do. Lear is a king whose follies result in the clash of armies, but he is also a father who has wronged his daughter and an old man who goes to his grave lamenting his loss. Macbeth's ambition is no different from a modern politician seeking public office, a worker aspiring to union leadership, or a minor executive maneuvering to climb the corporate ladder. The questions of the play are, how much of our humanity must we leave behind in that climb, and what may become of one who finally reaches the goal? Richard II, as he is about to fall from that pinnacle, assures his followers that he is, after all, but a man, one who must "live with bread like you, feel want / Taste grief, need friends." And Henry V concludes that kings and peasants are much the same, separated only by "thou idol Ceremony."

It may seem presumptuous to isolate a play's theme and propose what Shakespeare means by it. But actors, directors, critics, and scholars must do so all the time. All attest to the remarkable diversity of the plays and the limitless possibilities of portraying a Hamlet or a Lear, but in the end any stage production must find a core of meaning in a play or character and remain true to it. To do so does not reduce a work or restrict its range—we're just trying to make sense of it. Certainly one person's "sense of it" will not be the same as another's, but all seek somewhere to stand in coming to terms with the words and actions they are witness to, and they are not much helped by constant reminders that Shakespeare is ambiguous, contradictory, ambivalent, or undecided about the characters and events he places before us. Life is unsure, justice uncertain, and human beings complex, but something may still be said of them.

In the pages that follow, the same characters and events will reappear in several chapters, because Shakespeare's figures are so multifaceted and his plots so encompassing. For example, Henry Bolingbroke, Duke of Lancaster and later the king of England, is a prominent figure in three of the history plays, *Richard II* and *Henry IV, Parts 1 and 2,* and he is mentioned frequently in other works because he comes to the throne by deposing an anointed king. But he is also a man driven by ambition for power, a monarch plagued by rebellious subjects, and a father disappointed in a wayward son. Lear is at once a reigning king, a father betrayed by ravenous daughters, a foolish old man, an oppressed human being raging at the lack of justice in the world, and a distracted madman. And Hamlet is cited in several chapters, each of which examines a different facet of this enigmatic figure. We encounter him as a tragic hero, a son troubled by his mother's remarriage, a human being unnerved by the visit of a ghost, a young man disappointed in love, and a sophisticated scholar with a biting wit. To see such figures whole, we must look at them in all their dimensions, and so their names will appear time and again in these pages as exemplary of different themes.

In the same way, certain passages will reappear in successive chapters, and again because they are capable of a variety of interpretations. Shakespeare's words have meaning at many levels. The seemingly unimportant warning by the Bishop of Carlisle that "the blood of English shall manure the ground" as a result of the deposition of Richard II is cited variously as an example of the cost of warfare, the belief in universal order, and evidence of the prophetic voice of clerics. If brief phrases reappear more frequently than their importance would seem to warrant—like Richard III's gleeful remark that the court of Edward IV offered fertile ground for him "to bustle in," or the request of the Chorus in *Henry V* to "piece out our imperfections with your thoughts"—it may simply be that I am inordinately fond of them.

I owe a debt of gratitude to my good friends and colleagues, Profs. James A. Butler and Kevin Harty of LaSalle University, and to my sharp-eyed publisher, Ivan Dee. They have, with equal measures of candor and compassion, shown me the error of my ways.

# Characters

AS A CONVENIENCE for readers, passages in which individual characters are discussed at some length are listed below. A more comprehensive index is available at the end of the book.

# A THEATERGOER'S GUIDE TO
## *Shakespeare's Themes*

# LOVE AND HATRED

IT HAS BEEN SAID that love and hate, like joy and sorrow, are two sides of the same emotional coin. Others insist, rather cryptically, that there is no hate without love. Whatever the case, there is enough of both in Shakespeare's works to recommend them as a source for study of all theories on the subject, as his characters swing abruptly from one to the other and back again in his plays. Indeed, love is the most pervasive of Shakespeare's themes, with hatred not far behind, and it appears in a rich array of relationships—man and woman, woman and woman, man and man, sister and brother, parent and child—and with a wide range of effects from comic to tragic. We shall leave the bond between servant and master to another chapter and dwell here on those that involve courtship, family, and friendship. The forms of love most frequently staged by Shakespeare are the courtly or chivalric, with its elaborate code and formal images as they were developed in medieval and Renaissance times, and what we may call, for want of a better word, the "romantic," more or less as it is understood in modern times.

The staging of love scenes presented a challenge for playwrights in Shakespeare's time. A modern filmmaker can dramatize a lovers' tryst with relative ease: The heroine enters at left, the hero at right. They stare at each other for a long moment, she her bosom heaving, he his jawline aquiver, until, as the strings of the sound track soar, they rush together and, to all appearances, attempt to devour one another. But any prolonged display of physical passion ran a risk on the Elizabethan stage. A lengthy embrace seriously strained the audience's willingness to suspend disbelief by drawing attention to the fact that beneath that golden wig and stiff brocade was the body of a twelve-year-old boy! Playgoers were perfectly happy to accept the illusion as long as the young actor didn't do something to violate it, for any slip in his impersonation of a woman would only prompt an undercurrent of suppressed laughter, especially among the earthy "groundlings" in the theater's pit, and at a moment when precisely the opposite effect was intended. A modest embrace or tentative kiss could pass, but anything more would only overburden the illusion.

So how do Shakespeare's lovers project their passion for one another? We find it in the poetry! Some of his most memorable lines capture moments of devotion so intense that a physical display would only diminish them, indeed would cheapen and drain them of dramatic effect. Thus Romeo, concealed in the garden below, utters a chaste wish as he gazes up at Juliet, who, unconscious of his presence, is leaning on the balcony rail, her head resting on her hand: "O that I were a glove upon that hand, / That I might touch that cheek." And as Othello is greeted by Desdemona after he survives a storm at sea, he exclaimed, "O my soul's joy! / If after every tempest come such calms, / May the winds blow till they have waken'd death." Antony is entranced by Cleopatra's perverse appeal: "Fie, wrangling queen! / Whom everything becomes—to chide, to laugh, / To weep"; and she is desolate at the thought of his impending departure for Rome: "O, my oblivion is a very Antony, / And I am all forgotten." In famous lines, Enobarbus later describes her paradoxical attraction:

> Age cannot wither her, nor custom stale
> Her infinite variety. Other women cloy
> The appetites they feed, but she makes hungry
> Where most she satisfies.

These few lines display as well the range of emotions that afflict those in love, from Romeo's longing to Othello's passion, Antony's perplexity, Cleopatra's despair, and the awe of Enobarbus. It can be a time, as Shakespeare's many lovers attest, of transcendent joy as well as crippling sorrow.

## Courtly Love

Courtly love evolved during the Middle Ages, when a knight in shining armor vowed eternal devotion to his "lady." The best-known example in our literature is the legend of King Arthur and his Knights of the Round Table, with its tales of Launcelot's passion for Queen Guinevere and the holy quest of the peerless Galahad. But the tradition began long before Sir Thomas Malory composed his moving *Morte d'Arthur* (1485). It all started, so it is told, some three hundred years earlier under the pleasant skies of southern France. There troubadours, poets and singers, moved from court to court entertaining the nobility with tales of fierce warriors reduced to speechless awe by the mere sight of a lady, to whom they imme-diately pledged their lives to the performance of deeds that would prove them worthy of her regard. They would venture forth to slay dragons, to slaughter Turks, to right wrongs, and especially to champion and protect the virtue of maidens endangered by lusting, predatory villains.

It was an impossibly idealistic notion, but it caught the imagi-nation of the time—and we can imagine why. Life in the eleventh and twelfth centuries was barbarous, even in the agreeable climate of southern France. It was an era when the idea of a spring fling for the lord of the manor was to plunder the fields and villages of a neighboring baron. Thus it was a significant accomplishment for his lady to persuade him to remain by the fire and listen to tales of love, which he was content to do only so long as they were liberally laced with episodes of martial valor. In time, as society grew more settled and courts of the nobility more sophisticated, the tradition pre-vailed, elaborated upon during long evenings of cultivated discussion of the troubadours' songs. The lords and ladies evolved a complex and daunting code of chivalric love, dictating the proper conduct of a knight toward his lady. There was less talk of her attitude toward him, except that she should maintain a discreet distance and coolly acknowledge his devotion, thereby encouraging it the more. His vows were often silent, though no less heartfelt; and if the lady took notice of his achievements, he was inspired to even higher deeds—more dragons slain, more Turks slaughtered, more maidens rescued.

It was all artifice, but chivalry had a profound effect upon the upper classes during the Middle Ages. Many modeled their lives by its injunctions, the best known perhaps Pierre du Teraill, seigneur de Bayard (c. 1474–1524), called "the knight without fear and without reproach" chiefly because of his courage in battle and the courtesy of his bearing. Indeed, this sensibility has surfaced from time to time in our own age, during the latter decades of the nineteenth century, for example, and survives today in the lyrics of many a country and western song. Women were worshipped and protected from the harsh realities of the world, whether the unsavory practices of merchant classes or the dangerous intrigues of ambitious men to secure a medieval crown.

Several episodes come to mind in which Shakespeare portrays this theme, instances in which husbands involved in great events are unwilling to confide in their wives. In *Henry IV, Part 1,* the fiery Hotspur is at the center of an alliance of Welsh, Scots, and English nobles conspiring to overthrow the king, and his wife demands to know why he has been distracted of late—so much so, it seems, that she has been denied his bed. He attempts to ignore her, but she is so insistent that he finally replies, rather harshly: "I must not have you henceforth question me / Whither I go, nor reason whereabout. / Whither I must, I must." Again, the noble Brutus is deep in a plot to assassinate Julius Caesar when his wife, Portia, pleads with him to confide in her: "You have some sick offense within your mind, / Which by the right and virtue of my place / I ought to know of."

He resists her pleas until she shows him a wound she has inflicted on her thigh to demonstrate, as she puts it, "strong proof of my constancy." He is shaken by the sight, and in awe at her nobility promises to share with her all "the secrets of my heart." Even the murderous Macbeth, once having mounted the throne, is reticent with his wife about his plot to have Banquo killed, though she has been his closest, indeed his only confidante in his rise to power. "Be innocent of the knowledge, dearest chuck," he cautions, "till thou applaud the deed."

Shakespeare's tale of chivalric love is *The Two Noble Kinsmen,* and a close look at the play will reveal additional aspects of the tradition. It is in fact an old story, retold by Geoffrey Chaucer in his fourteenth-century classic *The Canterbury Tales.* In his version, "The Knight's Tale," the setting is ancient Greece, where two cousins, Arcite and Palamon of Thebes, are wounded and captured in battle by the legendary Athenian ruler, Theseus. Nursed back to health, they are held in prison atop a tower overlooking the palace gardens. When Emily, Theseus's sister, comes out one morning to gather flowers, they spy her, fall immediately in love, and begin to squabble over who saw her first, that is, whose lady she will be. In time Arcite is released and returned to Thebes, where he pines away, complaining that he is deprived of the sight of Emily and envying Palamon who, though still imprisoned, is able to see her daily.

But Arcite does not remain in Thebes. His sorrow reduces him to a shadow of his former self. He grows pale and emaciated, so much so that he can return unrecognized to Athens, where Theseus engages him as a servant to Emily. Palamon escapes from prison, and the cousins meet by chance in a nearby wood, where they prepare to fight to the death over who will have her. Theseus and Emily come upon them, stopping the fight, and the duke demands an explanation. They confess that they are contending for the hand of Emily, much to her surprise since she has no idea who they are. Theseus decides that since this is the case, the issue will be resolved in the proper fashion, at a public tournament. Each will return in a year accompanied by a hundred knights and engage in battle to decide who will claim the prize—marriage to Emily.

They reappear at the appointed time, and Chaucer devotes long passages of poetry to the prayers of the three on the night before battle. Arcite prays to Mars for victory, Palamon to Venus for Emily's love, and she, not especially excited by either of them, to Diana, the chaste, pleading only that she be given to the one who loves her best.[1] In the fight, Palamon is dragged to a designated stake and Arcite emerges victorious; but as he is about to claim the prize his horse bolts, unseating him. He is fatally injured in the fall and with his dying breath gallantly releases Emily to Palamon. Thus all three in effect have their prayers answered.

Shakespeare is faithful to Chaucer's plot with one or two exceptions: Arcite does not pine away in Thebes until he is unrecognizable. He remains robust, returns to Athens in disguise, participates in the traditional games, wins them all, and is rewarded with a position in Emily's service. Further, in deference to the limitations of the Elizabethan stage and the number of players available, each of the cousins returns with three, not a hundred, knights.

Chaucer's work highlights several additional aspects of the courtly love tradition, elements that Shakespeare makes ample use of, to both comic and tragic effect. The knight in some cases perceives the lady as far above him, unattainable in her station and virtue. Until Emily encounters the cousins in the forest about to duel to the death for her hand, she has no idea they even exist, Arcite being known to her only as one of many in her service. His status is entirely satisfactory to him, however, for the courtly knight sought only to "serve" the lady, and he was content if she acknowledged him from time to time with a gracious smile or a word of thanks for some service. In his mind she was a creature to be worshipped from afar, and he had no aspirations that she would ever re-

---

1. These are Roman, not Greek gods, apparently better known to Chaucer's audience.

turn his ardor. One of the most famous of such relationships was Dante's love for Beatrice, the wife of a Florentine merchant, who by his own account he saw only twice in his lifetime and with whom he never exchanged a word. Nevertheless she became a ruling passion of his life, and even her death at a relatively young age did not cool his devotion. Indeed, it seems that he revered her more than when she was alive. Beatrice achieved the stature of a spiritual guide in Dante's life, a role he portrayed in his *Commedia,* where it is she who escorts him through the spheres of Heaven.

The spiritual dimension of Dante's devotion to Beatrice serves notice that the courtly knight's adventures in laboring to be worthy of his lady's regard were shaped by Christian teaching. He was pledged to live a blameless life, to champion the poor and the helpless, to succor the meek and poor in spirit, to protect the chastity of young maidens, and to oppose evil in whatever guise it appeared. His unflinching devotion bore some of the marks of the worship of the Virgin Mary so prominent in the late Middle Ages, when many of the great cathedrals of Europe were raised in honor of *"Notre Dame."* At the same time the knight-errant of the era was a model of the *miles christus*, or Soldier of Christ, further pledged to oppose the forces of evil wherever met, whether on the field of battle in the distant Holy Land or in the human heart. His vows were a form of religious conversion, enlisting him in the armies at war with the Antichrist.

Another of the characteristics of the courtly lover illustrated by Chaucer's "Knight's Tale," and freely adopted by Shakespeare, was the pitiable state of the young man deprived of the favor of his lady. In Chaucer's tale (though, as mentioned, not in *The Two Noble Kinsmen*) Arcite, once released from prison, is deprived of the daily sight of Emily and as a consequence is so afflicted by sorrow at the loss that his entire countenance is altered. His transformation reflects the etiology of what was called the "lovesickness" or "love disease," a condition brought about by outright rejection by the object of his worship, her apparent neglect or preference for an alternate suitor, or in the case of Arcite by the absence of any opportunity to "serve" her. The symptoms of this deplorable state have been vividly described by the distinguished scholar Maurice Valency in his consummate study of the tradition, *In Praise of Love:*

> In the initial states the symptoms were not unbecoming—sleeplessness, loss of appetite, loss of flesh, and the characteristic pallor of the lover, together with love of solitude and a tendency to weep, particularly when music was played. But we are told, unless the disease was cured, it became dangerous—the lover might pass into a melancholy, waste away, and die.

And, further:

> The lover sighed incessantly. Since each sigh came from the heart and cost him a drop of blood, his face grew pale, betraying his anemia. For lack of spirit, his bodily members failed. He froze and burned with love's fever, trembling constantly, consumed inwardly with excessive heat, outwardly chilled. In addition he suffered psychic tortures beyond description—jealousy, doubt, and fear, and incessant inner debate. He cut indeed a pitiable figure in the eyes of the world.[2]

Shakespeare reflects this tradition of the lovesickness throughout the comedies, at times dwelling on it at some length. In *As You Like It,* Rosalind, disguised as the young man Ganymede, challenges Orlando's contention that he is in love. She insists that he neither acts nor looks like a lover, since he bears none of the characteristic marks of one:

> A lean cheek, which you have not; a blue eye and sunken, which you have not; an unquestionable spirit, which you have not; a beard neglected, which you have not (but I pardon you for that, for simply your having in beard is a younger brother's revenue); then

2. Maurice Valency, *In Praise of Love* (New York: Macmillan, 1958), pp. 154–155.

your hose should be ungarter'd, your bonnet unbanded, your sleeve unbutton'd, your shoe untied, and everything about you demonstrating a careless desolation. But you are no such man, you are rather point-device[3] in your accoustrements, as loving your self, than seeming the lover of another.

Again, in *The Two Gentlemen of Verona,* the servant Launce observes that his master, Valentine, is in love. Valentine asks him how he can tell, and receives the following answer:

Marry, by these special marks: first, you have learn'd, like Sir Proteus, to wreathe your arms, like a malcontent; to relish a love-song, like a robin redbreast; to walk alone, like one that had the pestilence; to sigh, like a schoolboy that had lost his A B C; to weep, like a young wench that had buried her grandam; to fast, like one that takes diet; to watch, like one that fears robbing; to speak puling, like a beggar at Hallowmas.

The plight of Chaucer's heroes illustrates yet another characteristic of Shakespeare lovers: they always fall at first sight. This phenomenon troubles playgoers little, since this is the way it happens to most of us anyway. Older readers will recall the lyrics of the popular song from the Rodgers and Hammerstein's musical *South Pacific* (1949): "Some enchanted evening, you will see a stranger, / You will see a stranger across a crowded room." So it goes in our time and so it went in Shakespeare's, as it has typically in the long chronicle of human history. In his "two hours' traffic of our stage," however, there was little time for the poet to trace the growth of love from first attraction to final consummation, or to record the tortuous progress of a courtship. His concern was to bring his lovers quickly to a spontaneous passion for one another so that he could then explore the comic, or tragic, consequences of their condition.

A few instances, of many that could be cited, will illustrate how

3. Neatly dressed.

pervasive this theme of instantaneous attraction is in Shakespeare. When Romeo first spies Juliet at the Capulet ball, he is immediately stricken: "O, she doth teach the torches how to burn! . . . I ne'er saw true beauty till this night." And at the sight of him she is equally startled by the sudden surge of emotion. Though she has yet to learn his name, she is certain of her fate, exclaiming, "if he be married, / My grave is like to be my wedding-bed." In *As You Like It,* Rosalind first sees Orlando as he prepares for a wrestling match, from which he emerges victor. She is immediately enchanted and in a charming scene approaches to congratulate him. He in turn is struck comically speechless during the encounter and can only stare dumbly at her, so as she leaves she must be content with a coy confession: "Sir, you have wrastled well, and overthrown / More than your enemies." In *The Tempest,* an innocent Miranda is overcome by her first sight of Ferdinand, "I might call him / A thing divine, for nothing natural / I ever saw so noble," as he is by her: "Most sure, the goddess / On whom these airs attend." Examples of this mysteriously abrupt blossoming of love abound, and in each instance Shakespeare simply says, this is how it happens, so let's get on with the play.[4]

Shakespeare reflects the general tenor of his time in mining courtly love for comic effect, joining in his contemporaries' delight in composing parodies of the whole notion. Perhaps the best-known satire of the tradition is Miguel de Cervantes's *Don Quixote* (1605), in which the self-appointed knight-errant undertakes absurd chivalric missions to demonstrate his devotion to "Princess Dulcinea," a young woman from a neighboring village who takes no notice of him whatsoever. Seeking adventures to prove himself worthy of her,

---

4. See, further, Antony's first sight of Cleopatra on her barge where "she did lie / In her pavilion—cloth of gold, of tissue— / O'er picturing Venus where we see / The fancy outwork nature." Angelo is troubled by his meeting with Isabella in *Measure for Measure*: "What, do I love her? / That I desire to hear her speak again? / And feast upon her eyes? What is't I dream on?" as is Olivia in *Twelfth Night* when she first meets Viola, who is disguised as the page, Cesario: "How now? / Even so quickly may one catch the plague."

he assaults windmills he imagines are giants and challenges innocent merchants in her name. Shakespeare employs the tradition to
less satiric effect, however, content simply to make fun of young
men who fall hopelessly, and at times ridiculously, in love.

Two examples will suffice to illustrate Shakespeare's comic
treatment of courtly love, one in a tragedy, the other in a comedy. In
*Romeo and Juliet* the hero is in love for the entire play, though in the
first act it is not with Juliet. He pines rather for the unresponsive
Rosaline who has rejected him, leaving the young man subject to
the melancholy symptoms of the "lovesickness" and the object of
good-natured ridicule from his friends. A sympathetic Benvolio reports on Romeo's wandering in the night and love of solitude, but
the high-spirited Mercutio scoffs at the spectacle in the time-
honored manner of those that "never felt a wound." Searching for
his friend, he calls out "Romeo! humors! madman! passion! lover!"
Romeo himself rambles on inanely about his groans and sighs, and
the peerless virtues of Rosaline: "The all seeing sun / Ne'er saw her
match since first the world begun."

Shakespeare's most consummate parody of the code of courtly
love comes in *As You Like It*, where the lovesick shepherd Silvius
pleads his passion for the resolutely indifferent shepherdess Phebe,
who wants nothing to do with him. He claims that she has wounded
him with her eyes, an injury that can prove fatal according to the
tradition, and he begs plaintively that she should "pity" him because of his distress (the dying words of Chaucer's Arcite are "Mercy,
Emily"). He is desolated by Phebe's coldness; and when it appears
that he has a rival for her heart, he happily agrees to deliver her letter to him, ecstatic to be of service. He does not begrudge her attentions elsewhere but is content, he says, to "glean the broken ears
after the man / That the main harvest reaps" so long as she will
"loose now and then / A scatt'red smile, and that I'll live upon." Silvius is in a sorry state indeed, "a tame snake," as a skeptical Rosalind puts it, though as it happens she is suffering from the same
affliction because of her passion for Orlando.

# *Romance*

For our purposes, the phase of love's history that follows the declaration of mutual passion will be called "romance," though admittedly the word has implications that fall well outside the boundaries of such a definition. "The course of true love never did run smooth," not in Shakespeare or anywhere else for that matter. The lovers find they are forced to overcome obstacles to their desire, especially the pain of separation. Having declared themselves, they soon discover that hours or days apart are like an empty gap, a suspension of time, in their lives. The normal activities of everyday existence, which had consumed their attention before, are now tiresome, so many meaningless tasks to be endured until the moment they meet again. They just want to *be* with one another. Thus Rosalind laments in *As You Like It:* "I tell thee, Aliena, I cannot be out of the sight of Orlando." Othello requests that his newly wedded bride, Desdemona, accompany him on his campaign against the Turks. He does so with proper deference to the court of the Duke of Venice, but the passion beneath his dignified exterior is evident—he wants her with him. Anxiety mounts when lovers find that they must be apart. Juliet, on learning that Romeo has been banished, is desolate: "There is no end, no limit, measure, bound / In that word's death." And Cleopatra, after Antony's departure for Rome, asks frantically, "O Charmian! / Where thinkst thou he is now? Stands he, or sits he? / Or does he walk? Or is he on his horse?"—while in Rome, Enobarbus predicts that he will not be long separated from her: "He will to his Egyptian dish again."

The most pervasive obstacle that Shakespeare places in the path of true love is the objection of an irate father. His was a patriarchal society in which the father ruled as head of the family in keeping with the universal order of things. As God reigns over the universe, the sun over the heavens, the king over his subjects, and the lion over all beasts, just so, it was thought, the father should preside over his household. Among well-to-do families it was his prerogative, indeed his obligation, to provide suitable husbands for his daughters, and it was their duty to submit to his will.[5] He exercised this prerogative whenever possible to enhance the fortunes of the family. A merchant might arrange for the marriage of a daughter with the son of another wealthy and powerful commercial house. A duke would find a prospective husband from among the nobility of his own social rank. And kings, whenever possible, married their princesses to princes.

Given the precarious commercial and political circumstances of the time, it may be said that the custom was justified in a practical sense, preserving peace between rival merchants, jealous noble houses, and contentious kingdoms. At the national level, treaties of peace were fragile agreements at best, fragments of paper that monarchs felt free to tear up whenever it suited them. But a union of two royal families was thought to create a more permanent bond and was the occasion for much rejoicing, especially among the common people who suffered the most from depredations by the marauding armies of feuding monarchs. In Shakespeare's *King John,* the kings of England and France arrange for the marriage of Lewis, the French dauphin, to John's niece, Blanch of Spain, in hopes of healing the breach between the two nations. The young couple seem content with the match, but as is often the case the amity between the nations is short-lived. In *Henry V* the French king gives his daughter, Katherine, in marriage to Henry in hopes that "neighborhood and Christian-like accord" will then prevail between the two kingdoms. Again, it doesn't last.

These decisions were made, however, with little or no concern for the feelings of the daughter, who might as a result be torn between her obligation to the family welfare and the dictates of her heart. Many of Shakespeare's plots, those of the comedies in particular, revolve around the schemes of young lovers to evade the parental

5. See pp. 148–150.

design. In *The Taming of the Shrew,* for example, the father, Baptista, announces that his younger daughter, the beauteous Bianca, may not marry until someone agrees to take the quarrelsome Katherina off his hands. The edict forms a bond between Bianca's suitors, young Hortensio and the ancient Gremio, who venture forth arm in arm to find a prospective bridegroom for "Katherine the curst." Yet a third suitor appears on the scene, the visiting Lucentio. He and Hortensio disguise themselves as tutors in music and language (Gremio is too old to be anything but himself) in order to pay court to Bianca without her father's knowledge. Again, in *The Merry Wives of Windsor* the parents of young Anne Page are at odds over a suitable husband for their daughter, the father favoring the dim-witted but wealthy Abraham Slender and the mother an irascible French physician, Dr. Caius. Anne finds them both distasteful, preferring the attentions of the more attractive Fenton, whom both parents disapprove of because of his reputation for carousing with Prince Hal and his riotous companions in London. In a wildly comic final scene the lovers evade her parents' schemes and dash off to marry secretly.

At times the father's disappointed wrath can be daunting. In *Cymbeline* the king banishes Posthumus upon hearing that he has married his daughter, Imogen, whom he had intended for his distasteful stepson, Cloten. Florizel, the young prince of Bohemia in *The Winter's Tale,* is enamored of Perdita, a shepherd's daughter. His father discovers the attachment and, finding it totally unsuitable, warns Perdita that she is never to see the prince again on pain of death. With the help of a sympathetic nobleman, the lovers flee to Sicily, where it is discovered that she is actually the long-lost daughter of the king there, which serves to reconcile the father to the match. In *A Midsummer Night's Dream* the father, Egeus, is especially harsh. Lysander and Hermia are determined to wed, but Egeon has already chosen Demetrius as a husband for her. When his daughter remains defiant, he demands the penalty for her disobedience called for in Athenian law, death or lifelong confinement in a convent. To escape her father's anger, the lovers plan to seek refuge with Lysander's wealthy aunt; but, of course, they get no further than the nearby forest, where the well-meaning fairies manage to complicate their lives. Egeus remains adamant to the end, demanding that Duke Theseus enforce the law and punish Lysander, but the sympathetic duke, himself about to be married, overrules him.

On most occasions Shakespeare manages to work things out so that the lovers are joined to everyone's satisfaction. In *The Merchant of Venice* an obedient Portia is faithful to her father's wishes, well after he is dead, that she should marry only the man who chooses the right casket from three presented him. Fortunately a procession of unsavory suitors fail the test, and the highly attractive Bassanio picks the right one. And in *The Taming of the Shrew,* Bianca marries Lucentio, the man her father had agreed to anyway. Shakespeare's attitude toward the custom is perhaps to be found in the advice Beatrice gives Hero in *Much Ado About Nothing:*

> Yes, faith, it is my cousin's duty to make curtsy and say, "Father, as it please you": but yet for all that, cousin, let him be a handsome fellow, or else make another curtsy and say: "Father, as it pleases me."

These are the comedies, however, in which the lovers end up happily united, or reunited, in the lawful union they most desire. In the tragedies this circumventing of the father's wishes in an unsanctioned marriage often ends badly. Othello and Desdemona wed in secret, infuriating Brabantio, who is grudgingly forced to acknowledge the marriage but warns, "look to her, Moor. If thou hast eyes to see; / She deceiv'd her father, and may thee." Later the villainous Iago reminds Othello of Brabantio's warning—"She did deceive her father, marrying you"—in persuading the Moor that Desdemona is engaged in an illicit affair with Cassio. And Juliet resists her father's plan for a desirable union with Paris, "a kinsman of the prince." Unaware that she is already married to Romeo, Montague interprets her refusal as willful disobedience and angrily threatens to disown her: "Hang thee, young baggage! Disobedient wretch. Out! Out!" and "Hang! Beg! Starve! Die in the streets!" Both pairs of lovers are doomed, of course, by a series of events arising from their challenge to the custom of the parental prerogative.

Mention should be made of unfaithful lovers, wives, and husbands, in which Shakespeare's plays abound. In the comedies infidelity serves to complicate the plot, setting up scenes ripe with misunderstandings, schemes to evade jealous husbands, and embarrassing disclosures; but all parties are reconciled in the end. In Elizabethan England the cuckolded husband was a figure of fun, as he is even in our own day. He was, in the well-known sense, "always the last to know," the object of ridicule, gossip, and sly innuendo, always with the implication that he was inadequate as "a man," that is, unable to satisfy his wife. In popular legend he was said to wear "horns" growing out of his forehead, of which he is unaware though they are visible for anyone else to see. Shakespeare makes jest of the images, as in *As You Like It,* where the woodland company sing of "the horn, the horn, the lusty horn," and the clown Touchstone insists that a husband's horns are "the dowry of his wife, 'tis none of his own getting." And in the final scene of *The Merry Wives of Windsor,* Falstaff is persuaded to wear a ridiculous set of horns on his head. The tradition is hilariously reversed here, since the fat knight fails to seduce either Mistress Page or Mistress Ford. These clever wives trick him into the absurd attire with promises of an assignation and humiliate him in the end. It is he, not their husbands, who has been cuckolded.

Unfaithful lovers populate Shakespeare's comedies. *The Two Gentlemen of Verona* are the lifelong friends Valentine and Proteus. Valentine travels to Milan to learn something of the world, and Proteus soon follows, but not before bidding farewell to his love, Julia, and vowing his "true constancy" to her during his absence. Arriving in Milan, he finds that Valentine has fallen in love with Sylvia, and he immediately develops a passion for her himself, forgetting Julia, whom he claims "is dead." Meanwhile she, impatient at the separation, disguises herself as the page Sebastian and goes in search of him. Proteus presses his suit on Sylvia, who spurns him. He even asks Julia/Sebastian to carry gifts to her, which she dutifully, though sadly, agrees to do. In the end Julia reveals her identity, Proteus is properly contrite for his "inconstancy," and the two are happily reunited.

Perhaps the most notorious lover's desertion appears in *Troilus and Cressida.* In Shakespeare's biting satire of love and war, the two pledge their love and are led off by her uncle, Pandarus, to consummate it. But Cressida's father, the Trojan priest, Calchas, has defected to the Greek camp and is anxious to have his daughter join him. He persuades the Greeks to exchange a prisoner for her, and she is forced to part from Troilus, though not before they declare tearful vows of mutual devotion. When she arrives among the Greeks, this proper Trojan maiden promptly turns vamp and hurries off in the company of Diomedes, with whom she betrays Troilus, who is a concealed witness to her inconstancy. In all fairness to Cressida, however, it must be said that her situation is perilous. She has been dumped unceremoniously into a circle of burly Greek warriors far from home, the only woman, as far as is evident, in the camp. She disarms them all by flirting with each and then puts herself under the protection of Diomedes, who has been her escort from Troy and seems the most civil and courtly of the lot. Cressida laments her fate: "Ah, poor our sex!" Or otherwise: "What's a girl to do?"[6]

Women are more forgiving of their lovers' faithlessness, as in the instances of the "bed trick" in such plays as *Measure for Measure* and *All's Well That Ends Well.* Angelo, the puritanical deputy of the

---

6. In variations on the theme of lovers' betrayal, in *A Midsummer Night's Dream* Demetrius and Lysander, after the fairies apply drops from "a little western flower" to their sleeping eyelids, awake to shift their amorous attentions promptly from Hermia to Helena. And in *Cymbeline,* Posthumus is tricked into believing that his loyal wife, Imogen, has been unfaithful; in retaliation he vows to kill her.

Duke of Vienna in *Measure for Measure,* develops a sudden passion for the virtuous Isabella, and offers to spare her brother, Claudio, whom he has sentenced to die, if she will submit to his lascivious advances. Isabella refuses, but the duke, disguised as a holy friar, conceives of a plan involving Mariana, whom Angelo had agreed to marry some five years earlier but had coarsely rejected when a shipwreck deprived her of a dowry. Isabella, he counsels, is to agree to the assignation with Angelo on the condition that the lovemaking will be brief and in the dark, but that Mariana will take her place. The substitution is a success, and in the end the duke discards his disguise, reveals the switch, orders Angelo to marry Mariana, and takes Isabella as his bride.

In *All's Well That Ends Well,* Bertram, the young Count of Rossillion, is forced to marry Helena against his will; and he scornfully deserts her to seek his fortune in the wars of Florence. He vows that he will never accept her as a wife until she can "show me a child begotten of thy body that I am father to." Helena follows him to Florence, where she encounters Diana, a young woman whom Bertram lusts after. At Helena's urging, Diana agrees to an assignation, instructing Bertram to come to her house after dark, stay but an hour, and speak not at all. Helena takes Diana's place with her husband; and sometime later, back at Rossillion and one would assume obviously pregnant, she confronts him with evidence of his impending fatherhood. They are reconciled, and all ends well.

Such episodes raise serious questions about what it is that attracts Shakespeare's young women to such singularly unsuitable men. What in the world do they see in them—Mariana in the unbending Angelo, who had rejected her years before because she was to come without dowry, or Helena in the scornful, philandering Bertram? The same puzzling pattern of questionable taste appears elsewhere in the comedies. We can well understand Perdita's attraction to the handsome young Prince Florizel in *The Winter's Tale.* And Portia's partiality toward Bassanio in *The Merchant of Venice* is perhaps justified, even though he is irresponsibly profligate, having squandered a fortune and sunk himself heavily in debt. It may be that he presents a favorable alternative to the ridiculous bores she has to put up with before he appears on the scene. But what is it about the silly-ass Duke Orsino that Viola finds so endearing in *Twelfth Night?* And how can Julia patiently accept Proteus in *The Two Gentlemen of Verona* after he has so heartlessly abandoned her? Shakespeare accepts a young maid's heart as an eternal mystery, it seems, and he dares not attempt to explain it.

In the tragedies the consequences of infidelity are more serious. In *King Lear,* Goneril develops a passion for Edmund and plots her husband Albany's death. Both the wife and her lover are dead by the play's end. *Othello,* of course, is the tale of a man who unjustly suspects his wife of adultery and murders her, finally taking his own life when he discovers his error. His fatal jealousy adds a tragic dimension to the plight of the cuckolded husband, so often a figure of ridicule in his society. Othello agonizes that he could not bear the stigma of having an unfaithful wife; it would be the end of his life's work. "Farewell!" he rages, once convinced of her betrayal, "Othello's occupation's gone."

In offering a survey of love in his plays, Shakespeare does not shy from portraying naked lust. The clown Touchstone, in *As You Like It,* has designs on the simple but resolutely virtuous shepherdess Audrey, and finds that he can have his way only if he marries her. He arranges for a performance of the rites by an unauthorized preacher, Sir Oliver Martext, admitting to Jaques that he does so because if they are not joined legally, "it will be a good excuse for me thereafter to leave my wife." Touchstone has been called "the scapegoat of Arden" because he represents the basic urges that lie beneath the surface of the other, more idealized, attractions in the play. When he joins the company of young couples in the closing scene of the play, he addresses them wryly as "country copulatives."

Underlying all of the chivalric vows of "service," the rigid rites of courtship, and the romantic avowals of undying devotion, Shakespeare tells us, will be found the elemental passion of a species in perpetual pursuit of sexual gratification. Bertram, in *All's Well That Ends Well*, pursues Diana with all the ardor of a soldier far from home; and Angelo's infatuation for Isabella in *Measure for Measure* is motivated, he admits, by unrepentant physical desire. *Pericles* has its Pandar, Bawd, and Boult; *Measure for Measure* its madam, Mistress Overdone; *Henry IV, Part 2* its Doll Tearsheet; and even *The Comedy of Errors* a Courtezan, all attesting to the "rampant heterosexuality" of the race, as a sardonic colleague once remarked.

## Men and Men, Women and Women

Among the upper-class English of Shakespeare's time, the young of both sexes had to use ingenuity to find occasion for unsupervised socialization. Only men and boys received formal schooling, and anxious parents carefully guarded the virtue of marriageable daughters, whose chastity was a necessary condition for an auspicious match. Their vigilance was not, however, an insurmountable obstacle for young lovers intent upon an amorous assignation. The poet John Donne courted and secretly married sixteen-year-old Ann More, a ward of his patron, but with the consequence that he was imprisoned briefly for the affront and lost all promise of preferment in government service. Such exceptions notwithstanding, men and women formed friendships in different worlds, the former consumed in matters of commerce, warfare, and politics, the latter with child-rearing and household management.[7] Under such circumstances it should not be surprising that deeply emotional bonds would develop between members of the same sex.

The language of that bond is erotically suggestive to modern audiences, however, especially as it was expressed between men in the plays, who often describe their attachment in terms of love and

7. Shakespeare has some striking exceptions to this general rule, however, such as Lady Macbeth, Cleopatra, and the fiery Queen Margaret of the *Henry VI* plays, who leads armies in support of her husband.

the movements of the heart. In his speech to the Roman public after Caesar's assassination, for example, Brutus addresses the crowd as "Romans, countrymen, lovers" and insists that he "loved" the man he has slain. Today, of course, no matter how committed an advocate might be, it would certainly be inappropriate for any public figure to profess that he "loved" Bill Clinton or George W. Bush. Hamlet confides in Horatio that he wears him "in my heart's core, ay, in my heart of heart"; and in *Twelfth Night,* Antonio says of Sebastian: "But come what may, I do adore thee so, / That danger shall seem sport, and I will go." In *The Merchant of Venice* it is remarked of Antonio that "he only loves the world for" Bassanio. Indeed, many of Shakespeare's sonnets, which include some of the most memorable love lyrics in the language—those such as "Shall I compare thee to a summer's day?" "That time of year though mayst in me behold," and "When, in disgrace with Fortune and men's eyes"—were addressed, it is said, to a man, the third Earl of Southampton.

Shakespeare's women are equally expressive in declaring their love for one another. In *As You Like It,* Duke Frederick's daughter, Celia, is willing to accompany her friend Rosalind into exile because of "the love / Which teacheth thee that thou and I are one." And Helena plaintively recalls her attachment to Hermia in *A Midsummer Night's Dream*: "And will you rend our ancient love asunder, / To join with men in scorning your poor friend?"

There is a great deal of cross-dressing in the plays, women disguised as men, and, though less often, men as women. We examine the device elsewhere as a means of disguise,[8] but a glance at the frequency with which Shakespeare makes use of it will confirm his fondness for the practice. The list includes Viola as Duke Orsino's page, Cesario, in *Twelfth Night*; Portia as Balthasar (as well as Nerissa and, briefly, Jessica) in *The Merchant of Venice*; Rosalind as Ganymede in *As You Like It*; Julia as Sebastian in *The Two Gentlemen of Verona*; and Imogen as Fidele in *Cymbeline*. The only instance that comes to mind of a man dressed as a woman is Falstaff as "the old

8. See pp. 124–126.

woman of Brainford" in *The Merry Wives of Windsor,* devised only to make him ridiculous. Characters assume and maintain the disguise for a variety of reasons, but each does so in one way or another in the name of love.

Instances of emotive language and cross-dressing have suggested to some that Shakespeare is implying a homosexual attraction between the characters in those instances, for example, where one woman falls in love with another who has assumed a male persona, as Phebe is drawn to Rosalind (as Ganymede) in *As You Like It,* and Olivia to Viola (as Cesario) in *Twelfth Night.* Are these women enamored of the thinly disguised female qualities of the characters? This is a plausible reading, but it is not necessarily an indication of homosexual attraction. It could as well be that the women unconsciously detect in them a sentiment lacking in the men of their experience. There are indeed gay allusions in plays—the legendary relationship between Achilles and Patroclus in *Troilus and Cressida,* and in *Richard II* the close affinity between the king with his courtiers, Bushy, Greene, and Bagot, an attachment strongly implied by Bolingbroke's accusation that they have "made a divorce betwixt his queen and him, / Broke the possession of a royal bed." But none of these affairs is blatantly overt, as, for example, is the passion between the king and Gaveston in Christopher Marlowe's *Edward II.* In Shakespeare's time homosexuality was considered an affront to both God and nature. Men loved men, surely, and women, women; but any untoward display of homoerotic affection on the public stage would only have invited the condemnation of the censor, the church, or the court. Shakespeare's same-sex lovers are either minor figures or suffer for their preferences. Achilles does not appear prominently in *Troilus and Cressida* and is an unprincipled buffoon in the bargain, and Richard II loses his crown because he rules over a dissolute court.[9]

9. As does Marlowe's Edward II.

# The Family

It was of critical importance for a family to have many children in Shakespeare's time. Sons would inherit and daughters provide a prosperous union with families of the same, or higher, social standing, cementing alliances and reducing the threat of discord between jealous noble houses. In the lower classes children were a promise of more hands to till the soil and bring in the harvest, and among the nobility they gave assurance that an ancestral line would survive. With kings, a mature son and heir standing ready to assume the throne enhanced a monarch's stature and presaged a peaceful transfer of power. A house filled with children attested to a father's energy and virility. Titus Andronicus boasts of twenty-five sons, twenty-one of whom died in the service of Rome, proud testimony of his devotion to the empire. A further advantage to prolific parents, of course, was the promise of a secure old age, protected by a circle of loyal offspring.

Children could be a trial, however. Childbirth itself was a trying and dangerous ordeal. Subject to the primitive medical practices of the time, many women died in the process and more than half their children failed to survive infancy.[1] Lusty husbands spread their seed widely, and neglected wives found others to share their beds, producing a brood of envious bastards, whom Shakespeare occasionally features in a play. The Earl of Gloucester in *King Lear* places trust in his illegitimate son Edmund, who persuades him that "legitimate Edgar" is plotting his death to inherit the title. Gloucester lives to regret his misplaced confidence; it costs him his title and his eyes. In *King John,* Lady Faulconbridge confides in her son, Philip the Bastard, that during one of her husband's lengthy absences she had

---

1. The poet John Donne had twelve children during his sixteen-year marriage to Ann More, but only seven survived childhood, and the last took the mother as well. John Milton lost two of his three wives in childbirth, and three of his five children died in infancy.

DANVILLE PUBLIC LIBRARY
DANVILLE, INDIANA

lain with King Richard I and that he was the product of the union. Fortunately for the Bastard, he bears a striking resemblance to his father, who has since died in an Austrian prison, and Queen Elinor, the king's mother, takes him into her service.

The custom of primogeniture provided that only first sons could inherit. It was a practical matter, ensuring that large estates remained intact rather than become fragmented among surviving heirs; but it could result in a disgruntled group of second or third sons entirely dependent upon the generosity of their elder brother. The younger sons could marry a richly dowered wife, of course, or they could pursue careers in the ministry or the military; but they could inherit a title only if their elder brother died without offspring. The conditions resulted in families ripe with discord and intrigue, fertile ground for Shakespeare's imagination.

The elder brother's generosity was not always forthcoming. In *As You Like It,* Oliver inherits his father's wealth, but he keeps his younger sibling, Orlando, in a condition of poverty and servitude, denying him even the small portion their father had left him. Orlando demands of his brother why "you have train'd me like a peasant, obscuring and hiding from me all gentleman-like qualities." Oliver, it seems, is fiercely jealous that his brother is "enchantingly beloved" by his people, and the contrast between the two leaves him "altogether mispris'd." He engages a wrestler, Charles, who is scheduled for a match with his brother, to kill him during the bout. Orlando defeats Charles but, warned that Oliver still plots his death, he flees to the Forest of Arden.

The plays have their share of loving children and devoted parents, including a number of dutiful daughters. In *The Merchant of Venice,* Portia is faithful to her father's involved scheme for choosing her husband, even though he is long dead. Fortunately for her, Bassanio chooses the lead casket (rejected by a series of haughty suitors), which contains Portia's portrait and thus wins her hand. King Lear disowns his youngest, Cordelia, because she refuses to debase her love for him when he requires his daughters to express their devotion to him in a public ceremony. The King of France accepts her as his wife even though Lear has dismissed her without a dowry. She nonetheless continues to love her father and returns to England with a French army to rescue him from the scornful neglect of her sisters, Goneril and Regan, losing her life as a result.[2]

We also find obedient, even loving, sons: In *King Lear,* the Earl of Gloucester orders his son Edgar captured and put to death under the mistaken impression that the young man is engaged in a plot to kill him. To escape detection, Edgar assumes the disguise of "mad Tom" and seeks shelter in a hovel on the barren heath. Later Gloucester attempts to protect Lear and is apprehended by the villainous Duke of Cornwall, who accuses him of treason and in punishment gouges his eyes out. Edgar finds his blind father wandering helplessly about the heath, defeats his effort to end his life, and stays by his side until his eventual death.[3]

Children and their elders do not always get along in Shakespeare's plays, however. The plots are complicated by resentful children chafing under parental restraint, and by princes impatient to sit upon a throne occupied by a father or stepfather. Yet truly vindictive daughters are rare in Shakespeare, the most prominent example being, of course, *King Lear's* Goneril and Regan. Lear favors his youngest, Cordelia, and her elder sisters bitterly resent his partiality. Goneril is especially envious, muttering sourly, "he always lov'd our sister most," and their later actions reveal an animosity toward him that runs deep. They take pleasure in stripping him of his retinue of a hundred knights, and Regan cruelly shuts her doors to the old man when in his rage and disappointment in his "ingrateful

2. In another instance, Ophelia breaks off her affair with prince Hamlet in obedience to her father, Polonius, causing great distress for them both.

3. Among other dutiful sons, young Prince Hal in *Henry IV, Part 1* finally accepts the responsibilities his father urges upon him and proves his devotion on the field of battle by coming to his aid when the king is confronted by the formidable Scots warrior Douglas. And in *Titus Andronicus,* Lucius obeys his father's order to leave Rome and return at the head of an army of Goths to avenge the rape and mutilation of his sister, Lavinia, by the dissolute sons of the empress Tamora.

daughters" he wanders out onto the heath battered by a raging storm.

Treacherous sons are not much in evidence either, the most conspicuous exception being Edmund, the bastard son of the Earl of Gloucester, again in *King Lear*. As the play opens Edmund schemes to replace Gloucester's legitimate heir, his half-brother Edgar, in his father's favor. Later, however, he discovers that Gloucester has been in collusion with the French forces who have invaded England to rescue the aged king. Edmund decides to aim higher in his aspirations by betraying his father to the Duke of Cornwall, and he is rewarded when the duke appoints him Earl of Gloucester in his father's place. It is Edmund who voices the heartless theme of such betrayals: "The younger rise when the old doth fall."

As we have seen, the plays are crowded with daughters who defy their parent's marriage choices, but it is uncommon for a son to openly challenge a father. In one instance, Titus Andronicus commits his daughter, Lavinia, to marry the emperor Saturninus. She is already betrothed to another, however, and the couple flee. Titus, in a rage at their disobedience, rushes to intercept them, and one of his sons, out of loyalty to his sister, bars his way. Titus slays him for his insolence, needlessly as it happens, since Saturninus decides to marry the Gothic queen Tamora instead. We are more likely to encounter sons seeking vengeance for a father's death. Laertes vows to avenge Hamlet's murder of Polonius, for which, he says, he would gladly "cut his throat i' th' church." And the entire play traces the history of Hamlet's abortive efforts to seek revenge for his father's "foul and most unnatural murder."[4]

The plays feature devoted siblings, conspicuously Laertes and Ophelia, Viola and Sebastian in *Twelfth Night,* and Polydore and

---

4. In other instances, the Duke of York kills Old Clifford in battle and his son vows vengeance in *Henry VI, Part 3*. Later, in retaliation, young Clifford stabs York's son Rutland and assists in killing the captured duke himself. And Edgar kills his half-brother Edmund in *King Lear*, accusing him of disloyalty "to thy gods, thy brother, and thy father."

Cadwal in *Cymbeline*. But they also include some very unpleasant brothers, prominent among them the aforementioned Edmund, who works Edgar's downfall in *King Lear*. Among others, in *As You Like It*, Duke Frederick overthrows his brother, Duke Senior, and later leads an armed expedition in an effort to root him out of his refuge in the Forest of Arden; and Oliver despises Orlando to such a degree that he plots his death. "False Clarence" joins his brother's Lancaster enemies for a time in *Henry VI, Part 3*, though in the end he switches back. Clarence falls victim to another brother in *Richard III*, when the treacherous Gloucester arranges to have him imprisoned and ultimately drowned in a barrel of wine. And in *The Tempest*, Prospero recounts to Miranda how his devious brother Antonio deposed him to become Duke of Milan.[5] Malicious sisters are less in evidence, Goneril and Regan the most memorable, of course, in *King Lear*. They eye Cordelia jealously in the opening scene but have no opportunity to do her harm. Later in the play they have a falling out in competition for Edmund's love. Goneril plots her husband's death, poisons her sister, and finally takes her own life when her crimes are discovered. There is no love lost between any of these siblings.[6]

Mothers are conspicuously absent from many of the plays. They are not to be found in a number of the histories: *Henry IV, Parts 1 and 2*, for example, and *Henry V* (except for a brief appearance of the French queen in the final scene). Nor do they appear in several tragedies: *Julius Caesar, King Lear, Othello*.[7] And they play no part in many of the comedies: *As You Like It, The Merchant of Venice, Two*

5. Claudio is more feckless than he is treacherous in *Measure for Measure*. When told that his sister Isabella must surrender her virtue to save his life, he is at first highly indignant but promptly decides that it is not such a bad idea after all.

6. Kate fits the description in *The Taming of the Shrew*. She binds and beats her sister Bianca in a jealous fit.

7. Lady Macbeth mentions that she has "given suck," but there is no other evidence of her children in the play. Lady Macduff and her son appear briefly and are murdered.

*Gentlemen of Verona, The Tempest* (except for brief mention of Sycorax), *The Two Noble Kinsmen, The Taming of the Shrew, Twelfth Night,* and others.

When mothers do appear, it is in a variety of roles, none of them happy ones. In Shakespeare they for the most part worry, wait, suffer, or mourn. Some are deeply concerned about their children. Their sons worry them: Gertrude is anxious that Hamlet seems to be sunk into a deep melancholy, little knowing that her marriage to Claudius is the chief cause of it. Lady Montague questions Benvolio about Romeo's strange behavior, keeping strange hours and avoiding all company. The young man is in love, of course, and with a woman who wants no part of him. Queen Elizabeth agonizes over the threat to her sons in *Richard III,* so much so that she seeks religious sanctuary for herself and her youngest. And mothers worry as well about their daughters: Lady Capulet, unaware of the true cause of Juliet's sorrow, is distressed that she seems unduly upset by the death of her cousin Tybalt. In *Henry VIII,* Queen Katharine, abandoned by the king, pleads with him to protect their daughter Mary. And in *The Merry Wives of Windsor,* Mistress Page is concerned that her daughter Anne has taken a liking to Fenton, a young man with the unenviable reputation of carousing with the Prince of Wales and Poins in London's Eastcheap.

Shakespeare occasionally introduces that familiar figure, the mother ambitious for a son. Volumnia in *Coriolanus* has raised hers to be a fearsome warrior so that he may gain renown in Rome. In *King John,* Constance believes that her son Arthur is the rightful heir to the English throne, and she secures the aid of the French king in an effort to unseat John. The queen in *Cymbeline* is eager to establish her son Cloten as heir to the throne through marriage to the king's daughter Imogen. When she marries Posthumus instead, the queen attempts to poison her.

Resolute mothers come to the defense of their children. Tamora rages at Titus Andronicus, pleading for the life of her eldest son, taken captive in the Gothic wars; but Titus insists that he must be sacrificed so that the spirits of his own sons, killed in the same wars, may rest in peace. Tamora vows revenge, and when she marries the emperor Saturninus, she is in a position to carry it out. In *Richard II,* Bolingbroke forces Richard to surrender his crown, and he mounts the throne as Henry IV. Loyal supporters of the deposed king immediately plot to unseat Henry, a conspiracy that includes his cousin Aumerle, the son of the Duke of York. The duke discovers the plot and rushes out to inform the king, a revelation that would condemn Aumerle to death. The Duchess of York manages to reach Henry first, however, and she falls on her knees, pleading with him to pardon her son, begging the king to do so even before he learns of Aumerle's crime. The king, exasperated perhaps, or embarrassed by the spectacle of his stately and revered aunt kneeling before him, finally agrees; and the duke arrives belatedly on the scene to find that his son has already been forgiven.

Other seek vengeance for the death of their children. Aside from Tamora, the fierce Queen Margaret in *Henry VI, Part 3* avenges the murder of her son Edward by the Yorks when her forces take the duke captive. After subjecting him to mocking taunts, she joins others in stabbing him. In *Richard III* she revels in the fact that the York faction has suffered the same humiliations and sorrows she has, at the hands of the scheming Gloucester.

Mothers are often helpless victims, caught up in a web of events beyond their control. In *Richard III* the king confines the two young princes, Edward, the heir to the throne, and his younger brother Richard, in the Tower of London—for their protection, he insists. Their mother, Queen Elizabeth, is denied access to them and, anxious for their safety, stands helplessly outside the Tower, pleading "pity, you ancient stones, those tender babes / Whom envy hath immur'd within your walls." Her fears are realized when, according to Shakespeare, King Richard has them murdered to remove a threat to his throne. Later she and the Duchess of York lament the recent deaths, which they were powerless to prevent. Both have lost two sons, the queen her two princes, and the duchess the late King Edward and his brother Clarence. Hermione, the Queen of Sicilia in *The Winter's Tale,* is an innocent victim of the irrational jealousy of her husband, Leontes. Her son dies of grief, and her infant daughter is left abandoned on a deserted shore while she goes into seclusion for sixteen years, leaving the impression that she has died, in order to escape his wrath.[8]

From all this we can only conclude that a mother's lot was not an enviable one in Shakespeare's time. Living in a patriarchal world, women could only wait anxiously while their husbands and sons, fired by ambition, marched off to war, and grieve when they failed to return. They had no recourse but patient submission when husbands deserted the marriage bed or when children became innocent pawns in the pitiless dynastic struggles of their day. We find very few happy or even contented mothers in these plays, and only in the comedies, and then only in the last scene—as in the case of Hermione, who is reunited with her daughter Perdita at the end of *The Winter's Tale,* or Mistress Page, who good-naturedly accepts the marriage of her daughter Anne to her lover Fenton at the close of *The Merry Wives of Windsor,* or the austere Abbess in *The Comedy of Errors,* who turns out to be the wife of Egeon and the mother of the twin Antipholi.

Two plays in particular explore the relationship between mothers and sons, both warranting special attention. In *Coriolanus,* Volumnia is clearly the dominant influence in her son's life, raising him to be a famed warrior. She exults when Coriolanus returns from a campaign with new wounds to show, and delights when he leaves to garner more. Her influence has left him inordinately proud of his achievements, however, and scornful of those unwilling to defend Rome with a devotion comparable to his own. When the senate nominates him for consul, he adamantly insists that he deserves the honor because of his deeds alone and is arrogantly abusive to the Roman citizens when, as required by custom, he must solicit their

8. The list of victimized mothers is long. Henry VIII casts aside Katharine, his wife of twenty years, when he becomes infatuated with the younger Anne Boleyn, and the queen pleads with him to care for their daughter Mary. Macbeth, enraged at the witches' confirmation that Banquo's heirs will inherit the Scottish throne, turns his wrath on the family of the absent Macduff, ordering his innocent wife and children murdered.

approval. Banished for his insolence, he returns at the head of the Volcian forces, threatening to lay waste the city in revenge for his humiliation. He refuses an old friend's entreaties; but when confronted by his kneeling mother, he is moved to dismiss his soldiers. In the end the Volcian leader kills him for breaking his pledge to them. Volumnia is the embodiment of the ambitious mother and Coriolanus the model of the dutiful son, molded by her for fame but doomed in the end when he is ruled by her.

Hamlet's relationship with his mother is more complex. Of the many events in Elsinore that trouble him, Gertrude's marriage to Claudius grates the most. And it is their union between "incestuous sheets," as he calls it, that, according to some interpretations, lies at the heart of his inability, or reluctance, to avenge his father's death by killing the king. Authority for this reading leans heavily on the theories of Sigmund Freud, especially his explanation of the Oedipus complex. Freud suggests that the young male child goes through a stage when he feels an especially strong bond with the mother and a concurrent resentment of the attention she pays to the father, so intense that at times the child wishes him dead. This desire for his death is accompanied by an equally strong sense of guilt at such a thought. The normal child, Freud contends, soon outgrows these conflicting emotions of desire, hatred, and guilt, and is eventually seen swaggering about in a juvenile imitation of his father. But if for any number of reasons—an overattentive mother, for example, or an absent or indifferent father—this natural development is arrested, the son may grow to maturity plagued by the same impulses, all repressed in his subconscious mind. This shameful desire for his mother, Freud concludes, can make it difficult for him to engage in a normal relationship with any woman. When Hamlet unleashes his tirade on Ophelia, for example, his abuse targets the falseness in all women as much as it does in her alone: "If thou wilt needs marry, marry a fool, for wise men know well enough what monsters you make of them." Hence, it is said, Hamlet is unnaturally harsh with her, scorns marriage, and later in a tumultuous scene demands that his mother abandon her husband's bed.

More important, it is suggested that the profound and again subconscious sense of guilt that accompanies Hamlet's desire for his mother and resentment of his father restrains him from taking action against a father figure, in this case his uncle, until events force the deed upon him. Of course, the notion of twisted love is only one of many interpretations of this challenging figure; but the play has been frequently so staged, receiving its most compelling dramatization in Laurence Oliver's film version (1948).

What are we to make of this contradictory passion, of hatred where there should be love and love where we would expect to find hatred, of the paradox that Romeo calls, "O brawling love, O loving hate"? It is a painful contradiction echoed by Juliet when she learns that he has killed her cousin Tybalt; Romeo is at once her "beautiful tyrant, fiend angelical" and "a damned saint, an honourable villain." What of lovers at one moment elated with soaring hope and the next consumed by despair? And what of this parade of family bonds: faithful couples whose union is tainted by the shadow of suspicion; inconstant wives and husbands; brothers at each other's throats; poisonous sisters; mothers, some helpless victims, others fierce and resolute in their children's behalf; and fathers who, despite a lifetime of compassionate care, suddenly turn on their sons and daughters in unreasonable rage? And yet in the same plays we witness loving couples, loyal siblings, and devoted parents and children. Shakespeare portrays them all and passes judgment on none. His theme is that this is how we are, human beings blessed or damned by our contentious nature. We are, in Hamlet's words, "the beauty of the world; the paragon of animals," and at the same time "remorseless, treacherous, lecherous [and] kindless." Human relations are messy, Shakespeare seems to say, especially when love and family are involved; but this varied pageant, he assures us, can also be cause for hope and laughter.

# WARFARE

❧

ASIDE FROM LOVE, war is the most pervasive theme in Shake-speare. It forms the backdrop to all the tragedies, with the exception of *Romeo and Juliet,* where the conflict between two families is con-fined to the streets of Verona.[1] Save for *Henry VIII,* war is a central theme in the history plays; and soldiers populate the comedies as well—*Troilus and Cressida, Cymbeline, Much Ado About Nothing,* and *All's Well That Ends Well.* Episodes of individual combat abound in the plays. Angry duels are fought in countless scenes, where men in the heat of passion contend for a crown or defend their honor.

Shakespeare does not oppose war in his works, however much we may wish he had, nor does he favor it. He simply stages it as it is, with its rewards for the victor and sorrows for the vanquished. He places before us an image of what we are—both constant and treacherous, noble and common, faithful and disloyal, valiant and cowardly. He shows us war's captains and kings as well as the com-mon soldiers who endure the heat of battle. He records the suffering that war imposes on a wasted land, its heartless unconcern for human life, and the extraordinary courage and sacrifice of ordinary men who, having survived the boiling cauldron of combat, look back on their deeds with quiet pride. He explores the inner thoughts of men on the eve of battle as they contemplate the threat

1. It is the war between Venice and the Turks that brings Othello to Cyprus, and at the end of *Timon of Athens,* Alcibiades commands an army that lays siege to Athens.

of death and ponder the fate of their immortal souls, anxious over the justice of their cause in the eyes of God. He holds a mirror up to our contentious nature, in which we see reflected all the folly and grandeur flesh is heir to.

When Shakespeare was writing his plays, it had been more than a century since England had been ravaged by war. Not since 1485, when Henry Tudor defeated Richard III at Bosworth Field, had her downs and pastures been troubled by marching feet. The century had not been entirely peaceful, surely, but England's victories had come at sea, raiding the fat Spanish galleons that lumbered across the Atlantic, their holds heavy with gold and silver from the New World, and scattering the mighty Armada that threatened her shores in 1588. English soldiers were deployed across the narrow Channel to oppose the formidable power that Spain had marshaled to subdue the embattled Dutch, but the country had been spared large-scale internal conflicts, which were not to be renewed until the brutal civil wars of the mid-seventeenth century.

It had not always been so. In Shakespeare's first plays he reached back to a time of terrible civil strife in England, and he later returned to an even earlier time when Englishmen fought Englishmen, bathing the land in blood. Shakespeare's first four history plays, *Henry VI, Parts 1, 2, and 3,* and *Richard III,* known as "The First Henriad," record the long fifteenth-century struggle between two noble houses, York and Lancaster, for the crown of England. In this War of the Roses, as it was called, York prevailed; but Lancaster returned in the person of Henry Tudor, Earl of Richmond, who defeated Richard III in 1485 and inaugurated the long reign of the Tudor monarchs.[2] A more mature Shakespeare then returned to the beginning of that contentious century and composed four more plays, *Richard II, Henry IV, Parts 1 and 2*, and *Henry V,* called appropriately "The Second Henriad." Although *Richard III,* the last of the

2. These monarchs (and the years of their reign) were Henry VII (1485–1509), Henry VIII (1509–1547), Edward VI (1547–1553), Mary I (1553–1558), and Elizabeth I (1558–1603).

first group, is justly admired, these later works are more highly regarded, giving evidence of the poet's growing skill as a playwright.
In all these plays Shakespeare's pen explores with consummate insight the cause and consequence, the folly and glory, the loss and
gain of warfare. Men have always fought, he tells us, either one-on-
one or as soldiers in vast armies, and thus armed conflict is a pervasive theme in his plays.

## The Stage

We shall pursue Shakespeare's image of warfare in a variety of his
plays, especially the histories, and conclude with a survey of his
most complete portrayal of the theme, in *Henry V.* But first, mention should be made of the limitations under which Shakespeare la-
bored in presenting scenes of combat on the bare Elizabethan stage.
He was unable to provide the spectacle of great armies locked in
battle, a luxury enjoyed by modern filmmakers who can amass a cast
of thousands to duplicate the noise, fury, and confusion of an armed
encounter. So limited, the staging of such furious battles as Tewkesbury, Shrewsbury, Bosworth Field, and Agincourt was reduced to
the entrance of a half-dozen actors in blue uniforms from the left
and a like number in red from the right, waving banners similarly
tinted, and armed with safely dulled swords and pikes of the period.
They clashed briefly until one side was hailed the victor. Bosworth
Field, for example, occupies but a short scene and a half in *Richard
III,* though it contains one of the play's most memorable lines, the
king's "A horse! A horse! My kingdom for a horse!" The Chorus in
*Henry V* apologizes for this inadequacy, urging the audience to
"piece out our imperfections with your thoughts." When we see a
single man, we are asked to imagine him as a thousand, and when
we hear of horses we should picture them "printing their proud
hoofs i' th' receiving earth."

As a consequence of these limitations, Shakespeare was more

likely to stage scenes of individual combat, such as those, to mention but a few, between Macbeth and Macduff, Hamlet and Laertes, Prince Hal and Hotspur in *Henry IV, Part 1,* Achilles and Hector in *Troilus and Cressida,* and Edmund and Edgar in *King Lear.* And, with only a limited ability to portray combat itself, he was inclined to dwell on events leading up to the clash of arms, filling his lines with long speeches before battle. These speeches take various forms— kings urging their soldiers to show courage, ferocity, and devotion to the cause, and heralds or envoys moving back and forth between camps to offer terms of peace, recite grievances, or issue haughty challenges. To reduce the tedium of such occasions, Shakespeare occasionally introduced supernatural visitations on the night before battle, such as the spectral procession of his victims that troubled Richard III's sleep and the appearance of Caesar's ghost to Brutus on the eve of Philippi. But these speeches should not be dismissed, since they are occasionally marked by passages of stirring poetry, and they frequently include the essence of Shakespeare's vision of war.

These episodes before battle also demonstrate the use of deception and duplicity in warfare. A soldier will employ any means at his disposal before and during battle to gain advantage over his opponent. He will lie, cheat, break his word, and prey upon an enemy's weakness in an effort to deceive him, render him vulnerable to surprise, or trick him into submission. The *Henry IV* plays illustrate the role of duplicity. In a parlay before the battle of Shrewsbury in *Part 1,* the king urges his rebellious nobles to dismiss their forces, promising them friendship and forgiveness. The Earl of Westmoreland, Hotspur's uncle, mistrusts the king, fearing that once they have disarmed, he will surely punish them for their revolt, and he decides not to tell his nephew of the offer. Later events prove him justified in his fears. In *Part 2* the rebel army once more faces the king's forces, commanded by the king's son, Prince John (Hal is in the west subduing the Welsh). In a parlay before battle, John offers a similar amnesty and promise of friendship, proposing that both sides dismiss their soldiers as a mark of amity. This time the rebels agree to the arrangement, but John secretly keeps his army intact. Once the rebel forces have disbanded, he hunts down their leaders and has them executed for treason.

In *Antony and Cleopatra,* Octavius Caesar tricks Mark Antony into a battle where Caesar's forces have the advantage. The two emperors had been allies in the war against the Roman Senate, defeating Brutus and Cassius at Philippi. But Antony, a seasoned warrior, has always been openly dismissive of the youthful Octavius, who is some twenty years his junior. Before the battle of Actium, where the forces of the western and eastern empires clash, Octavius, aware that his western navy is superior to the enemy's, challenges Antony to a contest at sea rather than on land, where the eastern armies have the edge. Octavius is confident that Antony's pride will not permit him to ignore a taunt from "the boy," as he calls him,[3] and indeed, despite the urgings of his generals, Antony agrees, because as he says, "he dares us to't." In the battle Octavius wins a stunning victory, and Antony is compelled to retreat to Alexandria.

There Octavius displays his skill at duplicity. Antony mounts a stubborn defense of the city, and Octavius attempts to divide the enemy forces. He sends an envoy, Thidias, to Cleopatra, instructing him to promise her anything she wants if she will abandon her husband. Octavius has no intention of honoring such promises, since he plans to display her as a prisoner on his triumphant return to Rome. Cleopatra, herself subtly skilled in such matters, pretends to be receptive to the offers but sees them for what they are and confirms her devotion to Antony.

There is little evidence of fair play and chivalric courtesy in Shakespeare's wars. Such niceties have no place, he seems to say, in modern conflict; and he found the concept more apt for comic treatment.[4] Hector is a parody of the chivalric knight in *Troilus and Cres-*

---

3. Cleopatra calls him "the scarce-bearded Caesar."
4. See the discussion of Shakespeare's comic use of chivalric love, pp. 7–13.

*sida.* Troilus faults him for having "a vice of mercy" because instead of killing fallen enemies he is more inclined to "bid them arise and live." The noble Hector replies simply that " 'tis fair play," to which a more practical Troilus answers that it is "fool's play." The folly of Hector's code is evident in Shakespeare's version of his legendary duel with Achilles, which bears no resemblance to Homer's. Achilles has been sulking in his tent for some time, refusing to enter the battle; and when the two finally clash, the Greek falters, explaining that his long absence from the field has left him a bit out of shape. In the interest of "fair play," Hector gallantly permits him to retire to catch his breath; Achilles returns, backed by a band of his Myrmidons, who descend upon and slaughter the hapless Trojan.[5]

In *The Two Noble Kinsmen,* Shakespeare stages another ludicrous parody of chivalrous fair play. Arcite encounters his cousin Palamon, who has just escaped from prison with the help of the jailer's daughter. They are rivals for the affections of Emily, the sister of Duke Theseus, though she has no idea they exist; and these cousins, who have been devoted friends and comrades in arms, decide that the only way to resolve the matter is to fight it out for her. But first Arcite releases his adversary from his shackles and brings him food to restore his strength. He later arrives with suits of armor and weapons, and in a farcical scene helps to dress Palamon, solicitous all the while as to the fit. "Do I pinch you?" he asks, and "is't too heavy?" and he urges him to be sure to wear the gauntlets, even offers to exchange swords with him. Only when he is assured that Palamon is entirely satisfied with the preparations do they square off to fight. Fortunately, before they can do one another harm, they are interrupted by Theseus and Emily, who is unpleasantly surprised to find that they are fighting over her. All of this chivalric courtesy

---

5. Again, in *Twelfth Night* Shakespeare reduces the duel over slighted honor to a mockery when the ridiculous Aguecheek and Viola, disguised as the page Cesario, are tricked into a swordfight. Since neither of them is skilled in the martial arts and both are led to believe they are facing a fearsome warrior, the two of them do everything in their power to avoid each other.

to an opponent, Shakespeare seems to say, is a bit out of date—and was absurd to begin with.

When a chivalric sentiment does arise, it is often dismissed. In *Henry IV, Part 1,* as the opposing armies face each other before the battle of Shrewsbury, the rebel leaders meet with the king to voice their grievances. Prince Hal, in a burst of youthful exuberance, offers to resolve their differences in single combat with Hotspur "to save the blood on either side." His father quickly vetoes the chivalric gesture, unwilling, quite understandably, to risk his crown in a contest between his young, untried son and a seasoned warrior like Hotspur.

## The Cause

Shakespeare's wars break out for a variety of reasons. It may be a simple matter of repelling an invasion—the Britons defending against an incursion of the Romans in *Cymbeline,* or the English against the French in *King Lear* and again in *King John,* or Coriolanus defending Rome against the Volcians. Then too, in the plays England is constantly troubled by uprisings by her warlike subject nations. Both the Duke of York in *Henry VI, Part 2* and Richard II lead expeditions against the Irish, and the Welsh and Scots are a constant thorn in England's side, joining in the rebellion against Henry IV, for example.

The cause is at times more complex. Wars break out because of resentment against an intemperate, a tyrannical, a corrupt, or a weak king. There are no scenes of battle in *Richard II,* but Bolingbroke sets armies on the march to unseat a monarch. Richard is overly impressed with the splendor of the crown and has been profligate in ornamenting his court, expenses which have impoverished the royal coffers. To support his extravagance, among other unlawful acts he has imposed arbitrary taxes on his subjects, a source of growing resentment. Particularly galling is his practice of confiscating the estates of his noble uncles upon their death. After the murder of the Duke of Gloucester, which it is widely suspected he had a hand in, he reduces his surviving duchess to penury. As she complains sadly to her brother-in-law old Gaunt, the Duke of Lancaster, she will retire to her castle, now stripped of possessions by Richard, leaving only "empty lodgings and unfirnish'd walls, / Unpeopled offices, untrodden stones." It is the seizure of Gaunt's estate on his death that angers the duke's son, Bolingbroke, whom Richard had earlier banished from the kingdom. In defiance to the king's decree, Bolingbroke returns to claim his inheritance as Duke of Lancaster and finds himself joined by a parade of disaffected nobles, resentful of Richard's intemperate demands. Backed by their forces, he confronts the king and replaces him on the throne.

In *Henry IV, Part 1,* the irascible Hotspur is infuriated by the king's contemptuous treatment of his kinsmen and himself. Hotspur erupts angrily with a litany of complaints about the indignities the king has heaped on the house of Northumberland. After his family supported Bolingbroke in securing the crown, he rages, the king betrayed them, having,

> Disgrace'd me in my happy victories,
> Sought to entrap me by intelligence,
> Rated mine uncle from the Council-board,[6]
> In rage dismiss'd my father from the court,
> Broke oath on oath, committed wrong on wrong.

Incensed by Henry's high-handed manner, Hotspur leads a conspiracy to dethrone him. The plot fails and he is killed in battle, but Henry IV is plagued by civil broils throughout his reign.[7]

Ancient animosities have a way of surfacing in succeeding generations as proud nobles recall old wrongs. In the *Henry VI* plays,

---

6. The Earl of Westmoreland.

7. Again, in *Macbeth,* Malcolm and Macduff lead an army into Scotland to rid their homeland of the tyrant. And Henry VI is so ineffectual a king that the nobility fall to squabbling over his crown.

the rivalry between the houses of York and Lancaster surfaces in the War of the Roses. One cannot escape the impression that these two neighboring domains in northern England have long been at odds and that the war offers an opportunity for them to settle old scores. The rivalry between France and England, so prominent in the history plays, had ancient roots, and indeed persisted into the Napoleonic wars of the nineteenth century. The long struggle between east and west for control of the Mediterranean world forms the backdrop of such plays as *Othello* and *Antony and Cleopatra.* And *Troilus and Cressida,* like *The Iliad,* enacts an episode in the ten years' conflict between Greece and Troy.

War erupts also as a consequence of a brazen play for power by ambitious spirits. In the first of the *Henry VI* plays, a boy king presides over a court of contentious nobles, whose feuds a stronger monarch would have kept in check. The avaricious Bishop of Winchester plots against his brother, the Duke of Gloucester, who has been appointed Lord Protector of England during Henry's minority, and he is eventually responsible for the duke's death. Of even more importance is the simmering animosity over succession to the throne between the houses of York and Lancaster. In a famous scene, one apparently invented by Shakespeare, Richard, Duke of York, confronts the Lancastrian Duke of Somerset in the gardens of the Temple in London.[8] York, in a gesture of defiance, plucks a white rose from a bush, and Somerset, in angry response, a red one. The powerful lords in attendance each pluck one or the other, symbolizing their allegiance to either the York or the Lancaster cause, creating dangerous factions that are later to contend in the destructive War of the Roses. The Earl of Warwick, who attempts to mediate their differences, utters the prophetic lines,

> This brawl to-day,
> Grown to this faction in the Temple Garden,

8. In fact they are both earls at the time but are elevated shortly thereafter. The Duke of York is Richard III's father.

Shall send between the Red Rose and the White
A thousand souls to death and deadly night.

In a dozen plays, then, from *Macbeth* to *Pericles* to the Roman tragedies, the action revolves around conspiracies to unseat a ruling figure, be he king, duke, or dictator, and for any number of causes, just or unjust, mean or noble.[9] In the comedies, on the other hand, dynastic wrangling of this sort is more likely to precede the action, and we learn of it in the opening scenes of the play. In *The Tempest*, Prospero has lost his dukedom to his treacherous brother Antonio long before the curtain rises; and Duke Frederick has already deposed Duke Senior when *As You Like It* opens.[1] Shakespeare, it seems, felt that weighty political intrigues should not be allowed to intrude on his comic plots, which are all about love anyway.

The justice of the cause is a matter of no small concern in the plays. Of course there are those who conceal their ambition under a cloak of justice. As we have seen, Henry Bolingbroke in *Richard II* insists that his sole purpose in raising an army is to claim his lawful rights as Duke of Lancaster. He is well aware, however, that, having confronted the monarch with armed men to force his claim, he has committed an act of treason and must either gain the crown or lose his head. In *Henry VI, Part 3,* Edward IV, returning to England, is similarly deceptive. He has been defeated in battle by his Lancaster foes and is compelled to seek refuge in France. He persuades the French king to support his claim to the throne and returns to England with an army of borrowed soldiers. He finds, however, that the gates of York are closed to him, and in a parlay with the mayor he maintains that the only reason for his return is to reassume his rights as Duke of York. He will no longer assert his claim to the throne, he insists, and argues that it is inconsistent of the mayor to

9. The civil wars in Rome in *Julius Caesar* and *Antony and Cleopatra,* for example, are fought by proud men wrestling for control of an empire.

1. Before the action of *Much Ado About Nothing,* Don John raises a revolt against his brother, Don Pedro. In the first scene, Don Pedro and his army are returning from a successful campaign to put down the rebellion.

deny the Duke of York entrance to the city of York. Once inside, however, he is quick to reassert his right to the crown.

The gallant Lord Talbot, in *Henry VI, Part 1,* like many soldiers in Shakespeare, finds cause enough to take up arms in the medieval code of fealty that the lower nobility owed the higher. As a loyal "servant in arms to Harry King of England," he attempts to preserve the fruits of Henry V's victories in the face of the resurgent French, newly inspired by Joan la Pucelle. Trapped by a French army, he calls for aid from the dukes of York and Somerset, whose loyalties, as we have seen, lie elsewhere in the service of their own ambitions. They refuse to march to his relief and he is overcome, dying beside his fallen son John. And with him dies, Shakespeare seems to say, the ancient bond of loyalty between servant and master that offered a measure of order to the scattered medieval world.[2]

Others, discussed at greater length elsewhere, deserve brief mention here among those who go to war for a variety of reasons. Joan of Arc, according to Christian legend, was inspired by divine voices to come to the aid of the French dauphin; or alternately, according to the English, as Joan la Pucelle she joins the battle in league with underworld "fiends."[3] And King Duncan's son, Malcolm, marches on Macbeth to free Scotland from his tyrannical reign.[4]

A just cause was of critical importance to both kings and their subjects in this age, not only because a war must appear righteous in the eyes of the people, but because it must also be righteous in the eyes of God. It is common today to suspect any reference to the deity in public affairs as so much hypocrisy, but it was not so in Shakespeare's time. In those days belief was strong in an immanent God, one who played an active role in human affairs. He made his

2. Shakespeare was fond of the theme. In *As You Like It,* Orlando praises his old servant, Adam: "How well in thee appears / The constant service of the antique world, / Where service sweat for duty, not for meed [profit]!"

3. See p. 135.

4. See p. 166.

will known in many ways, not the least of which was to strengthen and protect one side or the other in battle, on the basis of which of the combatants fought for truth and the right. It was a conviction sanctioned by Scripture in accounts of the Old Testament God who made his presence felt with some frequency in the wars of the Israelites. Out of this belief came confidence in the "trial by combat," which was said to reveal the judgment of God: If two states, or two individuals, contended on a field of battle, it was thought, the deity would ensure that the righteous side achieved the victory, demonstrating conclusively that the vanquished were in the wrong.

Shakespeare includes a number of scenes that enact this "trial by combat." In *Richard II*, Bolingbroke accuses Mowbray of murdering the Duke of Gloucester, one of the king's powerful uncles, and Mowbray defies him. The two challenge each other in the traditional manner by throwing down a glove (a "gage") and daring the other to pick it up.[5] In the absence of evidence one way or the other, Richard proclaims that the issue will be decided by a ceremonial fight to the death between them. The two appear in the arena fully armored at the appointed time and engage in ritualistic speeches, each declaring his devotion to the king and accusing the other of treason. At the last minute, however, the king cancels the contest, for reasons that become evident later in the play. Many strongly suspect that Mowbray is indeed guilty, and moreover that he has carried out the murders on orders from Richard himself.[6] Thus it may be concluded—though Shakespeare never says as much—that the king's anxiety arises from a fear that should Bolingbroke emerge the victor, Mowbray's crime will be confirmed and his own role in the murder will become more than a mere suspicion.

5. Readers will be familiar with the later custom of issuing a challenge by slapping the face of an adversary with a glove, but the medieval "gage" was a sturdy garment, often decorated with metal studs. A slap in the face with it might well draw blood prematurely.

6. Lady Gloucester is convinced of Richard's complicity in her husband's murder and pleads with his brother, the Duke of Lancaster, to avenge his murder—to no avail.

Another instance is the ritualistic duel between Edgar and Edmund in *King Lear,* where the opponents observe the elaborate ceremony required by tradition. The Duke of Albany announces the arrest of Edmund for "capital treason." The two throw down their "gages," Albany to emphasize his charge and Edmund to defend his "truth and honor." Edmund asserts his right to have his innocence decided by combat, and a herald is called for, who declares formally that if "any man of quality or degree" will maintain that Edmund is a "manifold traitor," he should appear when the trumpet sounds three times. On the third note Edgar enters in full armor, his helmet hiding his identity, and the two exchange accusations, Edgar that Edmund has been "false to thy gods, thy brother, and thy father," and he in turn that he will "toss these treasons to thy head." They fight and Edmund falls, a dramatic illustration of the belief that right makes might and that the just cause will prevail in battle.

# The Soldiers

We find many young men eager to enter the fray, whatever the cause. Bertram, the Count of Rossillion in *All's Well That Ends Well,* looks on enviously as his fellow lords in the court of the French king march off to make a name for themselves in the wars of Florence, while he is forbidden to join them. Forced to marry Helena, much against his will, he defies the king's command and deserts her on their wedding day to seek fame in those same wars. A thoroughly despicable husband, he turns out to be a fairly competent soldier, eventually appointed to command the Florentine cavalry.

The Bastard, Philip Faulconbridge in *King John,* is the penniless son of an English knight who leaves his estate to his legitimate son Robert. Taken into the service of Queen Elinor, he looks forward to making a name for himself in battle and is delighted when the opportunity arises. The kings of France and England are embroiled in a controversy over the succession to the English throne, one that results in a confrontation between their opposing armies. To the disappointment and disgust of the Bastard, they arrive at a peaceful resolution to their disagreements, depriving him of the occasion to demonstrate his martial prowess. He scorns their timidity, condemning them for their surrender to "commodity," excessive self-interest or expediency, which has reduced them, he scoffs, "from a resolv'd and honorable war / To a most base and vile-concluded peace." Fortunately for him, the peace doesn't last, and when France invades England he is put in command of the defending forces.

In contrast to these aspiring young men, the Duke of Gloucester (later Richard III) has already achieved fame as a formidable fighting man, battling the forces of Lancaster to depose Henry VI and raise his elder brother to the throne of England as Edward IV. In the famous opening soliloquy of *Richard III*, Gloucester complains of his "winter of discontent" because of the "weak piping time of peace" that has followed the War of the Roses. He is, he says, ill-suited to court life because of his physical deformity—tradition has it that he had a hunched back and a withered arm. As a result he is not one to caper "nimbly in a lady's chamber / To the lascivious pleasing of a lute" or "strut before a wanton ambling nymph." In consequence, he concludes, with a touch of gleeful malice, "I am determined to prove a villain." The field of battle is an agreeable environment for all these aspiring figures.[7]

The lower ranks of the army, understandably, had a slant on war quite different from that of their contentious superiors. Some joined the forces willingly, moved to do so by an inspiring leader or a national cause, but others were motivated by less enviable concerns. The Roman legions were loyal to their commanders, a Pompey or a Caesar, because they were rewarded generously for their service with pay, or citizenship, or titles to land. And there was always profit to be had in the sacking and looting of cities. One of the most lucrative

---

7. Then, too, there is young Fortinbras, who in search of fame sets an army on the march to annex a worthless piece of Poland with a determination that arouses the envy of the introspective Hamlet.

opportunities for gain was the practice of ransoming prisoners. In the Middle Ages the nobility fought under the protection of a form of life insurance—they were worth more alive than dead. If a soldier could capture a well-heeled enemy, his life could be spared if he was able to pay for his release. At the battle of Poitiers (1356), Edward III captured the French king, John II, and escorted him back to London. He was treated there with every respect due his station, but his countrymen had to impoverish France to raise the enormous ransom required for his release, which they felt honor-bound to do.

By rights all prisoners taken in battle were the property of the king, who rewarded the captor in one way or another and then demanded a tidy ransom for the captive's freedom. In *Henry IV, Part 1,* a violation of this custom sparks the rebellion. Hotspur, fighting in the north, takes a number of Scots prisoner but initially refuses to turn them over to the king's agent. Later, taken to task by King Henry for his neglect, he explains that he was at the time "breathless and faint" from the exertion of battle and "smarting with my wounds being cold" when a court fop appeared, "neat and trimly dress'd, / Fresh as a bridegroom [and] perfumed like a milliner," demanding the prisoners. He lost his temper, he explains, and sent the dandy packing. The king is unmoved by the account, observing angrily that "yet he doth deny his prisoners" and warning Hotspur to deliver them "or you shall hear in such a kind from me / As will displease you." The volatile Percy is furious at the slight to his honor and vows vengeance for the affront.[8]

There were no standing armies in Shakespeare's time. The rulers recruited their forces when the occasion demanded, either to repel invasion, undertake a conquest, or put down a rebellion, and they were disbanded when the crisis had passed. Feudal lords were under an obligation to answer a king's call to arms, and they did so by marshaling their own lower nobility, who were similarly obligated

8. In *Henry IV, Part 2,* Falstaff takes Coleville of the Dale prisoner and turns him over to Prince John, asking that the prince give "a good report" of him in court. And in *Henry V,* as we shall see, the practice of ransom is a central concern.

to them. But somewhat different measures were employed to fill the ranks with foot soldiers. A "king's press" was proclaimed and captains dispatched to towns and villages, armed with lists of eligible men and funded with "coat and conduct" money, the "coat" to provide uniforms and the "conduct" to sustain them on the march to a rendezvous. This "press" was open to corruption, however, and acquisitive captains often seized the occasion for gain. A well-to-do landowner or merchant could either appoint a servant to be conscripted in a son's place or bribe the captain to release him from service.[9]

Shakespeare dramatized the practice in the *Henry IV* plays. Falstaff, appointed to raise "a charge of foot," in *Part 1*, admits in a soliloquy that he has "misus'd the King's press damnably." He has pocketed bribes from prospective recruits and been forced to empty the jails and drag beggars from the streets to fill his ranks. As a result he has a company of men, as he says, "as ragged as Lazarus," among whom "there's not a shirt and a half," this because he has neglected to supply them with "coats." When Prince Hal comes upon Falstaff's troops en route to the battle, he is shocked: "I have never seen such pitiful rascals." The fat knight shakes off his concern with callous bluster: "Tut, tut, good enough to toss, food for powder, food for powder; they'll fill a pit as well as better."

In *Part 2* we actually witness Falstaff in the process. Appointed once again to raise soldiers to oppose a later rebellion, he comes to Gloucestershire for the purpose and is assisted by Justice Shallow, who has corralled a group of eligible recruits. Falstaff enlists them all but then releases those who have the funds to buy their way out. The names of those finally "pressed"—Wart, Shadow, and Feeble— emphasize the fact that they are singularly unfit for military service.

In the plays, a victory is often hailed as ushering in a new era of peace and brotherhood for embattled subjects who have filled the

---

9. The practice of buying a way out of service was not limited to Shakespeare's time. The first American conscription act, passed in 1863 during the Civil War, made it legal by exempting any who could pay a fee of $300.

ranks of contending armies. Henry Tudor, after defeating Richard III, predicts that the death of the tyrant ensures that England will henceforth enjoy "smooth-fac'd peace, / With smiling plenty, and fair prosperous days." Edward IV is more exuberant after the final victory of the War of the Roses: "Sound drums and trumpets! Farewell foul annoy! / For here, I hope, begins our lasting joy!"

Just as often, Shakespeare lends emphasis to the cost of wars in the blood of common soldiers. When Bolingbroke unseats the king in *Richard II,* the Bishop of Carlisle warns that his impious deed will draw the wrath of God down upon England: "The blood of English shall manure the ground. / And future ages groan for this foul act," he rages, and "children yet unborn / Shall feel this day as sharp as thorn." The bishop proves prophetic, as Shakespeare foreshadows the War of the Roses, in which the toll in lives is indeed daunting. In *Henry VI, Part 3,* the victorious Edward IV observes with some satisfaction that on the Lancastrian side the casualties among the nobility alone include "three Dukes of Somerset," "two Cliffords," "two Northumberlands," the Earl of Warwick, and his brother Montague, to which may be added Henry VI and his son, Prince Edward. The king himself lost his father and young brother, Rutland. No mention is made of casualties among the lower ranks on either side, but the losses among the common soldiers, it is implied, were equally devastating.

# Henry V

Shakespeare's most complete survey of the grandeur, the banality, and the terror of war is *The Life of Henry V.* The play summarizes many of the aspects of armed conflict touched upon in his other works, and as such deserves close attention as his ultimate treatment of the theme. Some features are less in evidence. Chivalry, for example, is dead, except as displayed by the shallow French, who represent the fading era of the mounted knight, finally eclipsed by the sturdy English longbowmen. Further, there is no evidence of "the king's press" in the play; the soldiers we encounter are willing volunteers, though their motives for enlisting are sometimes questionable. And duplicity is restricted to the French, who bribe English nobles close to the king to assassinate him as he is about to embark on the campaign, a conspiracy fortunately discovered before it can be consummated.

But other qualities of war briefly addressed in other plays are more fully explored, those such as the persistence of ancient animosities, the cause, the ransoming of prisoners, the quality of soldiers, and the cost. And new dimensions are added: the use of terror and the destruction of a people's fabric of life.

*Henry V* is a controversial work. Many years ago the renowned scholar John Dover Wilson wrote that it "is a play which men of action have been wont silently to admire, and literary men, at any rate during the last hundred and thirty years, volubly to contemn." To one group Henry is an inspiring leader who unites his subjects in a grand enterprise and raises them to new levels of courage and resolve. To another he is a self-serving military adventurer intent upon personal glory, callously indifferent to suffering caused by his ambition. Wilson goes on to quote William Hazlitt, the nineteenth-century critic, who thought Henry "a brute and a hypocrite," and the Irish poet William Butler Yeats, surely no friend of English conquest: "He has the gross vices, the coarse nerves, of one who is to rule among violent people. . . . He is as remorseless and undistinguished as some natural force."[1] The play in fact can support either interpretation, and such extreme responses only attest to just how compelling a figure Henry V is.

The animosity between France and England had ancient roots. When William, the Duke of Normandy, conquered England in 1066, under the medieval system of feudal obligation he owed fealty

1. John Dover Wilson, ed., *King Henry V. The New Shakespeare*, general editor John Dover Wilson. (Cambridge: Cambridge University Press, 1968), pp. vii, xv–xvi.

to the French king, a duty subsequent monarchs of that country were not likely to forget. The two nations, separated by the narrow English Channel, were constantly in contention. In the 14th century, the English Edward III, Henry V's great-grandfather, laid claim to the French throne and invaded the country at will to assert his rights, humiliating the French at the battles of Crecy (1346) and Poitiers (1356). He eventually surrendered the demand, in exchange for several French provinces; and it is this claim that Henry V seeks to reassert.

*The Cause.* In the play, Henry V's motives for invading France are ambiguous. His fiery nobles urge him to undertake the expedition, but the youthful king feels the need of assurance that the cause is just. It is the Archbishop of Canterbury who finally sways him with a long, legalistic argument confirming that he has a sacred right to the French throne. Persuaded, he announces grandly that "by God's help" he will "put forth / My rightful hand in a well-hallowed cause."

Any conclusion about Henry's motives is complicated, however, by certain practical considerations that bear on the decision. There is some evidence in the play that he intends to enter into a war with France from the very beginning and is simply manipulating his subjects to agree to it. The reign of his father, Henry IV, was plagued by rebellious nobles and constant uprisings by the Scots, Irish, and Welsh; and in *Henry IV, Part 2,* the king, with his dying breath, advised his son "to busy giddy minds with foreign quarrels." Further, early in his reign Henry V expressed an intention to appropriate certain church lands. Canterbury commits a substantial sum to support the campaign, with the implication that he does so to distract the king from his threat. In the end the archbishop declares the cause just, but his motives raise a troublesome question: Is the king blackmailing the anxious church, or is the church bribing the youthful king?

As mentioned earlier, political leaders today who undertake an enterprise claiming that it is "the will of God" can well be suspected of hypocrisy or fanaticism, at least in the Western world; hence Henry's declaration of divine sanction may fall on modern ears as so much pious bombast. But in Shakespeare's era it was not so. An incident later in the play strongly implies that Henry's concern about the justice of his cause is a serious matter to him, an issue of vital importance not only to the king but to his soldiers.

On the night before the battle of Agincourt, the king roams through the English camp in disguise to reassure himself about the morale of his army. He comes upon a group of common soldiers and engages two of them, John Bates and Michael Williams, in conversation. Faced with the strong possibility that they may not survive the following days' encounter with the vastly superior French forces, they are contemplating the fate of their immortal souls should they be killed. Bates observes that "there are few die well, that die in battle: for how can they charitably dispose of any thing, where blood is their argument?" He comforts himself with the thought that if the king's "cause be wrong," their obligation to obey him "wipes the crime of it out of us," and that he will have "a heavy reckoning to make . . . at the latter day" when he must face divine judgment. Henry, of course, unwilling to bear this spiritual burden, argues against the notion and finally convinces them that "every man that dies ill, the ill upon his own head, the king is not to answer it."

This encounter, in which Bates raises the issue of the king's cause and expresses the belief that he is responsible not only for his soldier's lives but for the fate of their souls for all eternity, casts light on Henry's earlier concern about the justice of the enterprise and helps explain why he consults the Archbishop of Canterbury, the voice of God in the kingdom, on the matter. Later when he kneels to pray, he is anxious that in retribution for his father's role in the death of Richard II, God will not favor him in battle. "Not to-day, O Lord / O not to-day," he pleads, and lists the many measures he has taken in penance for the crime. All these factors would seem to indicate that when, after the battle, Henry declares, "O God, thy arm was here: / And not to us, but to thy arm alone, / Ascribe we all," he is uttering not just hollow, pious rhetoric but sincere belief. His cause was indeed just, and the victory confirms it: God was on his side.

*The Soldiers.* Aside from Bates and Williams, who appear to be sober and responsible young men, the common soldiers in *Henry V* are far from admirable. The king's speeches are indeed grand, and his allusion to his army as "we few, we happy few, we band of brothers" is quite moving. But Shakespeare gives us warfare whole, in all its splendor and brutality. The reality, he seems to say, is that the ranks of Henry V's army held their share of cowards, thieves, and shameless braggarts. The soldiers we see most frequently are a group of the king's old drinking companions from the Boar's Head Tavern, his accomplices in the pranks of a supposedly misspent youth (Falstaff, we learn, has died).

The chief comic character of *Henry V* is Pistol. He is an "ancient," or ensign-bearer, a rank somewhere between captain and the lower ranks, perhaps akin to a petty officer in the modern navy or a warrant officer in the army.[2] He plays the role of a *miles gloriosus,* a boastful soldier, quick to draw his sword and just as quick to put it away when in danger of injury.[3] Like his mentor, Falstaff, he enters the service for gain, planning to act as a "sutler" to the forces, selling provisions to soldiers at a substantial profit. As they leave, he exhorts his comrades: "Let us to France, like horse-leeches, my boys, / To suck, to suck, the very blood to suck." At the end of the play he receives a sound and much-deserved beating from Captain Fluellen, suffering injuries which, he says, he will later claim are marks of his valor at Agincourt. He survives the battle and Fluellen's beating, and decides to desert: "To England will I steal, and there I'll steal."

Pistol's companions are less fortunate. Bardolph and Nym are

2. Iago is Othello's ancient.
3. Parolles is another, in *All's Well That Ends Well.*

hanged for looting, which the king had expressly forbidden, and the Boy is killed in a French raid on the English encampment. It is the Boy who takes the proper measure of the lot. Bardolph, he says "is white-livered and red-faced . . . but fights not"; Nym "never broke any man's head but his own, and that was against a post, when he was drunk"; and Pistol "hath a killing tongue, and a quiet sword." "They will steal any thing, and call it purchase," he concludes, and so "I must leave them, and seek better service."

In the king's stirring speech, urging his soldiers to attack "once more unto the breach" blown in Harfleur's battlements, he ends observing that "I see you stand like greyhounds in the slips, / Straining at the start." But in the very next scene, in an ironic comment on his expectations, we see his straining "greyhounds," Pistol, Nym, Bardolph, and the Boy, making every effort to avoid the dangerous "breach." The Boy wishes he "were in an alehouse in London" rather than in the heat of battle, and Pistol agrees: "If wishes would prevail with me, . . . thither would I lie."

We are also introduced to the captains of the army, who, unlike Falstaff, seem to be competent professionals. Shakespeare gives them all distinct personalities. The chief figure is the pedantic Welshman Fluellen, a by-the-book soldier who complains that the campaign is not being conducted in accordance with "the disciplines of the pristine wars of the Romans." Among them are the sturdy Irishman, Macmorris, who chaffs at inaction—"we talk, and, be Chrish, do nothing, 'tis shame for us all"—the loyal Scot Jamy, and the levelheaded Englishman Gower. They represent the various ethnic groups that had so troubled the reign of Henry's father, and their presence in the army in relative amity is evidence of his son's achievement in uniting them in common cause.

On the eve of Agincourt, as the king wanders through his camp, providing his soldiers with "a little touch of Harry in the night," Shakespeare gives us a quick glance at all the levels of his army. Henry starts out with brief words for his royal brothers, Gloucester and Bedford, and then encounters Sir Thomas Erpingham, who represents the loyal nobility in his service. Next he comes upon the pompous Pistol, an ancient, and then moves on to overhear an exchange between two of his captains, Fluellen and Gower. Lastly he enters into conversation with the common soldiers Bates and Williams. Thus in *Henry V,* Shakespeare offers a panoramic view of a medieval army, staging the defiant speeches of the king, the loyal dedication of captains and nobility, the solemn commitment of some soldiers, and the shameless cowardice of others.

*Ransom.* The practice of ransoming prisoners, alluded to briefly in *Henry IV, Parts 1 and 2,* figures more prominently in *Henry V.* The play features a number of long speeches before battle. In two of them, the French herald Montjoy asks the king to name his ransom beforehand. It is an arrogant taunt on the part of the supremely confident French, but it has a practical purpose. Henry's soldiers know full well that a man of his station is worth more alive than dead, hence is likely to survive the battle; and Montjoy's suggestion is designed to loosen the bond of loyalty between the king and his men. Henry answers the herald evenly: "My ransom is this frail and worthless trunk." But when Montjoy returns with the same taunt, the king seizes the occasion to deliver a defiant speech, directed not so much to the herald as to his own troops, rousing them with the prospect of victory: "Good God!" he exclaims, "why should they mock poor fellows thus?" and goes on:

> We are but warriors for the working day:
> Our gayness and our gilt are all besmirched
> With rainy marching in the painful field.
> . . . . . . . . . . . . . . . . . . . . . . . . . . . . .
> But, by the mass, our hearts are in the trim.

"Come no more for ransom, gentle herald," he concludes, "they shall have none, I swear, but these my joints."

The French herald's mocking suggestion that the king name his ransom has apparently reached the ears of some of his soldiers, however, and seems to have had the desired effect. At the close of his conversation with Bates and Williams, the disguised Henry remarks that he heard "the king say he would not be ransomed." The practical-minded Williams has his doubts on the matter: "Ay, he said so, to make us fight cheerfully: but when our throats are cut, he may be ransomed, and we ne're the wiser." The retort angers Henry, and the two come near to blows. But they agree to postpone their argument until after the battle and exchange "gages" (gloves), symbolic of a challenge to fight over the issue.

The very next scene following Henry's dismissal of the herald is a parody of the practice of ransom, an ironic comment on what has just transpired. Pistol takes a French prisoner and threatens to kill him unless he pays for his release. It is a comic interlude in which the ancient mangles the Frenchman's language and must call upon the Boy to translate for him. The prisoner pleads that he will pay two hundred crowns in ransom, so Pistol relents—"I will some mercy show"—and leads him off. The Boy concludes the scene with another observation about the posturing ancient: "The empty vessel makes the greatest sound."

The incident may cast some light on a controversial episode in the play, one that Shakespeare adopted from the chronicles of the time. On the day of the actual battle, the French formed into three lines, each of which outnumbered Henry's entire army. The English managed to repel the assault of the first two, but the third showed signs of preparing to renew the attack. As the play is staged, we see Henry only twice during the battle, and on both occasions he gives a startling command. The first occurs when he observes that "the French have reinforced their scattered men" and appear to be preparing for another assault. Fearing that his exhausted soldiers may not prevail if faced with a fresh attack, the king orders each of them to "kill his prisoners." According to modern codes of war, such an act would constitute a "crime against humanity," but under the circumstances at the time the order may appear justified. Many of the English, like Pistol, had probably taken prisoners and marched them to the rear, where in expectation of ransom they stood careful guard over their investment. The king desperately needed every man on line to meet the anticipated attack; but if he simply ordered his men back to their battle positions, he would leave a dangerous body of enemy soldiers roaming freely on his rear flank. If he wanted his soldiers back in their ranks, he had no alternative but to have them kill their prisoners.

When we next see Henry, he repeats the order, but under different circumstances entirely. During the battle a force of French cavalry raids the English camp, killing all the boys left to guard it. When the king comes upon the scene, he is enraged and orders his men to cut the throats of all their prisoners and any others that may surrender, vowing that "not a man of them that we shall take / Shall taste my mercy." In one case, the order may be justified as a desperate measure demanded by the fortunes of battle; in the other, it is given in anger, a brutal response to an atrocity by committing another in reprisal. And yet both are in the text of the play! A modern director can take his pick, it seems, depending on whether he chooses to portray Henry V as the model of a Christian king or, to recall the judgment of William Hazlitt, as "a brute and a hypocrite."

*The Cost.* Shakespeare balances his celebration of this famous victory of Henry V with vivid descriptions of the barbarous conduct of warfare in the Middle Ages and the destruction it inflicted on the land and its people. The siege of Harfleur and the battle of Agincourt in 1415 were actually only the opening events in a five-year campaign that ended in 1420 with the Treaty of Troyes. In the play, Shakespeare skips over the intervening years and goes directly from the battle to the peace treaty, in which the elderly French king is forced to declare Henry his heir and relinquish control of his country to the English. But those years between were devastating for France.

The most vivid portrayal of the heartless brutality of war is

Henry's speech to the governor of Harfleur at the end of the city's siege. Harfleur held out for several months and opened its gates only when it became evident that the French king did not intend to come to its aid. Sieges were a common occurrence in medieval wars, when towns and castles were protected by formidable walls built to discourage attack. Cannon were still primitive weapons, largely ineffective against sturdy embattlements, and the chief tactic against fortified cities was to mine them, burrowing under the walls to plant explosives that shattered their foundations.[4] Besieging forces were often as distressed as the citizens of the defending city. Armies compelled to remain static for long periods were soon rife with disease because of insufficient supply and the lack of disciplined sanitation. Once he has successfully reduced Harfleur, Henry decides to curtail his campaign for the year and return to England because of his army's deterioration. With "the winter coming on, and sickness growing / Upon our soldiers," they will conduct a march through Normandy to the English-held port of Calais and embark for home.

The king urgently needs to reduce Harfleur, and he has no qualms about using terror as a weapon in his effort to do so. In a parley with the governor he paints a frightening picture of what will happen to its citizens should the city refuse to surrender. When there was obviously no possibility of relief, besieged cities had two alternatives: They could open their gates under a promise of "Quarter," an arrangement under which the commander of the occupying forces agreed to keep his soldiers under control. If continued resistance forced the besieging army to take the city by storm, however, it would receive "no Quarter," that is, the soldiers would be free to "sack" it, to rape, burn, and plunder at will. It was often the prospect of such an opportunity that attracted fair-weather soldiers like Pistol, Bardolph, and Nym to enlist in the first place.

Henry threatens the governor of Harfleur with just such a sack-

4. In *Henry V* the pedantic Fluellen complains that the mining of Harfleur is not being conducted properly, that is, "not according to the disciplines of the war."

ing should he fail to surrender, and the words Shakespeare gives him
are chilling:

> The gates of mercy shall be all shut up,
> And the fleshed soldier, rough and hard of heart,
> In liberty of bloody hands, shall range
> With conscience wide as hell, mowing like grass
> Your fresh virgins, and your flowering infants.

These depredations did not necessarily take place because a commander condoned them, or even because he chose to turn a blind eye
on the actions of his "fleshed soldiers." In storming a fortified city,
officers would almost always lose control of their troops, whose
blood lust was fueled by danger and the spectacle of destruction.
Henry urges surrender "whiles yet my soldiers are in my command,"
and charges that the governor himself will be responsible for the
consequences of further resistance. And he describes what will occur
in even more lurid detail. The lines defy paraphrase:

> . . . why, in a moment look to see
> The blind and bloody soldier with a foul hand
> Defile the locks of your shrill-shrieking daughters:
> Your fathers taken by the silver beards,
> And their most reverend heads dashed to the walls:
> Your naked infants spitted upon pikes,
> Whiles the mad mothers with their howls confused
> Do break the clouds.

The governor wisely submits. But we may well ask if this
paragon of a Christian prince would have permitted such a holocaust. As mentioned, the sack of a city was not an uncommon occurrence in his era, and he may have been unable to prevent it anyway.
For the threat to have any force, the governor must have been convinced that Henry was fully capable of such brutality, and we may
be assured of it as well.

The cost in battle casualties receives special attention in the play. Henry recites a long list of "French / That in the field lie slain," numbering some ten thousand and including an impressive catalog of their nobility. Shakespeare reduces the number of English losses to four lords and "but five and twenty" others, a significant undercount since the chronicles of the war place the figure at a more realistic sixteen hundred. But the ten thousand French dead is faithful to contemporary accounts. They never did learn how to deal with the English longbowmen. Stubbornly committed to the supremacy of the mounted knight, they insisted on riding heedlessly into a hail of arrows. The cream of French chivalry fell to Crecy, Poitiers, and Agincourt.

Shakespeare included yet another passage describing the devastation of war. At the peace treaty the Duke of Burgundy acts as mediator between the French and English monarchs. He urges them to end the conflict, painting a sad picture of the effect a five-year military campaign can have upon the land and people of the contested territories. Again, the impact of these moving lines would be lost in a paraphrase:

Burgundy asks:

What rub, or what impediment there is,
Why the naked, poor, and mangled Peace,
Dear nurse of arts, plenties, and joyful births,
Should not in this best garden of the world,
Our fertile France, put up her lovely visage?

He goes on to describe the effect of war on the land:

Alas, she hath from France too long been chased,
And all her husbandry doth lie in heaps,
Corrupting in its own fertility.
Her vine, the merry cheerer of the heart,
Unprunéd, dies: her hedges even-pleached,
Like prisoners wildly over-grown with hair,
Put forth disordered twigs: her fallow leas

The darnel, hemlock, and rank fumitory
Doth root upon; while that the coulter[5] rusts,
That should deracinate such savagery.

And the people:

And as our vineyards, fallows, meads, and hedges,
Defective in their natures, grow to wildness,
Even so our houses, and ourselves, and children,
Have lost, or do not learn, for want of time,
The sciences that should become our country;
But grow like savages, as soldiers will,
That nothing do but meditate on blood,
To swearing, and stern looks, diffused attire,
And everything that seems unnatural.

These final lines conjure up modern images of grinning twelve-year-olds proudly displaying their rifles in Beirut, the Congo, the jungles of Myanmar, and the mountains of Afghanistan.

Whatever effect Burgundy's moving words may have on Henry, he has no intention of winning the war and losing the peace. Indeed, if peace is what the French want, he answers coolly, it can be bought only "with full accord to all our just demands."

The causes of wars, then, are as varied as the figures that embrace them. Some fight in defense of their homeland, others in pursuit of power and conquest, and still others are spurred by ancient grudges handed down mindlessly from generation to generation. Some mount wars in angry resentment, others to rid their country of a tyrant. Zealots embark on sacred missions, ambitious nobles aspire to a crown, loyal servants dutifully follow their masters, and young men enlist to test their manhood. There is no single cause of war in Shakespeare or elsewhere. It's just not that easy.

5. The plow.

Thus Shakespeare gives us warfare whole. We witness the exhilaration of the victor and the despair of the vanquished. We encounter both brave men and cowards, both loyal soldiers and parasites, some devoted to the cause, others no more than pompous charlatans. We hear of the glories of conquest as well as the barbarity of marauding armies. The spectacle is at once splendid and banal, evoking both admiration and horror.

But Shakespeare does not venture to say whether it should or should not be thus.

He simply says—it is.

# MADNESS AND
# MELANCHOLY

❧

THE YOUNG SHAKESPEARE had only to pass by the walls of Bedlam Hospital (St. Mary of Bethlehem) to know that the human
mind can be twisted beyond recognition. As he left London through
Bishopsgate on his way to attend performances at the Theatre or the
Curtain in Shoreditch, he could not help but hear the anguished
cries of inmates in the nearby lunatic hospital. That huddled mass of
deranged minds was not his only evidence, however, that there are
those among us not quite right in the head. Every village seemed to
house its own idiot, generally harmless, whom the citizens not only
condoned but nurtured, in the belief that he was a gift from God or
a being endowed with otherworldly insight.

Our response to an encounter with the insane is mixed. We look
upon them somewhat fearfully as creatures capable of unpredictable,
potentially harmful behavior. But we also pity them as human beings who have lost the sacred gift of reason, a blight more tragic
than the loss of sight or hearing or limb. We are inclined to avoid
them, however, turning aside with a revulsion that transcends any
impulse of Christian charity, too well aware that the delicate balance
of any brain can be upset by events beyond its control. It is with
these conflicting emotions of fear, pity, and revulsion that any theater audience will respond to the spectacle of insanity on the stage.

In Shakespeare, madness is marked by unnatural or erratic behavior and outwardly incoherent speech; and it arises largely from three causes. The first is an accumulation of sorrows that the spirit cannot continue to bear. The second is the superstitious belief that the forces of darkness can possess the mind and transform it into an agent of evil. The last is the conviction that a state of melancholy, if not relieved, can decline into madness. Some of Shakespeare's characters actually do go mad, as is the case with Lear and Ophelia. Some feign madness for one reason or another, as do Edgar in *King Lear* and Titus Andronicus. And others are accused of possession by demons, as are Malvolio in *Twelfth Night* and Joan of Arc in *Henry VI, Part 1.* Hamlet deserves special consideration, since Shakespeare leaves the balance of his mind open to question.

The word "mad" occurs frequently in the plays, but more often than not in contexts that have nothing to do with insanity. In some instances it is uttered in affectionate approval of comic behavior. The gravedigger hands Hamlet the skull of Yorick, his father's jester, with an appreciative chuckle: "A pestilence on him for a mad rogue! 'A pour'd a flagon of Rhenish on my head once." On other occasions the word is used to admonish someone who seems to have temporarily taken leave of his good sense. When Artemidorus approaches Julius Caesar in the Forum to deliver a letter warning of the conspiracy to assassinate him, the great man dismisses him imperiously: "What, is the fellow mad?" And at times it merely connotes anger, as in *Henry IV, Part 1,* when Hotspur taunts the Welshman, Glendower, and Mortimer cautions him: "Peace, cousin Percy, you will make him mad." In these instances "mad" refers to behavior that is either antic or rash or wrathful; but our concern here is the theme of real or feigned insanity.

# Madness

The chief cause of insanity in Shakespeare's plays is grief. There are other contributing factors, of course, but essentially the spirit cannot survive the impact of a succession of emotional blows, and the mind, unable to accept the realities confronting it, retreats into fantasy. King Lear endures a series of painful revelations about his position in his family and kingdom, and his mind seeks refuge in insanity rather than acknowledge the truth of them. First, his favorite daughter, Cordelia, refuses to profess her love for him in a public assembly, and he flies into a rage, disowning her: "I have no such daughter!" Next, having divided his kingdom between Goneril and Regan, the two daughters who have so eloquently confirmed their devotion, he finds that they turn against him. They heartlessly press upon him the realities of his state—he has grown old and, having surrendered his kingdom, no longer wields the power of the crown. Finally, when they refuse him shelter during a raging storm, he wanders aimlessly on the heath, where the elements themselves seem to assault him in pitiless mockery of his helpless state.

Lear's Fool, with his riddles and quips, attempts to force reality on the old king. It was folly, he insists, to give his daughters "the rod, and put'st down thine own breeches"; and he concludes "thou shouldst not have been old till thou hadst been wise." But Lear rejects the facts that stare him in the face, aware, it seems, that to accept them will overwhelm his spirit. When he contemplates his injustice to Cordelia—"I did her wrong"—and the apparent ingratitude of his other daughters, he thrusts the thought from his mind: "O let me not be mad, not mad, sweet heaven!"

Indeed, it is Lear himself who foreshadows his own descent into madness. When Goneril and Regan deny him his train of a hundred knights, an unmistakable sign of his loss of royal authority, he refuses still to accept the fact that he is powerless. He rages at them, threatening some unspoken revenge, but finally falls into despair: "O fool, I shall go mad!" As he suffers the assault of swirling wind and rain, he accuses the elements of conspiring with his daughters to destroy him, "a poor, infirm, weak, and despis'd old man." The storm leaves little doubt of his helpless condition, and as reality encroaches upon his consciousness, he realizes that the truth will shatter him: "My wits begin to turn." He is obsessed by the thought of his abusive daughters: "The tempest in my mind / Doth from my senses take all feeling else / Save what beats there. Filial ingratitude!" Again realizing the danger, he vainly attempts to expel the thought: "O, that way madness lies; let me shun that!"

In a masterful instance of Shakespeare's command of dramatic action, Lear is finally thrust over the edge when he is confronted by insanity itself. Gloucester's son Edgar has assumed the guise of a madman, a "Tom o' Bedlam," to escape his father's wrath; and he suddenly appears before Lear, uttering gibberish about his affliction by "the foul fiend." The king's wits turn at the sight of "poor Tom," in whom he sees a kindred spirit, one, he exclaims, who could have been brought "to such a lowness" only by the betrayal of "his unkind daughters." He resists the urgings of the loyal earls of Kent and Gloucester to seek shelter, insisting that he would rather "talk with this philosopher," this "learned Theban" and "good Athenian" in whose deranged ramblings he detects a sympathetic mind.

Ophelia is driven mad by a similar series of unsupportable blows. First, her father forces her to reject the amorous advances of Prince Hamlet, who, it would appear, has captured her affection. She is further unsettled by his strange behavior toward her, and then she is compelled to take part in a scheme in which she acts as bait for the prince. She is placed where he is bound to encounter her while her father and the king hide to observe his reaction to her. When they meet, she must submit to Hamlet's torrent of abuse. "Get thee to a nunnery," he rages, and,

> I have heard of your paintings,[1] too, well enough. God hath given you one face, and you make yourself another. You jig, you amble, and you lisp, you nickname God's creatures, and make your wontonness your ignorance. Go to, I'll no more on 't; it hath made me mad.

1. Cosmetics.

Ophelia is distraught by his tirade: "O, woe is me, / T' have seen what I have seen, see what I see!" Her tender spirit is finally shattered when she learns that her former lover, whom she has been forced to reject, has murdered her father. She may not know how or why, but this latest assault on the balance of her mind is too much for it to bear.

Shakespeare endows his mad men and women with a degree of wisdom, as if to say that the loss of reason strips away a layer of pretense, allowing the demented mind a penetrating insight into the human condition that the sane are blind to. Lear in his madness is particularly gifted in this regard. His first illumination comes when he sees the apparently deranged Edgar, dressed perhaps only in a loincloth, his body and hair matted with mud, babbling inanities about "the foul fiend." Lear gazes on his naked squalor and observes: "Thou art the thing itself; unaccommodated man is no more but such a poor, bare forked animal as thou art." Lear in his madness recognizes a melancholy truth of the human condition and attempts to enact the role of an "unaccommodated man," tearing at his own clothing. "Off, off, you lendings! Come, unbutton here."

In the scenes that follow, Lear reveals a heightened sensitivity to creatures of the natural world—the mouse, the wren, "the small gilded fly," the fitchew (polecat), and the horse—and he exhibits a new awareness that they share the globe with mankind. It is a sensitivity that survives his return to reason, as when he speaks of his imprisonment with Cordelia: "We two alone will sing like birds i' th' cage." Later cradling her dead body, he mourns the fact that "a dog, a horse, a rat have life, / And thou no breath at all."

And Lear gains insight into the role of a king, one of whose functions is to administer justice. He recognizes that judges must look with compassion on the failings of human nature and dispense mercy with their justice. Condemn a man to death for adultery? No, look about you, he says: "The wren goes to 't, and the small gilded fly," as does the fitchew and the horse. In his newfound wisdom, he perceives that those who judge are often as guilty as those they punish: "See how yond justice rails upon yond simple thief . . . which is the justice, which is the thief?" He urges an officer charged with punishing a whore to "strip thy own back," since "thou hotly lust'st use her in that kind / For which thou whipp'st her." Further, he observes that wealth protects the mighty from penalties that the poor must suffer for the same offense: "Through tatter'd clothes small vices do appear; / Robes and furr'd garments hide all." In Shakespeare, insanity and wisdom are never very far apart.

Lear and Ophelia portray insanity in very different ways, most obviously in the fact that he recovers from his fit and she does not. Lear emerges from his madness under the tender care of his daughter, Cordelia; but Ophelia is beyond comfort. She enters the court in a distracted state, singing songs about the losses that have reduced her to this pitiable condition. She alludes to Hamlet's harsh rebuke—"How should I your true love know / From another one?"— and the death of her father—"He is dead and gone, lady, / He is dead and gone." But her sorrows also seem to have endowed her with insight. The stunned members of the court, immobilized by pity, can only look on as she distributes flowers among them, each one of which has a special significance. Rosemary is for remembrance and pansies for thought. She offers the queen rue, symbolic of sorrow, and remarks cryptically, "you may wear your rue with a difference." Of particular significance, she gives the guilty Claudius a daisy, the emblem of faithlessness, and regrets that she has no violets, flowers of the faithful, since "they wither'd all when my father died." Ophelia dies when she falls into a brook where, either unmindful or uncaring of the danger, she drowns. The queen describes death brought on by madness in lines of incomparable poignancy:

> Her clothes spread wide,
> And mermaid-like awhile they bore her up,
> Which time she chanted snatches of old lauds,
> As one incapable of her own distress,
> Or like a creature native and indued
> Unto that element. But long it could not be
> Till that her garments, heavy with their drink,

Pull'd the poor wretch from her melodious lay
To muddy death.

We should not forget the figure who is perhaps the best-known madwoman in all literature, Cassandra, Priam's daughter in *Troilus and Cressida*. The myth has it that she was beloved by Apollo, who bestowed on her the gift of prophecy; but then she rejected him, and in retaliation he imposed the condition that no one would ever believe her. She makes two brief appearances in the play, the first during a debate among the Trojans over whether they should return Helen to her husband, Menelaus, and end the war. She enters raving: "Cry, Trojans, cry! A Helen and a war! / Cry, cry! Troy burns, or else let Helen go." They disregard her, of course; Troilus insists that "Cassandra's mad," and Helen stays in Troy. Later she attempts to persuade Hector to avoid entering battle. She seems more composed on this occasion, and others urge upon him her prediction that should he arm himself and go forth, all will "cry, Hector! Hector's dead! O Hector!" He rejects her pleas, however, and in that day's battle he encounters Achilles and his Myrmidons, who slay him. Shakespeare's Cassandra may or not be mad—the actress can play it either way—but she is certainly disturbed by her visions and upset that no one pays her heed.[2]

Thus madness in Shakespeare is a form of escape from emotional blows too harsh for the mind to bear. But it has a way of clearing the mind as well, allowing it to penetrate the façade of supposed justice and virtue with which we seek to mask the less admirable qualities of human nature. Shakespeare's mad men and women, having lost the ability to perceive reality as we know it, gain a kind of second sight which enables them to see the truth behind it.[3]

2. When Troy falls, Agamemnon claims Cassandra as a prize and carries her back to his palace in Argos. She warns him that his wife, Clytemnestra, will kill him, but again he dismisses the prediction. Clytemnestra does, and she dispatches Cassandra as well, events dramatized in *Agamemnon* by Aeschylus.

3. In later pages we shall consider yet another character who suffers madness, the jailer's daughter in *The Two Noble Kinsmen,* who succumbs to lovers' melancholy.

# Feigned Madness

Of Shakespeare's characters who only appear to have lost their wits, two assume the guise of madness and one has madness thrust upon him. Titus Andronicus engages in bizarre behavior, to all outward appearances reduced to a distracted state by the loss of his sons and the rape and mutilation of his daughter Lavinia by the Empress Tamora's two sons. His remaining son, Lucius, is marching on Rome at the head of a powerful army of Goths, intent upon avenging his family's disgrace. Tamora conceives of a plot to lure Lucius to his father's house, where he can be dealt with treacherously. She calls upon Titus disguised as the symbolic figure of Revenge and accompanied by her sons who are costumed as Rape and Murder. Titus recognizes them but, assuming the role of a man demented by grief, he pretends to accept their mythic identities and to believe the fiction that they have been "sent from th' infernal kingdom" to work vengeance on those who have caused his suffering. He agrees to Tamora's scheme to invite Lucius to a parlay in his house when she proposes to deliver the emperor, his wife, and her sons into his power.

Titus, still pretending to be taken in by the disguises, arranges for Lucius to attend, but then he insists that Rape and Murder remain with him while Revenge lures the imperial family to his house. Tamora, convinced that she is dealing with a madman who is completely deceived by their disguises, agrees to his demands and leaves confident that she has entrapped Lucius. The charade of insanity bears fruit when Titus kills the two sons, bakes their bodies in a pie, and offers it to Tamora and the emperor at a dinner served during their meeting with Lucius.

Perhaps the best-known instance of feigned madness is the aforementioned masquerade of Edgar as "Tom o' Bedlam" in *King Lear.* His father, the Earl of Gloucester, has been misled by his half-brother Edmund into believing that Edgar is plotting his death so

as to inherit the title. When the earl angrily orders his son apprehended and executed for his supposed treachery, Edgar assumes the
disguise of the demented Tom to evade capture. The result, as he
puts it, is that "Edgar I nothing am." Lear comes upon him during
the storm, where his imitation of madness is so convincing that it
deceives his father and convinces the king—who loses the last shred
of his sanity at the sight of Tom—that he is a sympathetic spirit.

Edgar's incoherent babbling is the most graphic example in
Shakespeare of the belief in demonic possession as a cause of insanity. He pretends to be a man who has sinned mightily: "Wine lov'd
I deeply, dice dearly; and in women out-paramour'd the Turk." In
punishment for his crimes, he raves, he has been possessed by the
"foul fiend," who has led him "through fire and through flame,
through ford and whirlpool, o'er bog and quagmire," finally reducing him to his present deranged state. Try as he might, he cannot
evade the fiend under whose influence he "eats cow-dung for sallets;
swallows the old rat and ditch-dog; [and] drinks the green mantle of
the standing pool." Demonic possession, in brief, compels him to
behavior that defiles his humanity.

In a comic twist on demonic possession, Malvolio, the officious
steward in *Twelfth Night,* is the victim of a trick devised by the
maidservant Maria, who convinces him that his mistress, Olivia, is
in love with him. Supremely confident of Olivia's affection, he appears before her garishly dressed in a fashion he has been led to believe she favors. But she is aghast at the sight of him and, convinced
that he has taken leave of his senses, entrusts him to the care of her
uncle, Sir Toby Belch, who despises the steward and is a party to the
deception. Sir Toby adopts the stance that Malvolio is possessed, and
he prescribes the customary treatment of the disorder, incarceration
"in a dark room and bound."[4]

Sir Toby enlists the aid of Feste, the "Clown," to plague Malvo-

4. Rosalind, as the skeptical youth Ganymede in *As You Like It,* prescribes
the same treatment for lovers: "Love is merely a madness, and, I tell you, deserves
a dark house and a whip as madmen do."

lio. Feste assumes the role of a cleric, Sir Topas, who speaks with the steward through a small barred window so that his identity is concealed. The clown impersonates a preacher fearful of the presence of a "dishonest Satan" in Malvolio, who has reduced him to madness. The steward complains that he is imprisoned in a dark room, but Sir Topas insists that "it hath bay windows" that let in ample light. Malvolio pleads his sanity, but Sir Topas finally abandons him: "Fare thee well. Remain there in darkness."

Shakespeare thus toys with the idea of insanity as a condition caused by demonic possession, a belief of the time sanctioned by Scripture.[5] The poet seems doubtful of the notion, however, since he attributes the distraction only to those who pretend to its effects or are unjustly accused of it.

## *Melancholy*

It was a common belief within the medical profession of Shakespeare's time, such as it was, that a prolonged bout of melancholy, if not remedied, could lead to madness. In the plays the malady is most frequently described as a consequence of lovesickness, the despair experienced by the rejected lover.[6] In *Hamlet*, Polonius is uncharacteristically succinct in his description of the prince's response to Ophelia's rejection:

> And he, repelled—a short tale to tell—
> Fell into a sadness, then into a fast,
> Thence to a watch, thence into a weakness,
> Thence to a lightness, and, by this declension,
> Into the madness wherein now he raves.

In *As You Like It,* Rosalind, in disguise as the youth Ganymede, undertakes the task of curing Orlando of his love; and she fabricates an

5. See, e.g., Matt. 8:16; Mark 1:34; Luke 7:21.
6. See pp. 9–11 for a more ample discussion of the "lovesickness."

account of her success with the therapy on a former occasion. She had worked upon a lovesick youth, she claims, until "I drove my suitor from his mad humor of love to a living humor of madness, which was, to forswear the full stream of the world and live in a nook merely monastic." Her remedy for the madness of love, it would appear, is the equally mad rejection of the world.

Again, in *Twelfth Night,* Viola, disguised as the page Cesario, enters the service of Duke Orsino, and he quickly takes her into his confidence. Her situation is complicated by the fact that she has fallen in love with the duke but cannot reveal her devotion. She must remain silent because his affections are engaged elsewhere in pursuit of his beautiful but unresponsive neighbor, Olivia. What's more, were she to admit to her identity she would be dismissed from his service and denied his company. In her sad dilemma she seizes upon an occasion when they are discussing love—the duke can talk of little else—to say something, if only by indirection, of what is in her heart. She invents the tale of her sister who was in love with a man but was unable to express it, and so pined away in silence:

> She never told her love,
> But let concealment, like a worm i' th' bud,
> Feed on her damask cheek. She pin'd in thought,
> And with a green and yellow melancholy
> She sat like Patience on a monument,
> Smiling at grief.

The distracted maiden of her tale, she implies, eventually died of her sorrow. The duke remains oblivious to her oblique confession, of course, his thoughts occupied only with Olivia; but Viola may have gained some release from the pain of her unrequited love simply in the telling of it.

In the medieval tradition of the lovesickness, upon which Shakespeare drew for his figures afflicted by melancholy because of rejected love, some driven to distraction, others to death, the principal victims of the malady are young men. As we have seen, several figures from the plays eloquently describe its effects; but the only one who comes to mind that actually descends into madness because of unrequited love is a woman, the jailer's daughter in *The Two Noble Kinsmen*. In Chaucer's "The Knights Tale," Shakespeare's source for the play, two cousins, Palamon and Arcite, fall in love with Emily, but they are in prison and know her only by sight. Arcite is released and declines into melancholy with all the debilitating symptoms of lovesickness because he is deprived of the sight of her. In adapting the tale for the stage, Shakespeare left Arcite hearty and hopeful and introduced Chaucer's theme of lovesick melancholy in the person of the jailer's daughter. She arranges for Palamon's escape because she has developed a passion for him: "I love him beyond love and beyond reason, / Or wit, or safety." She then follows him into the forest with food and clothing but cannot find him. Distressed by his apparent lack of gratitude for her sacrifice, she wanders about, increasingly distracted: "I am mop'd,[7] / Food took I none these two days— / Sipp'd some water. I have not clos'd mine eyes." Finally, concluding that Palamon has been "torn to pieces" by wolves, she goes mad, fantasizing that she witnesses a shipwreck in the middle of the forest. In later scenes she sings and speaks incoherently, but under the care of her father and a faithful lover she is finally nursed back to health.

Thus in Shakespeare it is chiefly women who sink from a lover's melancholy into madness or death, Viola's invented maiden "with a green and yellow melancholy" (perhaps a future she sees for herself if she cannot profess her love for Orsino) and the demented jailer's daughter. Hamlet's harsh rejection of Ophelia certainly distresses her, but she loses her mind only when he kills her father. It would be unwise, though, to conclude from this pattern that Shakespeare regarded women as more weak-willed than their male counterparts. The plays include too many resolute women who pursue their way-

7. Bewildered.

ward lovers and cleverly succeed in capturing or recapturing their affections. In *All's Well That Ends Well,* Helena follows the callously uncaring Bertram through Italy and France to claim him as her husband; Imogen endures countless dangers to return the foolish Posthumus to his senses in *Cymbeline*; and Julia adopts a disguise to win back Proteus in *The Two Gentlemen of Verona.*

No, there are too many clever, strong-willed women in Shakespeare's plays for us to entertain the notion that he thought them too delicate to endure the sorrows of melancholy. The reason that his male figures do not descend into madness may lie in the manner in which he portrays the melancholy induced by unrequited love. The desolate young man, mooning over his unresponsive mistress, is as much a figure of fun today as he was in Shakespeare's time. Romeo is comic in the opening scenes of the play, rambling on, to the ill-concealed amusement of his friends, about the peerless qualities of Rosaline; and in *As You Like It,* Silvius is endearingly pathetic in his pursuit of the scornful Phebe. The lovesickness in Shakespeare's male characters is not fatal—it is intended to provoke laughter. Madness is not amusing, however; it is more likely, as mentioned, to provoke feelings of fear, pity, and revulsion in an audience. Hence to reduce any of these delightfully addled young men to incoherent babbling would surely compromise the comic effect. Rosalind, in the guise of the practical-minded youth Ganymede, scoffs at the notion that a rejected lover is in danger of expiring from melancholy: "Men have died from time to time, and worms have eaten them, but not for love."

# *Hamlet*

Shakespeare leaves the balance of Hamlet's state of mind an open question. On the one hand, he suffers enough emotional blows in a short space of time to send any young man over the edge. In swift succession, his revered father dies; his mother marries his uncle with unseemly haste; her husband assumes the crown, denying the prince his inheritance; he is visited by his father's ghost, who reveals that his uncle, Claudius, now his stepfather, is a regicide, having murdered the king so as to marry his widow and seize the throne; the ghost pledges him to avenge the murder, a cause he undertakes with a mixture of righteous anger and reluctance; and on top of all this Ophelia rejects him. There is certainly enough turmoil in those few weeks to unhinge him.

Seen otherwise, Hamlet has an agile and resourceful intelligence and is quick to devise ingenious schemes to deceive his intended victims and defeat those who threaten his life. He pretends to assume an "antic disposition" to deflect any suspicion of his hidden intent; he alertly detects those who spy on him; he stages a play to "catch the conscience of the king"; and he uncovers a plot on his life, cleverly turning the instrument of his murder against the king's agents (who, however, are innocent of their role). He is physically vigorous and skilled with his weapon, defeating an opponent impressively in a duel. He is courageous, leading an assault on a pirate ship and then, once captured by the renegades, shrewdly enlisting them in his service. In brief, he seems to be a thoroughly competent young man, in full control of his faculties and intent upon avenging his father's murder.

The central question of the play is why he doesn't just do it. Stage productions attempt to answer the question in essentially two ways, presenting the figure as what we may call "the melancholy Dane" or alternately "the active Hamlet." Those who offer him as the "Dane" depict a man so overcome by the burden of his sorrows as to be paralyzed in his will, driven at times to demented behavior that gives every appearance of one who has taken leave of his senses. He is wracked with conflicting emotions, possessed with a fierce anger at the treacherous murder of his father but immobilized by some unnamed reluctance to kill his murderer. Alternately, in productions that offer "the active Hamlet" he is an energetic figure single-mindedly intent upon vengeance but thwarted in his efforts to get at the king, who is constantly surrounded by an attentive court.

The setting of the two best-known film versions of the play illustrate the different approaches to the figure. In Laurence Olivier's production (1948), Elsinore is a dark brooding castle with dimly lit corridors, hidden recesses, and immense pillars, providing concealment for any lurking assassin; but Hamlet, disabled by inner turmoil, cannot bring himself to act. In Kenneth Branagh's later film (1996), Elsinore is a spacious nineteenth-century palace, full of light and bustling activity. The king is constantly in the company of a crowded court, and a determined Hamlet is frustrated in his efforts to waylay him. Shakespeare offers both Hamlets, of course, and stage productions often seek a middle ground between them, leaning toward one or the other in accordance with the vision of the actor in the part and his director. The two interpretations intersect in the critical scene where the vengeful prince finally comes upon the king alone, absorbed in solitary prayer. Hamlet, at the very moment when he is about to honor his pledge to the ghost, pauses in the act, prevented by a sudden thought, or alternately by a subconscious reluctance to carry it out.

Our concern here is madness, so we shall dwell on that side of this enigmatic equation. The question is whether or not Hamlet's wits are turned by the sorrows heaped upon him. He is certainly not the man he once was. After her turbulent encounter with Hamlet, Ophelia sadly recalls his former stature:

> O, what a noble mind is here o'erthrown:
> The courtier's, soldier's, scholar's eye, tongue, sword,
> The expectancy and rose of the fair state,
> The glass of fashion and the mold of form,
> Th' observ'd of all observers, quite, quite down!

We catch hints here and there, especially from Horatio, of the high regard in which Hamlet is held, and Claudius remarks on "the great love the general gender bear him." It is evident that the Hamlet we see is not himself. He rages at or heaps scorn upon every significant figure he meets, except for the king, from whom he has reason to conceal his intent, and Horatio of course. As he acknowledges to Rosencrantz and Guildenstern, "I have of late—but whereof I know not—lost all my mirth, foregone all custom of exercise," with the result that "man delights me not—no, nor woman neither."

Hamlet displays irrational behavior on five occasions during the play, one that we hear of and four that we witness. It is safe to omit from the list his encounters with Polonius, since Hamlet obviously toys with the man, pretending to incoherent speech and then dismissing him contemptuously: "These tedious old fools!" Aside from these exchanges, he is wildly erratic in his encounters with the ghost of his father, Ophelia, his mother, Queen Gertrude, and Laertes, the son of Polonius.

Hamlet's demented behavior after seeing the ghost certainly startles his companions, as he demands that they swear on his sword to remain silent about the visitation. He scrambles back and forth from one side of the stage to another in response to the movement of a subterranean voice intoning "Swear!" a command that he alone may hear, leaving his companions all the more bewildered by his behavior. But to see a ghost is an unsettling experience in itself, and this one appears in the guise of his dead father, who relates a tale of treacherous murder, cause enough for Hamlet's wild words and actions. He cautions his friends that he may at times "put an antic disposition on" in the future, though whether this is a belated excuse for his unnatural behavior or a conscious design to conceal his purpose is a matter left in doubt. The remark certainly colors our perception of his later "antics."

Hamlet's encounters with Ophelia bear all the marks of a disordered mind. His first response to her rejection bears resemblance to the traditional symptoms of the lovesickness, the young man sunk in melancholy by unrequited love. She describes their encounter tearfully to her father:

He took me by the wrist, and held me hard,
Then goes he to the length of all his arm,
And with his other hand thus o'er his brow,
He falls to such perusal of my face
As 'a would draw it. Long stay'd he so.
At last, a little shaking of mine arm,
And thrice his head thus waving up and down,
He rais'd a sign so piteous and profound
As it did seem to shatter all his bulk
And end his being.

Hamlet's actions here seem no more than the customary anguish of the rejected lover, but when he next sees Ophelia, in a scene that we witness, he is something else entirely. "I did love you once," he says, and then cruelly, "I lov'd you not." He then flies into a rage, shouting over and over, "get thee to a nunnery" and raving, "I say we will have no more marriages" in resentful anger at her rejection. This is not the courtly lover, rambling on about the peerless beauty of his unresponsive mistress, wallowing in his melancholy, but the uncontrolled rage of the once-intimate suitor, stung by her betrayal.

The state of Hamlet's mind is open to interpretation, depending on how the scene is staged. If he is portrayed as aware that the king and Polonius are nearby, overhearing every word, it may be said that he puts "an antic disposition on" for their benefit. Staged thus, his frantic verbal assault on Ophelia may also be seen to arise from the anguished realization that she is playing a part in a conspiracy against him. His mother has betrayed him by marrying his uncle, and now his former lover betrays him by her apparent complicity in a scheme to entrap him. The pain of these revelations, when added to his secret knowledge of his father's murder, is too much for him to bear, and he lashes out at her in an intemperate outburst that poses a serious question about the balance of his mind. If, however, it is apparent that Hamlet is unaware of the eavesdroppers, we are left with an equally troubling spectacle of anger that seems far in excess to the rejection that has caused it—his wild words convey the impression that something else torments his distracted spirit. It is puzzling that, in sharp contrast to the tone of this scene, when Hamlet next meets Ophelia, at the performance of *The Murder of Gonzago,* he is far more composed. Rather than accept his mother's invitation, he chooses to sit by Ophelia and jests with her seductively about "a fair thought to lie between maids' legs."

The next instance of Hamlet's irrational behavior takes place in the scene where he attends his mother in her bedchamber, or "closet." He restrains her roughly and hears someone cry out from behind the room's wallhangings. Drawing his sword impulsively, he runs it through the fabric, only afterward discovering that it is Polonius he has killed. Seemingly indifferent to what he has done, he turns on his mother with uncontrolled rage, accusing her of betraying his father by marrying his brother so soon after her husband's death. The son is outraged that his mother shares a bed with her new husband and demands that she no longer do so, advising her disdainfully to "assume a virtue, if you have it not." This obsessive concern about his mother's sexual life echoes a sentiment we have heard earlier in the play. When we first see Hamlet, he is deep in melancholy, and the royal couple, convinced that he is grieving inordinately over his father's death, attempt to relieve his despair. When they leave him alone, we learn what is really bothering him—the hasty remarriage of his mother: "O, most wicked speed, to post / With such dexterity to incestuous sheets!"

The final episode in which Hamlet seems to lose control of his judgment takes place when he jumps impulsively into Ophelia's grave and wrestles with her brother, Laertes, who is embracing her for the last time. Stung by Laertes' display of grief, Hamlet challenges him wildly, shouting that he loved Ophelia more than "forty thousand brothers." He is so highly wrought that he demands of Laertes, "what is the reason that you use me thus? I lov'd you ever"—entirely unmindful, it would appear, that he has killed the young man's father. The shocked onlookers drag the two apart, and the troubling scene ends.

A judicious assessment of the balance between madness and sanity in Hamlet during these instances of apparently irrational behavior will necessarily note that four of his five outbursts are precipitated by encounters with the two women in his life, the single exception being the visitation of his father's ghost. His final tirade is triggered not by Laertes, whom he has no reason to dislike—as mentioned, he seems to have forgotten that he killed the man's father—but by the news of Ophelia's death. He is distraught by the loss, and perhaps by the agonizing realization that he may have been responsible for it.

The possibility that any imbalance of Hamlet's mind has something to do with his relationship with women has suggested to some that Hamlet is in the grip of a deeply repressed sexual desire for his mother, a desire that triggers his sharp anger at her remarriage. This interpretation draws heavily on Freud's theories, particularly his diagnosis of the Oedipus complex.[8] It offers some justification for Hamlet's irrationally explosive behavior at different stages of the play, his harsh treatment of both women, his violent reaction to the news of Ophelia's death, and his apparent inability, or unwillingness, to devise a plan to kill the king.

Is Hamlet mad, then? It is certainly safe to say that he is emotionally unstable and demonstrates the highs and lows of one under severe stress. He has moments when he loses control of his senses under the heavy burden of demands upon his spirit or of a passion he does not fully understand—but it cannot be said that he is mad. For one thing, Shakespeare was well aware that the death of a madman, that is, the loss of a human being who has already lost that which makes him human, will fail to arouse a tragic sense in his audience. We may feel pity, of course, as we do on the news of Ophelia's death, but not the stunned awe of those who witness the

8. See pp. 33–34.

needless destruction of a being much like themselves. To offset the impression of madness suggested by his grappling with Laertes in Ophelia's grave, the poet presents an uncharacteristically composed Hamlet in the opening episodes of the final scene, a man, one might say, very much his old self. Here he is as he once was, in full command of his emotions, confident in his skill at swordplay, witty, charming, and contemplative. He seems content to leave the outcome of his cause in the hands of fortune and falls to melancholy musings on the inevitability of death. "There's a special providence in the fall of a sparrow," he reflects, and then stoically: "If it be now, 'tis not to come; if it be not to come, it will be now; if it be not now, yet it will come. The readiness is all." He is calmly resigned to whatever fate has in store for him, and indeed fate decrees that "it will be now."

Shakespeare explores the theme of madness in all its dimensions. It may arise in men and women from any number of causes and is manifest in a variety of forms. It could result from unsupportable sorrows or unrequited love (he seems skeptical about the notion of demonic possession); it could be real or feigned, tragic or comic, fatal or transitory. And by some contradictory trick of nature, those who are out of touch with reality gain an insight denied the sane. It is as if a film drops from their eyes, one that familiarity grows there over the years, and they can finally see people and events for what they are. In his madness Lear discovers the reality of "unaccommodated man," finds sympathy for the natural world, and learns to temper justice with mercy. Ophelia detects the faithless one in the court of Elsinore; and Cassandra, though all believe her mad, voices the truth.

# THE PRINCE

❧

IN SHAKESPEARE, rulers come in many grades, though the great majority of them are either kings or dukes. But there are also princes (*Pericles, Romeo and Juliet*), emperors (the Roman plays), generals (*Othello, Coriolanus*), senators (*Julius Caesar, Coriolanus, Timon of Athens*) and a governor (*Much Ado About Nothing*). And they come in many guises, some benevolent or inspiring, some tyrannical, and others simply bungling.

This pageant of princes in Shakespeare's plays was enormously popular with the theatergoers of his time, most of whom may have caught no more than a brief glimpse of a monarch in royal procession. They were as fascinated by what went on in the halls of power as are modern citizens who consume intimate memoirs by recent White House aides or watch the currently popular TV series, "The West Wing." How do kings, queens, and learned counselors talk to one another, they surely wondered, and how do they arrive at nation-shaking decisions? It is a mystery how Shakespeare came to be acquainted with such matters. When, as an aspiring playwright, he was composing his *Henry VI* plays, it is doubtful that he had even seen the inside of a royal court. Yet his scenes have the ring of authenticity to them, even for modern audiences, few of whom, like their Elizabethan predecessors, can say they have ever addressed a king, or a queen, or a cardinal.

The term "prince" is used here in the Machiavellian sense of anyone who rules or aspires to rule over a city or state. In his fa-

mous, and infamous, little book, *The Prince,* Niccolò Machiavelli offered advice on two matters chiefly: how to gain power and how to
keep it. Shakespeare may not have read the work, since the first English translation was published twenty-five years after his death, but
he may have had access to it in other languages. He was certainly familiar with Machiavelli's demonic reputation, however. When the
Duke of York learns that Joan la Pucelle (Joan of Arc) is pregnant by
the Duke of Alençon in *Henry VI, Part 1,* he exclaims contemptuously, "Alençon! that notorious Machiavel!" And in *Part 3* the Duke
of Gloucester (later Richard III) is sardonically confident that he can
"set the murderous Machiavel to school." The references are somewhat anachronistic since *The Prince* was not published until 1532,
many years after the time frame of the plays, but the meaning is unmistakable.

Shakespeare found many of his plots in contemporary histories
like Raphael Holinshed's *Chronicles of England, Scotland, and Ireland*
(1577) and ancient works like Plutarch's *Parallel Lives of Greeks and
Romans.* But the plays abound in characters who seem to follow
Machiavelli's counsel on methods of attaining a crown, though
many of their princes appear to ignore his chapters on how to keep
it. It is perfectly reasonable to assume that in reading the histories
available to him, Shakespeare would have come to some of the same
conclusions about emperors, kings, and princes that Machiavelli did
in his time. The two have much in common, at any rate. In examin-
ing Shakespeare's rulers we shall therefore loosely adopt Machiavelli's concerns, though not his words, since, as mentioned, there is
some question whether the poet was familiar with them. So in this
survey of Shakespeare's theme of kingship we shall consider the
poet's pageant of the lives and deaths of rulers in terms of how they
gain power, how they keep it, and how they lose it.

# Gaining Power

To borrow the distinctions in Machiavelli's *The Prince*, let us first consider the various ways in which a ruler may come to power in a state. He can, of course, inherit the crown, much to be desired in maintaining the peace of a kingdom, but seldom the case in Shakespeare. The only peaceful transition in the plays seems to be that between Henry IV and his son, Prince Hal. The others are all troubled by the practice of primogeniture, which requires that the eldest son of the king, whatever his age, succeed to the throne. All too frequently in the plays, though, the heir is too young to rule, and as the citizen remarks in *Richard III*: "Woe to the land that's govern'd by a child!" Though not recorded in the play, Richard II assumed the throne at the age of eleven, and during his minority he was dominated by his powerful uncles, the proud warrior sons of Edward III. His resentment at the control they exercised over him may be felt in the play, however, by his apparent complicity in the murder of the Duke of Gloucester and his confiscation of the estates of both Gloucester and Lancaster upon their deaths. Henry VI, but nine months old when he inherited the crown of his famous father, became in his maturity an ascetic recluse, bewildered by the conflicts of ambitious nobles that swirled about him, and in his weakness he sowed the seeds of the War of the Roses. On the death of Edward IV in *Richard III*, his son of the same name succeeds him at the age of twelve, providing ample room for his uncle Richard "to bustle in."

Thus Shakespeare on the lawful succession of kings. He has more to say, however, about those who scheme to replace incumbent rulers. Henry Bolingbroke, in *Richard II*, is a classic example of one who seizes power by force. He returns from banishment on the death of his father on perfectly legal grounds, he says, and claims that he has no higher purpose than to claim his rightful inheritance as Duke of Lancaster, thus giving himself and those who flock to his cause legitimate cover for raising an army against the king. Richard, returning from his campaign in Ireland, is dismayed to find that his Welsh allies, tiring of his delay, have dispersed; and he is confronted with Bolingbroke at the head of a substantial body of armed men. The king is compelled to accede to Bolingbroke's claims, but by then it is too late for the restored Duke of Lancaster to settle for anything less than the crown. By coming with an armed force to assert his rights, he has committed an open act of treason, and were he to stop short of deposing Richard he would be inviting certain future retaliation. So he pursues his rebellion to the end, as he knows he must.

It is a cardinal principle of these dynastic struggles that the old king must die so that the new may confidently reign. No nation can escape civil strife with two contending monarchs within its borders. Shakespeare's Roman tragedies offer the most extensive dramatizations of the theme. Before the opening of *Julius Caesar*, Pompey and Caesar, each with his loyal army of legions and citizen supporters, alternately occupied the city of Rome. Caesar prevailed ultimately, and in the opening scene of the play, angry tribunes berate the fickle Romans, scolding them because not long before they had greeted Pompey with a "universal shout" and now celebrate Caesar's triumph. The conflict evolves into a struggle for power between the ruling Senate and a Caesar ambitious to reign as king, a controversy the senators resolve by assassinating Caesar. His heir, young Octavius, allied with Mark Antony, who had revered the great man, overpower the Senate. Determined to eliminate the body once and for all as a symbol of Roman rule, they embark on a merciless campaign of assassination and exile against the members and their families—even Cicero must die. And they crush the last remnant of the Senate's authority by defeating the forces of Brutus and Cassius at the battle of Philippi.

The victory leaves Octavius and Antony co-emperors of Rome, the arrangement in place at the opening of *Antony and Cleopatra*.[1] It

---

1. Lepidus, the third member of the so-called Second Triumvirate, is inconsequential, and Caesar soon disposes of him. Octavius is called "Caesar" in the play.

is an uneasy alliance. In an effort to patch over their growing animosity, it is agreed that Antony will marry Octavia, his fellow emperor's dearly loved sister. But after a period of relative calm, Antony deserts her to be reunited with Cleopatra, precipitating an irreparable breach between the two. Great armies then contend for the rule of Rome, and Octavius emerges from the wars as the "sole sir o' th' world." Even wide-ranging Rome proved too small for two emperors.

Again, two kings compete for the crown of England in *Henry VI, Part 3*. Edward, the Duke of York, defeats the Lancastrian Henry VI and mounts the throne as Edward IV. The deposed king is held prisoner in the Tower while the powerful Earl of Warwick undertakes a mission to France to arrange a dynastic marriage between Edward and the king's sister. Warwick is enraged when he learns that during his absence Edward has married Lady Grey. Stung by what he considers as an unpardonable betrayal, he persuades the French king to supply him with an army to unseat Edward. Warwick returns to England, defeats the Yorks, releases Henry, and restores him to the throne.[2] Edward escapes to the Continent, where he secures the aid of the Duke of Burgundy, returns to England with his borrowed soldiers, defeats Warwick at the battle of Tewkesbury, and resumes the throne. The York faction does not make the same mistake twice, however. They slaughter the Prince of Wales, Henry VI's son and heir, and imprison the king once more in the Tower, where this time, to forestall any further resistance, Gloucester (later Richard III) assassinates him. Having crushed all opposition, Edward IV then enjoys a peaceful reign, untroubled by any further Lancaster designs on the throne.

Thus when two contending figures aspire to rule, only one will prevail. This enduring principle raises a question about the ending of *The Tempest*. Prospero, by his "so potent art," arranges for his treacherous brother, Antonio, and Alonso, the King of Naples, who

2. Warwick was called "the king maker" because he was instrumental in Edward's success and then replaced him with Henry.

had conspired to depose him as Duke of Milan, to be shipwrecked on his magic island. The wizard casts a spell on them so that, as he remarks with solemn satisfaction, "at this hour / Lies at my mercy all mine enemies." But he then forgives them! Persuaded that "the rarer action is / In virtue than in vengeance," he absolves them of their crimes—Alonso, who had used him "most cruelly," and an unrepentant Antonio, "unnatural though they art." With Prospero restored to his dukedom, they agree to return to Italy as the curtain falls. But will Milan remain at peace for long with an envious brother a constant presence in the court? The havoc such a figure can cause is evident in *Much Ado About Nothing.* Don Pedro generously pardons his brother, Don John, for raising a rebellion against him, allowing the sullen malcontent complete freedom as they return from the war. Still resentful of his defeat, Don John schemes to subvert the prospective marriage between Claudio and Hero and almost causes a fatal duel between two of his brother's young officers.

The king must die; and those who fail to do away immediately with their deposed predecessors and their heirs soon live to regret their neglect. As we have seen, Edward IV is forced to fight his battles all over again to regain the throne from Henry VI because he failed to dispose of the king in the first place. In *Richard II,* Henry Bolingbroke compels the king to surrender the crown and mounts the throne of England as Henry IV. He has Richard imprisoned in the Tower but almost immediately finds himself the target of a plot to unseat him and restore the deposed king, a scheme that even involves a member of the royal family, his cousin, Aumerle, the son of the Duke of York. Exasperated by such conspiracies, he is heard to ask: "Have I no friend will rid me of this living fear?" Sir Pierce of Exton, who counts himself "the King's friend," interprets the remark as a royal sanction, and he assassinates Richard in his cell. History suspects Henry of collusion in the murder, but Shakespeare exonerates him. Exton, expecting reward, receives a rebuke instead. The king freely admits that "I did wish him dead" but goes on to voice regret for the deed: "I hate the murthurer, love him murthured," and piously commits himself to a pilgrimage to the Holy Land "to wash this blood of from my guilty hand."[3]

Thus those who rule or aspire to rule are well advised to dispose of a figure who may serve as a symbol around which potential opposition may rally. Brutus and Cassius resort to the assassination of Caesar. Richard III cuts down a string of relatives that stand in his way to the throne. He either kills, or has killed, Henry VI and his son, his own brother Clarence, the queen's brother and son, his wife Anne, and, having secured the crown, his young nephews Edward V and his brother. *As You Like It*'s Duke Frederick deposes and banishes his brother, Duke Senior; but he later thinks better of his leniency and leads "a mighty power" into the Forest of Arden to "put him to the sword."

Some who aspire to power, motivated by ambition or vengeance, or both, scheme to undermine the incumbent regime by inciting the people to rebellion. The most memorable instance of a successful effort to do so is Antony's speech to the Roman citizens, whom he addresses over the bloodstained corpse of Caesar. He makes his peace with the assassins, some of whom, conscious of his devotion to Caesar, want to kill him as well. But the noble Brutus, anxious that they be seen as "sacrificers, but not butchers," dissuades them and even allows Antony to deliver a eulogy for the dead man—on the condition, however, that he utter no criticism of his murderers. Antony agrees, opening his speech with the assurance that he comes "to bury Caesar, not to praise him," but he then proceeds to do just that. He sprinkles his lines with the reference to the assassins as "honourable men," but he does so with such frequency and with mounting irony that the words eventually take on their opposite meaning. He rouses the crowd to a frenzy, reminding them of Caesar's greatness and generosity, finally reading them his will in which

3. Others suffer because of the same neglect. Macbeth is unable to dispatch Duncan's son, Malcolm, who escapes to England and returns with an army to rid his homeland of the tyrant. And, of course, Antonio is forced to restore Prospero to his dukedom.

he leaves his wealth and property to the people. As they roar off in pursuit of the assassins on a rampage of burning and killing, Antony surveys his handiwork with sardonic satisfaction; "Mischief, thou art afoot, / Take thou what course thou wilt!"

In another instance the Duke of York is directed to raise an army to put down an Irish uprising in *Henry VI, Part 2.* Before he leaves, however, he incites an illiterate clothier, Jack Cade, to lead a peasants' revolt against the king by persuading him that he is the rightful heir to the throne. The rebels occupy London but are persuaded to disperse just as the duke returns from his Irish campaign. The revolt provides him with an excuse to keep his army intact and, backed by his soldiers and allies, he confronts the king and lays claim to the throne.

Shakespeare is not sympathetic to the clamoring mob that can be swayed this way or that by rousing oratory, pretense, or promise of gain. The people, he seems to say, are too easily misled. An eloquent old Clifford addresses Jack Cade's "rabblement," reminding them of their devotion to the king, while Cade answers him, urging them to pursue the revolt. They respond enthusiastically to whoever speaks last, greeting Clifford's words with shouts of "God save the king! God save the king!" and Cade's with "We'll follow Cade, we'll follow Cade!" Clifford is the more persuasive, and as the peasant army dissolves, Cade mutters in bewilderment, "was ever feather so lightly blown to and fro as this multitude."

One of the most outrageous, and successful, efforts to sway a crowd is the charade that the Duke of Gloucester (Richard III) puts on to persuade the citizens of London to accept him as king. In a performance stage-managed by Richard's loyal advocate, the Duke of Buckingham, he appears on a balcony above, prayerbook in hand and flanked by two bishops; and he piously rejects the offer of the crown, pleading that he prefers a life of spiritual contemplation. Finally persuaded to mount the throne, he asks the citizens to witness "how far I am from the desire of this." The mayor acknowledges his reluctance, "God bless your Grace! We see it, and will say it," and when Buckingham cries out, "Long live King Richard!" all respond, "Amen."[4]

In the plays, the shouted demands and rampaging violence of a mob of enraged citizens invariably have devastating consequences. Antony's speech, for example, precipitates fifteen years of civil strife in the empire, and York's claim to the throne sparks England's destructive War of the Roses. In another instance, when Coriolanus returns from his successful defense of Rome against the invading Volcians, the Senate proposes to reward him with appointment to the powerful office of Consul. The citizens at first accept him, but their tribunes, Sicinius and Brutus, citing his arrogant contempt for the common people, persuade them to invade the Capitol and arrest him. "This mutiny," as Brutus calls it, results in the banishment of Coriolanus, who in a towering rage joins the enemy Volcians and is given command of their army. He returns vengefully, threatening to destroy Rome.

Nor does the poet seem to have much confidence in the rule of a senate. It proves powerless to control the unruly mob, as we have seen in *Julius Caesar* and *Coriolanus,* and is often forced to submit to the rule of a dominant figure. In *Timon of Athens,* the Athenian Senate infuriates Alcibiades by refusing to pardon one of his officers who has slain a man in defense of his honor. Irritated by their general's insistence, the Senate banishes him, only adding fuel to his anger. In retaliation, he returns with his army, provisioned by Timon's gold, and lays siege to Athens. The Senate crumbles, opening the city gates to Alcibiades on condition that he execute only a "destin'd tenth" of its citizens, those who have wronged Timon and himself. In *Julius Caesar,* Antony and Octavius, employing

4. In like manner, Henry Bolingbroke seems determined to undermine the authority of Richard II with, as the king complains, "his courtship of the common people," to persuade them that "our England [is] in reversion his, / And he our subjects' next degree in hope."

exile and assassination, virtually eliminate the Roman Senate as a factor in the governance of the empire. Such bodies in Shakespeare prove to be, in the words of an anonymous wit, "a hotbed of cold feet."

## Keeping Power

Once in the seat of power, Shakespeare's princes discover that they must devote all their time and energy to keep it. They find they must be constantly on their guard against the envy of others no less ambitious than themselves, a threat that in their minds justifies resorting to any device, legal or illegal, honorable or dishonorable, to stabilize their reign. If, to gain a crown, they found it necessary to dispose of incumbents and potential competitors, they must be equally ruthless once on the throne. A prince who seizes power by force is a model for others to emulate—if it can be done once, it can be done again. In *Richard II,* Henry Bolingbroke, Duke of Lancaster, leads an army against the king and forces him to abdicate the throne. When Bolingbroke assumes the crown in Richard's stead, his reign is plagued by rebellions from within and without England. In *Henry IV, Part 1,* the Percies of Northumberland, Hotspur and his father the earl, who had been among his most staunch supporters in securing the crown, grow to resent his high-handed rule. Having learned perhaps from his example how easy it is to topple a king, they form an alliance with northern English nobles, the Scot Douglas, and the Welsh leader Owen Glendower, to replace him on the throne with their own choice, the Earl of March. The revolt fails only because of divisions within the rebel ranks.

Again, Macbeth gains the crown of Scotland by murdering King Duncan and is ever after convinced that others plot his death in turn. He keeps spies in the houses of all his thanes and visits a reign of terror on the kingdom by striking out at the families of any he suspects of disloyalty, indiscriminately ordering the murder of innocent women and children. He reasons, again, that if he can do it, others can as well.[5]

But how does a monarch retain his power in a land beset with ambitious adversaries and resentful nobles? In *Henry IV, Part 1,* the king advises his son and heir, Prince Hal, that he must gain the admiration of his people. He chastises Hal for consorting with his common subjects, the carousing thieves and drunkards of Falstaff's company in Eastcheap. The prince will never gain the respect of his people, the father tells him, by becoming "so common-hackney'd in the eyes of men, / So stale and cheap to vulgar company." Hal, he counsels further, should follow his own example in courting his subjects. He did so, he says, "by being seldom seen," so that when he did appear in public, "I could not stir but like a comet I was wond'red at." By keeping his presence "fresh and new," he "did pluck allegiance from men's hearts." Henry's advice runs somewhat counter to modern democratic practice, wherein elected officials are styled as "servants of the people" and mingle with their constituents at every opportunity; but it may have been appropriate for medieval monarchs. Later, in *Part 2,* the king on his deathbed, lamenting his "poor kingdom, sick with civil broils," advises Hal further on measures to avoid the factions and divisions that plagued his reign: "Be it thy course to busy giddy minds / With foreign quarrels," he urges his son, "to waste the memory of former days." It is counsel not unknown to modern presidents and prime ministers.

Hal seems to heed his father's dying advice when as Henry V he unites England in a campaign against France, but he appears to ignore the king's counsel to avoid the company of common people. In *Henry IV, Part 2,* he cannot resist the appeal of Falstaff and returns to the Boar's Head Tavern for more unrestrained gaiety in his company. Indeed, his ability to relate to his common subjects seems to enhance their affection for him. It strengthen his soldiers' loyalty to

5. The most able of monarchs will not shy from duplicity to strengthen their hold on power, e.g., Prince John in *Henry IV, Part 2* and Caesar in *Antony and Cleopatra,* for which see pp. 38–39.

him in *Henry V*, as he discovers while making his way among them in disguise on the eve of the battle of Agincourt, bestowing on each level of his command, as the Chorus tells us, "a little touch of Harry in the night." Pistol acknowledges that he reveres "the lovely bully," and the young soldier Bates confirms that he is determined "to fight lustily for" the king. His experience has taught him to appreciate the value of a dedicated captain like Fluellen, despite his rather stiff-necked pedantry: "Though it appears a little out of fashion, / There is much care and valor in this Welshman." And he is perfectly at ease when he sits down by a campfire with the ordinary soldiers of his army to converse with them about the impending battle and the justice of their cause.

Some of Shakespeare's princes win the love of their people. Duncan is so revered by his Scot subjects that Macbeth, contemplating the consequences of killing the king, fears they will be appalled at his death and "pity, like a naked new-born babe . . . shall blow the horrid deed in every eye, / That tears shall drown the wind." The play contains a glimpse of another beloved monarch, Edward the Confessor, the venerated king of England at the time. Malcolm reports that he has seen him dispensing "the king's evil," a public ceremony in which his touch is thought to cure his subjects' illnesses. Shakespeare alludes to the custom to contrast Edward's ability to heal his people with Macbeth's poisonous infection of his.[6]

Here and there in the plays, Shakespeare includes brief scenes illustrative of leadership techniques that a prince may employ to ensure the loyalty of his subjects. Prominent among them is the practice of rewarding those who serve him faithfully. Malcolm, for example, as he accepts Macbeth's recaptured crown, announces that all the thanes who joined him in overthrowing the tyrant will be elevated to the feudal rank of earl. Edward IV, having deposed Henry VI yet a second time, appoints his brothers, Richard and George, to

6. And Julius Caesar gains the allegiance of the Roman people with liberal gifts to them, a generosity that Mark Antony dwells upon in his speech to arouse their anger against his assassins.

be Dukes of Gloucester and Clarence. In *Richard III*, Gloucester promises the Duke of Buckingham that when he is king he will assign him the earldom of Hereford as a reward for his allegiance; and though he later breaks his word, Buckingham becomes indispensable in helping him to the crown.[7]

Another device is to appoint a subordinate to perform what might prove to be unpopular duties of his office. In *Measure for Measure,* the Duke of Vienna realizes that he has been lax in enforcing laws of the city. As a result, its citizens have become so indifferent to authority that, as he says, "liberty plucks justice by the nose." The time has come to restore respect for the law in Vienna, but he prefers it be done so that none of the consequences of a new rigid enforcement will be blamed on him. To that end he announces that he will travel abroad for a time. He deputizes the upright Angelo to act in his stead during his absence "to enforce or qualify the laws / As to your soul seems good." Angelo, an austere, puritanical, but loyal, servant to the duke, fulfills his charge by turning his attention to the moral laxity in the city and orders strict enforcement of the Viennese law forbidding fornication. He closes down the brothels in the suburbs and condemns to death a young man, Claudio, for impregnating his wife-to-be prior to the wedding. And he carries out this oppressive cleansing of the city, again according to his charge, without casting any discredit on the duke.

An astute prince, moreover, while appointing a deputy to take the heat for unpopular policies, will ensure that he himself receives full credit for any significant achievement in warfare or government. An equally astute subordinate will attribute his own triumphs to the skill and wisdom of his prince. Antony's general, Ventidius, defeats the Parthians in battle but refrains from pursuit of their retreating army. When urged to do so, he cautions that there is such a thing as being too successful: "Better to leave undone, than by our

7. These elevations do not always have the desired effect, however. When Henry VI restores the title of Duke of York to Richard Plantagenet, his generosity only serves to inflame the duke's ambition to replace his benefactor on the throne.

deed / Acquire too high a fame when him we serve's away." No, Ventidius says, he will permit the Parthians to retire and return to Athens, where he will credit the victory to Antony, whose "name / That magical word of war," he will acknowledge, inspired their success.

## Losing Power

Shakespeare's princes are toppled for any number of reasons. Some are foolish, some are too trusting, others neglect their office, and still others are simply inept. King Lear's folly in dividing his kingdom between his daughters Goneril and Regan is evident from the outset. The old man, some eighty years of age by his own admission, wants to "shake all cares and business" of the throne but still "retain / The name and th'addition to a king." The loyal members of his court dare not cross the powerful monarch in the matter, and it is left to his Fool to chide him for making "thy daughters thy mothers—for then thou gav'st them the rod and put'st down thine own breeches." Unlike Lear, who surrenders power, the folly of Titus Andronicus is to refuse it. He turns down the offer to serve as emperor of Rome in favor of Saturninus, whose lascivious appetites he is blind to. His refusal to accept the office precipitates a series of events that includes, by rough count, fourteen murders, two mutilations, a rape, a mother served her sons' bodies baked in a pie, and finally his own death.

Among those who trust too well is King Duncan in *Macbeth*. At the opening of the play, Scotland is under attack by a rebellion within and an invading army led by the King of Norway. Duncan is distressed to learn that the Thane of Cawdor, "a gentleman," he says, "on whom I built / An absolute trust," has betrayed him by allying himself with the Norwegians. Macbeth, Duncan hears, first put down the rebellion, and, turning on the invading forces, has defeated them as well. As a reward for Macbeth's valor, the king be-stows on him the title and lands of the disloyal thane, ironically leading to his betrayal by two perfidious Cawdors.

Henry V does not lose his crown, but he receives a harsh lesson on whom he can and cannot trust. In preparation for his invasion of France, Henry gathers his forces in the port city of Southampton, and there, on the eve of their departure, learns of a conspiracy on his life. Three of his trusted courtiers, tempted by French gold, plot to assassinate him in a scheme to prevent the invasion. He uncovers the conspiracy and has them put to death, but not before angrily condemning one of them, Lord Scroop, with whom he was especially close, a man, he rages, that "did bear the key of all my counsels, / That knew'st the very bottom of my soul." Scroop's treachery, in the king's eyes, is like "another fall of man." He can never again put his trust in another, since one in whom he has placed such unquestioned confidence has proven traitorous.

Some of Shakespeare's princes are simply inept. The prince is constantly beset with challenges to his rule, and if he fails to devote all his thought and energy to maintaining it, he will soon find himself deposed. Henry VI is hopelessly inadequate on the throne. He inherited the crown from his father as a nine-month-old infant and grew up under the domination of his warlike uncles. He is bewildered by his contentious nobles, little understanding that his own weakness encourages them to revive old animosities that divide his kingdom into warring factions. An unworldly and reclusive man, Henry can only plead with them to heal their differences. Confronted with his feuding uncles, the Duke of Gloucester and the Bishop of Winchester, he appeals to them ineffectually, "I would prevail, if prayers might prevail, / To join your hearts in love and amity," and piously, "blessed are the peacemakers on the earth." Later, in the face of the Duke of York's claim to his throne, he can only utter lamely, "O, where is faith? O, where is loyalty?" In the ensuing war, his allies persuade him to turn over direction of his army to his fiery queen, Margaret of Anjou. Returned briefly to the throne as a result of her efforts in *Henry VI, Part 3,* he promptly be-stows the reins of government on not one but two Protectors, a formula for even more dissension. He, himself, he announces, will retire "to private life, / And in devotion spend my latter days, / To sin's rebuke and my Creator's praise." He very shortly loses the throne once again, and ultimately his life.

In *King John* the monarch cannot make up his mind. Confronted with a threat to his crown by the French king, who favors young Prince Arthur as the legitimate heir, John invades France to assert his rights. Once there, however, he agrees to a marriage of convenience between his niece, Blanch of Spain, and Arthur as a means of resolving the controversy. The peace doesn't last, as is so often the case in Shakespeare, and in the ensuing war John takes Arthur captive. He pledges his faithful servant, Hubert, to put the prince to death, but later rescinds the order, directing that he be freed instead. John defiantly refuses to accept the Pope's choice for the powerful office of Archbishop of Canterbury: "No Italian priest / Shall tithe or toll in our dominions." But he later submits meekly to Rome's demands. When France invades England, John dissolves into a fit of impotent self-pity and retires to a monastery, leaving the Bastard Faulconbridge to defend the kingdom.

Governance, Shakespeare seems to say, is a full-time job, and a prince is well advised not to neglect his duties. In the opening scenes of *The Tempest,* Prospero explains to his daughter Miranda how they came to be marooned on their isolated island. He had been, he tells her, the Duke of Milan, but in time tired of the role. Preferring to devote himself to "the betterment of my mind," he entrusted the administration of the dukedom to his brother, Antonio, and "grew stranger" to his office, "being transported / And rapt in secret studies." Antonio promptly seized power and disposed of Prospero by setting the father and infant daughter adrift at sea in "a rotten carcass of a butt [tub]." It was only with the help of the good Gonzalo, who provided them with provisions and, of equal importance, his books, that they survived to be cast ashore on an island populated only by the pitiful Caliban and spirits of the air.

In a number of the plays a ruler's neglect may not result in his deposition, but his failure to enforce the law sometimes leads to tragic consequences for his subjects. In *Romeo and Juliet,* the prince forbids street brawls between the Montagues and Capulets under pain of death, but he relents and rather than carry out his decree merely banishes Romeo for killing Tybalt. He wonders at the time about the wisdom of the sentence, observing that "mercy but murders, pardoning those that kill." His clemency costs Verona the lives of three young citizens, Romeo, Juliet, and Paris, in addition to the two already dead, Tybalt and Mercutio. The prince admits that by "winking at their discords" he was partly at fault for the carnage. The comedies, of course, always end happily for all in a scene of harmony and reconciliation, but the rulers are at times remiss in their duties, leading to all manner of complications. As we have seen, in *Measure for Measure* the Duke of Vienna admits that he has been lax in his obligation to enforce the city's statutes. He acknowledges that " 'twas my fault to give the people scope," allowing "evil deeds [to] have their permissive pass / And not the punishment." He decides to retire temporarily, turning his responsibilities over to the puritanical Angelo, confident that he will restore respect for the law. Vienna soon feels the effects of Angelo's obsessive dedication as he strictly enforces the city's law against fornication, but complications arise when he becomes smitten with Isabella and schemes to break the law himself. The duke remains in Vienna, disguised as a holy friar, and in the end must reveal himself to unravel the muddle that has resulted from his laxity.

Some fair-minded princes accept their obligation to uphold the law, but, troubled by the necessity, they do so with obvious reluctance. In *The Merchant of Venice,* the duke is constrained to enforce the city's laws, even though they threaten the life of an honored citizen. Antonio has borrowed a sum of money from Shylock, and when he defaults on the loan, the vengeful Jew demands his "bond," the security agreed on—a pound of Antonio's flesh. In a painful dilemma, the duke attempts to reason with Shylock, but he remains adamant: "If you deny me, fie upon your laws!" Portia arrives, in the guise of a learned legal scholar, and appears to agree with Shylock: "A pound of that same merchant's flesh is thine. / The court awards it, and the law doth give it." Fortunately for Antonio, and for the troubled duke, she cites another, more obscure, Venetian law that prohibits Shylock from shedding "one drop of Christian blood," the penalty for which is the loss of all his "lands and goods." To the relief of all, the Jew desists.

In *A Midsummer Night's Dream,* Egeus in enraged when his daughter, Hermia, refuses to accept Demetrius, his choice for her husband, and is deaf to her pleas that she is in love with Lysander. Egeus brings the three of them before Duke Theseus and demands "the ancient privilege of Athens." She must either marry Demetrius, he insists, or go "to her death, according to our laws." Theseus is distressed by the need to uphold "the laws of Athens," which, he acknowledges, "by no means we may extenuate," and he counsels Hermia "to fit your fancies to your father's will" or pay the penalty. The duke draws Egeus aside in an apparent effort to reason with him, but the father remains adamant. To complicate matters, Hermia's friend Helena is in love with Demetrius, who of course prefers Hermia. The four steal into the forest, where, thanks to the magic properties of "a little western flower," Hermia gets her Lysander and Helena her Demetrius. When the four are discovered, however, Egeus demands that Lysander be punished: "I beg the law, the law, upon his head." But since the lovers seem to have worked out their difficulties to their own satisfaction, a sympathetic Theseus, who is about to be married himself, overrules Egeus, and the play ends with a joyous triple wedding. In the comedies, love conquers all, even the law.[8]

---

8. Again, in the final scene of *The Comedy of Errors,* Duke Solinus leads Egeon to his execution, which is required by law, though he is entirely sympathetic with the merchant's plight. The sentence is forgotten in the end, of course, and the play concludes with a series of happy reunions.

# Love versus Duty

A significant theme pervades Shakespeare's tales of princes who gain, keep, and lose power in the state—the internal conflict that any ruler faces between a concern for self, family, and clan and his loyalty to the obligations of high office. The human race has always felt the need for government of one kind or another, from the earliest primitive societies that found it necessary to appoint a chief to keep destructive elements within the tribe in check, to modern states that search for regional and world order in international bodies like the European Union and the United Nations. Those who assume the responsibility of public office often find that their duties conflict with personal obligations, and they return to private life, content to devote their time and energy thereafter to benefit their families. Legislators are continually confronted with decisions that call upon them to weigh their duty to a state or nation against a concern for the welfare of constituents back home.

Shakespeare portrays this conflict of concerns in several ways. Some princes simply refuse the office, as does Titus Andronicus, who, worn down by his wars, rejects the offer of the imperial crown. Some betray and corrupt it, as in the case of Macbeth, who mounts the throne of Scotland but then imposes a reign of terror on the subjects whose welfare is entrusted to his care. Some neglect the office, devoting too little attention to its duties, and, like Richard II, eventually pay the price. And some resign themselves to bear its burdens, regretting the sacrifice it entails. Henry V accepts the obligations of the crown, lamenting "what infinite heart's-ease / Must kings neglect."

A theme of the *Henry IV* plays is the personal sacrifice of friendship often required of those who rise to a seat of power. It may be said that Prince Hal "loves" Falstaff. The two certainly enjoy one another's company; even after Hal accepts the responsibilities of his royal office as Prince of Wales, he is drawn back to the Boar's Head

Tavern and the jolly fat knight. But it would not do for him to continue the association after he ascends the throne. Falstaff is outrageously irreverent, scoffing at all the civic values a monarch is obliged to uphold—honor, honesty, courage, loyalty, concern for his subjects, and respect for the law. Falstaff's mockery strikes a sympathetic chord with playgoers, fed by the media with a steady diet of the inadequacies of public figures. He is certainly eloquent and amusing in his derision of those in high places, and while we may agree that the mighty are often woefully deficient in one or all of these values, those who aspire to rule are expected to embody them. Hal knows he must sever his ties with such a man, no matter how close the bond between them, if he is to gain the regard of the English people. His public rejection of Falstaff is unequivocal—"I know thee not, old man"—but we must assume that he regrets the necessity of banishing this cherished companion of his youth.

The dilemma of those faced with a choice between public duty and personal obligation is illustrated dramatically by old John of Gaunt, the Duke of Lancaster, in *Richard II*. The king, confronted with highly charged accusations of treason exchanged between Thomas Mowbray, Duke of Norfolk, and Henry Bolingbroke, Gaunt's son, declares that guilt or innocence will be decided in a trial by combat. As the contest is about to begin, however, Richard calls it to a halt, convenes a quick meeting of his council, and announces that, rather than proceed with the fight, both men will be sentenced to banishment from the kingdom. Richard notices that the Gaunt is deeply saddened by the decision to banish his son, even though he had advised it as a member of the council. When the king questions him about the seeming contradiction in his sentiments, the loyal duke replies in a telling evocation of the conflicting sentiments that trouble those in high office: "You urg'd me as a judge, but I had rather / You would have bid me argue as a father."

The most frequent allusions in the plays to the conflict between personal desire and public duty are to be found in instances of a daughter's rejection of her father's choice of a husband for her. These marriages are arranged to benefit the family's dynastic or commercial fortunes, thus a daughter's resistance is angrily interpreted as a betrayal of the family bond. In the comedies, of course, love prevails: Anne Page marries her Fenton in *The Merry Wives of Windsor;* Lysander and Hermia are happily joined over objections of her father, Egeus, in *A Midsummer Night's Dream;* and Perdita and Florizel escape the wrath of the prince's father in *The Winter's Tale.* But the lovers' success in evading the parental design can at times be a mixed blessing. In *The Merchant of Venice,* the elopement of Shylock's daughter Jessica with the Christian Lorenzo brings home to the Jew his people's suffering over the centuries: "The curse never fell upon our nation till now; I never felt it till now." He is so angered that he determines to have revenge on all Christians by demanding his bond of Antonio's pound of flesh. The couple find happy refuge in Portia's Belmont, but the vengeful Shylock is stripped of his wealth and forced to deny his Jewish faith.

In the tragedies a daughter's insistence that she will have only the one she loves is perceived as a selfish disregard for the family's welfare and often leads to dreadful losses. In *Titus Andronicus,* Lavinia, already betrothed to Bassianus, refuses to obey her father's demand that she marry the emperor Saturninus. When the couple flee, Titus gives chase and her brother Mutius attempts to block his way, so enraging the father that he kills his own son. And Juliet's scheme to evade marriage to Paris by drinking Friar Laurence's potion, lending her the appearance of death, leads to comparable tragedy. Paris, thinking she has died of grief over the loss of her favorite cousin, Tybalt, challenges his murderer, Romeo, and is killed.

Men also at times rank their personal desire above their family or public duty. In *Antony and Cleopatra,* the uneasy alliance between Mark Antony and Octavius Caesar is threatened because Antony, besotted with the fascinating Cleopatra, neglects his duties. Soon the Parthians are ravaging Asia Minor unchecked, and Caesar is angered when Antony fails to dispatch promised legions to defend Rome, then imperiled by Pompey's son. But Antony is dangerously indifferent to these threats to his rule: "Let Rome in Tiber melt, and the wide arch / Of the rang'd empire fall," he declares, "here is my space" beside his Egyptian queen. Later Antony agrees to wed Caesar's sister, Octavia, in a marriage of convenience designed to create a family bond that, it is hoped, will heal divisions between the two emperors. But Antony abandons her to return to Cleopatra, and an angered Caesar vows that he will pay for the affront. Antony's indulgence ultimately costs him an empire.

In another instance the mercenary Angelo had renounced his betrothal to Mariana years before the time frame of *Measure for Measure,* apparently because tragic events left her without the dowry he had expected of her. Angelo is entrusted with the duty of enforcing the laws of Vienna. He focuses his attention on the city's statute against fornication, but his devotion to duty is seriously compromised when he develops a passion for the virtuous Isabella. In a scheme to evade him, she pretends to agree to his advances on the condition that he come to her bed at night, stay but an hour, and refrain from speaking. Mariana takes Isabella's place and, when the switch is revealed, Angelo is compelled to renew his vows.[9]

It is Shakespeare's women who most often place loyalty to family above public allegiance. In *Richard II* the Duchess of Gloucester attempts to incite old Gaunt to seek vengeance on the king for his complicity in the murder of her husband, Woodstock. Gaunt, though incensed by the death of his brother, replies that his obligation to the crown forbids him to do so: "God's is the quarrel [and] I may never lift / An angry arm against his Minister." And in *Coriolanus,* it is a mother who saves Rome by persuading her son to place the welfare of his family above his public ambitions. When Coriolanus is banished from Rome because of his arrogant contempt for the people, he joins his former enemies, solemnly pledging himself to their cause. The Volcians embrace him and in recognition of his fame as a warrior place him in command of their army, which he

---

9. For more on the "bed trick," see pp. 19–20 and 189.

leads back to Rome with every intention of sacking the city to avenge his humiliation at the hands of her people. He resists all entreaties to turn back until he is confronted with the kneeling figures of his mother, Volumnia, his wife, and his son. Volumnia pushes all the maternal buttons. She accuses him of "tearing / His country's bowels out." Should he persist, she says, he will "bravely shed his wife's and children's blood" and tread "on thy mother's womb / That brought thee to this world." She reminds him that "there's no man in the world / More bound to's mother" than he. Rejecting his efforts to silence her, she defends her words as "the duty which / To a mother's part belongs." Coriolanus finally submits, "O my mother, mother! O! / You have won a happy victory for Rome"; but he predicts that it will prove "most mortal" to her son. Thus shamed by Volumnia, he withdraws his army and, returning to the Volcian court, he is killed for betraying their trust in him.[1]

Perhaps the most intriguing instance of the conflict between public allegiance and private desire arises from Cleopatra's love for Antony. She is a queen of Egypt who loves an emperor of Rome, and for a time her duty to her realm and her personal passion are not at odds. But when Caesar and Antony have a falling out and marshal their armies to contend for the rule of the empire, the fate of Egypt and the survival of an ancient line of Ptolemy monarchs depends on which of them emerges victorious, and she is torn between loyalty to her kingdom and love for Antony. Plutarch's *Parallel Lives of the Greeks and Romans* offers no clues to her state of mind; and Shakespeare, following his source closely, leaves the matter unresolved.

Cleopatra's actions are certainly ambiguous. In the midst of the naval battle of Actium, the Egyptian ships suddenly raise their sails and abandon Antony. Did Cleopatra order their withdrawal in a mo-

---

1. In *Henry IV, Part 2,* Lady Northumberland and Hotspur's widow persuade the earl, "for all our loves," to abandon the rebellion against the king and retire to Scotland. And it is Lady Capulet who reacts most violently to news that Romeo has killed her nephew, Tybalt. She demands: "Prince, as thou art true, / For blood of ours, shed blood of Montague."

ment of panic when she thought Caesar's forces had gained the upper hand, or did she desert her lover to preserve her fleet? Later, when Thidias, an envoy from Caesar, presents the emperor's offer to allow her to keep her crown if she will abandon Antony, she receives him courteously and, as he prepares to depart, allows him to kiss her hand. Still later in Alexandria, at a critical moment in the battle between the two emperors, the Egyptian fleet deserts yet again, joining forces with Caesar.

Antony at first sees all these acts as betrayals and rages at her duplicity; but in each case she persuades him of her devotion anew and they are reconciled. He forgives her after the defeat at Actium—"Give me a kiss. / Even this repays me"—and following the audience with Thidias—"I am satisfied." After Antony's death she seems to accept Caesar's offer of clemency but confides in her attendants that she mistrusts him: "He words me, girls, he words me." She prefers to kill herself so as to rejoin Antony in death: "Husband, I come!" Shakespeare does not attempt to resolve the question of her response to her dilemma. He simply places it before us in all its complexity, so that we may decide whether it was love or duty that moved her most.

## Kingship

What, then, does Shakespeare have to say on this theme of kingship? His princes vary greatly in ability and temperament. As we have seen, some are bad, some are good, and some are simply incompetent. And indeed we find that Shakespeare's kings are more likely to fail than succeed.

This pageant of princes tells us something about Shakespeare's vision of the art of rule. Prominent among the "bad" kings are the tyrants, like Macbeth and Richard III, who concern themselves only with gaining and keeping power, and care little about how many innocent lives their ambition costs. At the outset, Macbeth is an upright thane, loyal to his king and, according to his wife, "too full o' th' milk of human kindness." At the end, encrusted with his crimes, he utters a sour regret at the course his life has taken. Richard III, on the other hand, is thoroughly wicked from beginning to end, and he has no such regrets. After a momentary lapse into self-pity— "There's no creature loves me"—he quickly shakes off the thought and calls for his horse. Both men, having gained power through treachery, suspect all about them of similar designs.

Some of Shakespeare's princes are weak or simply inept. Henry VI, bewildered by the factions in his kingdom, attempts vainly to persuade his nobles to cease their wrangling; but since he is unwilling or unable to assert the authority of the crown to bring them into line, they pay him no heed. Richard II is so enamored with the splendor of the throne that he gives little thought to the welfare of his subjects and exhausts the royal treasury to embellish his court. Both he and King John, when confronted with an armed challenge to their crown, dissolve into a fit of paralyzing self-pity, which leaves them completely ineffectual.

Some princes place their appetites above the welfare of the kingdom and in many cases their own self-interest. Edward IV unexpectedly marries the seductive Lady Grey, a self-indulgent act seen as a betrayal of trust by his longtime allies, Clarence, his brother, and the Earl of Warwick, who then turn against him. Henry VIII abandons Katharine, his wife of many years, for Anne Boleyn, though in Shakespeare his licentiousness has a glorious issue, the birth of Elizabeth. And Antony, of course, as a result of his infatuation with Cleopatra, loses an empire.

Some play the power game with Machiavellian skill, using duplicity and deception to achieve their ends, coldly exploiting their enemies' weaknesses. Henry Bolingbroke takes advantage of Richard II's preoccupation with his court and consequent neglect of his subjects by cultivating the favor of the English people and rallying the nobility against him. Later, as Henry IV, he offers the rebel leaders a promise of clemency he has no intention of honoring. On his deathbed he draws upon his long experience in the exercise of power in advising his son to "busy giddy minds with foreign quarrels" so as to avoid the insurrections that plagued his reign. Octavius Caesar participates in the bloodletting of the Roman Senate and later plots to preserve Cleopatra for his Roman triumph by making her promises that he fully intends to break. Bolingbroke and Caesar may indeed be devious, but they are not wickedly so. They are masters of the art of rule, which requires some skill in deception, and both succeed: Bolingbroke prevails and maintains his hold on the crown of England, and Caesar becomes the sole emperor of the known world.

The princes of the comedies are generally benign, dispensing mercy with their justice. Duke Theseus prevents Palamon and Arcite from mauling each other over his sister Emilia in *The Two Noble Kinsmen.* He proclaims that they will compete for her hand in a public joust, which turns out to resemble nothing so much as the childhood game of "capture the flag." In *A Midsummer Night's Dream,* this same Theseus overrules Egeus's objection to his daughter Hermia marrying Lysander once the two couples seem to have resolved their differences on their own. The Duke of Vienna suddenly reappears in *Measure for Measure* and absolves everyone of guilt for their transgression against the city's law that forbids fornication, including the incontinent Angelo, who had violated the very statute he was deputized to enforce.

Some kings in the comedies are subject to the same failings as their counterparts in the tragedies. In *The Winter's Tale,* King Leontes is seized by a fit of jealousy as intense as Othello's. When Cymbeline's daughter Imogen marries against his wishes, he flies into a rage as intemperate as Capulet's when Juliet refuses Paris. And Duke Frederick in *As You Like It* is intent upon revenge when his daughter Celia deserts the court to accompany her friend Rosalind into exile. In the comedies, however, all these princes come to their senses in the end. Shakespeare implies that our follies need not be fatal to us if we retain a redeeming sense of our mutual humanity.

Thus monarchs come in many guises. In view of the conflicting qualities of his various rulers, can it be said that Shakespeare at any time offers the image of an ideal king, one who is not only able but good, gladdening the hearts of his subjects? We have mentioned the brief allusion in *Macbeth* to England's Edward the Confessor, who cures his subjects' ills with "the king's evil," in contrast to the tyrant, who infects his with an epidemic of terror. And in some respects Shakespeare's Henry VIII is a "good" king. He is not the bloated monarch of the latter years of his reign, who made his way through six wives and sent the saintly Thomas More to the block. Shakespeare treats him sympathetically, as well he might the father of Elizabeth I and great-uncle of King James I. Henry agonizes over his divorce from his first wife Katharine, whom he praises as "the primest creature / That's paragon'd o' th' world," and obviously regrets what he is doing. He is loyal to his friends, defending his chancellor, Cardinal Wolsey, against the charges of his detractors until he is presented with proof that the cardinal has been taxing his subjects illegally and pocketing the revenues. He is equally as constant to Cardinal Cranmer, Wolsey's successor as Archbishop of Canterbury, when court factions seek to unseat him. And he is certainly appealing as the anxious husband and exultant father when Anne delivers Elizabeth. But Henry VIII cannot escape the judgment of history, no matter how sympathetic Shakespeare is to the father of Elizabeth I. The play defies our capacity to suspend disbelief.

Perhaps as close as Shakespeare comes to the image of an exemplary "good" king is his portrayal of Henry V. The brief, meteoric career of this "star of England" was viewed by the poet's contemporaries as "their finest hour." Henry momentarily joined the crowns of France and England, becoming the most powerful monarch in Christendom. His death, a short year after his triumph, was considered tragic, especially since he left a nine-month-old heir during whose reign the wrangling English nobles managed to lose all that he had gained. He was a figure of almost mythic stature, and Shakespeare spared no pains in portraying him as the ideal monarch.

The portrayal is not restricted to a single play. The career of Harry of Monmouth, Prince Hal, or Henry V, as he is variously called, is chronicled in *Henry IV, Parts 1 and 2,* and *Henry V.* It is the classic story of a young man coming of age. When we first see him, he is a carefree, fun-loving playboy who spends his time in thoughtless revelry with the common people of London's Eastcheap, delighting in the company of the dissolute knight, Sir John Falstaff. Shamed by his father, Henry IV, for his irresponsible behavior, he finally accepts his obligations as a prince of the realm and conducts himself honorably in putting down the rebellions that threaten the king's reign. He puts his misspent youth behind him—with some reluctance, it would appear—and on assuming the crown, banishes Falstaff and all he represents from his presence. He then goes on to rally his nation in an ambitious enterprise to conquer the kingdom of France, and after an arduous campaign succeeds in joining the two crowns.

Shakespeare describes him as a young man who develops into an ideal monarch under the influence of three figures who shape his early character. The first is the fiery Hotspur, Henry Percy, heir to the Earl of Northumberland, a renowned warrior who is the driving force behind the rebellion against Henry IV. He is known chiefly for his prowess in battle, and the king ruefully compares his wayward son to the admirable Percy, "who is the theme of honor's tongue." Hal overcomes Hotspur in single combat and thereby inherits the mantle of the fallen Percy as a formidable warrior.

The second influence on Hal is the king, his father, who is an example to him of a man devoted to his regal office. Henry IV presses upon the young prince the importance of public duty and deplores his choice of companions who, he charges, cheapen him in the opinion of his subjects. The king knows the burdens that the crown imposes on the man who wears it and scolds his son for his seeming indifference to the obligations that his royal birth place upon him.

The third influence, and certainly the most entertaining of those that shape the young man's character, is Falstaff, whose infectious wit and love of life are enormously appealing to the prince. The fat knight is always ready for a jest, even in the heat of battle, and never loses his lively sense of the absurdities of both high and low society. In the company of Falstaff, Hal is exposed to the day-to-day life of ordinary Englishmen.

The mature Henry V, we find, has adopted the finer qualities of each of the three, and has avoided their less admirable traits. Hotspur is headstrong, impetuous, and quick to take offense. Henry is even-tempered and carefully calculating, but he emulates the warlike Percy's courage, his driving energy, and his boldness in risking all for a cause. Before his elevation to the throne, young Hal leaves the frivolous pursuits of Eastcheap to match Hotspur's martial accomplishments. Lest he be misunderstood in his pursuit of fame in battle, it should be recalled that Henry V lived in an age when warrior kings were expected to take the field with their armies. He ruled in the tradition of his great-grandfather, Edward III, who with his formidable son, the Black Prince, scarred the fields of France for decades. Even the ineffectual Richard II leads an ill-fated expedition to Ireland, and Henry IV, until illness prevents him, fights alongside his soldiers. Those who shun the battlefield are soon deposed by more warlike enemies. This is the fate of pacific kings like Henry VI, who leaves the fighting to his nobles and his fiery queen Margaret, and loses his crown to the more able Edward, Duke of York.[2]

From his father, Hal learns to accept the responsibilities that his royal birth destines he inherit. He leaves his carefree life behind him but never adopts the aloof, staged manner that Henry IV assumes on the throne, rejecting his father's advice to avoid "vulgar company"

---

2. Monarchs were less likely to take the field in later times, but Charles II marched an army into England in 1651 and led a futile effort to break through Cromwell's lines at the battle of Worcester. England's last warrior king was William III, who in the 1690s commanded a combined English-Dutch army opposing Louis XIV's efforts to expand France's northern borders in Flanders at the expense of the United Netherlands.

and be "seldom seen." He does not neglect the dignity of the crown but, benefiting from his association with Falstaff, retains an abiding sympathy for those of his subjects less privileged than himself. To be in the company of the fat knight is to celebrate life, to affirm essential humanity. His unassailable optimism, his mischievous gaiety, and his love of a jest make him a delight to be with. He attracts the allegiance and affection of all those close to him, the common people who frequent the Boar's Head Tavern as well as a prince of the realm. It is this common touch that Hal inherits from Falstaff, an appreciation for the lives of his ordinary subjects, their need for a sense of purpose in their day-to-day struggle for survival, and the liberating effect of laughter in an otherwise dreary existence. As king, he never loses that delight in mischief, stage-managing the sentence of those who conspired to assassinate him and playing a seemingly heartless trick on the common soldier, Williams, after the victory at Agincourt. But Henry V rejects Falstaff's irresponsibility, his profligacy, his cowardice, and his cynical dismissal of the values of a civil society. He is, after all, an old reprobate, a thief, and a liar, however witty in his embellishment of the truth, and he willfully abuses his public duty for gain. Hal must in the end thrust him aside.

The madcap Prince Hal, then, puts his past behind him, though both friend and enemy continue to remind us of it. In *Henry V* the Archbishop of Canterbury remarks that "the courses of his youth" held little promise, and the French dauphin dismisses him as "a vain, giddy, shallow, humorous youth." But he emerges as a seasoned monarch who temperately seeks the advice of his council before embarking on the campaign against France. He is skilled in the martial arts and courageously endangers his life leading his armies in battle. He captures the hearts and engages the loyalty of noblemen and commoners alike, proving himself adept at dealing with archbishops, ambassadors, and barons, and at the same time reaching down to share the lives of ordinary soldiers with an instinctive sympathy for their lot. He embodies the qualities that an earlier age admired in a monarch and that later times have come to value in a modern senator.

Thus Shakespeare on the power of princes. What is so remarkable is the scope of his insight into the motives and strategies of the mighty. Machiavelli composed *The Prince* as a primer for Renaissance rulers or aspiring rulers, a guide on how to gain and retain power in a state. Shakespeare wrote his plays to fill theaters. Nonetheless his works might well serve as a handbook for those who seek to gain and keep a crown, a guide as rich and as valid as Machiavelli's little book. They are all here, those who fail and those who triumph, the despised and beloved, the feeble and the strong. Some revel in their royal robes, others regret they were ever born to wear them. We encounter rulers who are constant and those who are deceitful, the humble and the pompous, the loyal and the treacherous, the enlightened and the blind. And still they are human beings, driven by ambition but yet in need of the love of family and comfort of friendship, and in their need Shakespeare brings these lofty figures close to our own lives. Henry V sees in the treachery of a trusted companion "another fall of man" and ponders "what infinite heart's ease / Must kings neglect, that private men enjoy!" And Macbeth is painfully aware of what he has missed in his remorseless pursuit of power: "That which should accompany old age, / As honor, love, obedience, troops of friends, / I must not look to have."

# ILLUSION

❧

THE THEME OF ILLUSION—the difference between the way things are and the way they appear to be—pervades the plays of Shakespeare. He explores the theme in all its dimensions, in tragedy, comedy, and history, posing but never resolving the eternal question why things are not what they seem. Philosophers, theologians, and scientists have pondered the same question throughout the centuries, wondering whether the world as we perceive it may be a fantasy, an unreliable construct of our five fallible senses. In ancient times Plato imagined that what we call reality is no more than a procession of vague shadows projected on a cave wall. Scripture teaches that we can know the truth of our nature only as one who sees it "through a glass, darkly." Medieval astronomers firmly believed that the sun circled the earth since, well, one need only look to see the truth of the matter. And modern science proposes the existence of "alternate universes," whose unseen presence casts doubt on the substance of our own.

Playwrights are not alone, then, in pursuing the theme, but they do so with particular relish, since it is the very essence of their art. The most memorable of Shakespeare's references to illusion appear in those poetic passages where he compares the stage to the world. He is also fond of introducing plays within plays—illusions within illusions, if you will. And any number of his characters profess to be other than who or what they are by wearing masks or donning disguises of one sort or another. Still others pretend to qualities that hide their true nature or to motives that conceal their intent. Some deliberately pass themselves off as another person, and there are those who are unknowingly mistaken for others, often to their distress. And, of course, Shakespeare's otherworldly spirits can appear to mankind in any shape they choose.

## The Stage

The stage, of course, is the greatest illusion of all, as Shakespeare constantly reminds us. The playwright places before us a fantasy, a world populated by beings that have never walked the earth, or, if they have, do so in the plays only as his imagination directs their feet. When the fantasy is constrained by the physical limits of the stage, he calls upon his audience to imagine that small, enclosed space as a larger world. The genial chorus in *Henry V* asks the audience to "piece out our imperfections with your thoughts." "Let us," he says, "on your imaginary forces work" to transform the theater's bare boards into "the vasty fields of France" and to multiply the few soldiers he is able to crowd on the stage into great armies locked in mortal combat.

Some of Shakespeare's most memorable poetry pursues the image of the world as a stage. In *The Tempest* the wizard Prospero conjures spirits to perform a masque, a combination of music, dance, and poetry, to celebrate the betrothal of his daughter Miranda to Ferdinand, the prince of Naples. In the midst of the performance Prospero suddenly remembers the plot on his life hatched by his servant, the subhuman Caliban, and with an angry sweep of his arm he dissolves the vision. Observing that Ferdinand is stunned by the sudden disappearance of the spirits, he attempts to reassure the young man:

You do look, my son, in a mov'd sort,
As if you were dismay'd; be cheerful, sir.

> Our revels now are ended. These our actors
> (As I foretold you) were all spirits, and
> Are melted into air, into thin air.

He compares the final curtain of a performance to the dissolution of the world:

> And like the baseless fabric of this vision,
> The cloud-clapp'd towers, the gorgeous palaces,
> The solemn temples, the great globe itself,
> Yea, all which it inherit, shall dissolve,
> And like this insubstantial pageant faded,
> Leave not a rack behind;

. . . and life to a dream:

> We are such stuff
> As dreams are made on; and our little life
> Is rounded with a sleep.

Other figures, with a somewhat different vision, find our progress through life a series of performances. In *As You Like It,* the melancholy Jaques declares that "all the world's a stage, / And all the men and women merely players." They "have their exits and their entrances," he continues, in the seven acts of life, from the first as an "infant, / Mewling and puking in the nurse's arms" to the last, "second childishness, and mere oblivion, / Sans teeth, sans eyes, sans taste, sans every thing."

Macbeth, in the closing act of the play, learns of the death of his wife. Confronted by an approaching army marching to menace his crown, he can only mutter sourly that "she should have died here-after; / There would have been a time for such a word." His spirit, encrusted by the hard shell of his crimes, is incapable of mourning the loss of the only one who has stood by him during his troubled reign. All he can manage is the bitter observation that her death is no more than the final act in a meaningless existence:

Life's but a walking shadow, a poor player
That struts and frets his hour upon the stage,
And then is heard no more. It is a tale
Told by an idiot, full of sound and fury,
Signifying nothing.

And King Lear, driven mad by the heartless cruelty of his daughters, arrives at a melancholy wisdom: "When we are born, we cry
that we are come / To this great stage of fools."

These are certainly not happy thoughts. It does not gladden the
heart to hear that life is only a dream "rounded with a sleep" or a
mere performance in which we play a predetermined role, one moreover "signifying nothing." Shakespeare reminds us of one of the sad
truths of the human condition. His theme is our pitifully brief stay
upon this globe. We may entertain the illusion of permanence, but
our lives are as transitory, as ephemeral, as any of his plays with their
"two hours' traffic of our stage." And we will end our time on the
globe "sans teeth, sans eyes, sans taste, sans every thing." And that
is not a happy thought.

## The Play Within A Play

Illusion, then, is the very essence of the stage itself. And Shakespeare's plots have a way of reminding us that the play we are
watching is indeed but a play, a fantasy fabricated from bits and
pieces of the imagination, strung together into a tale either of
mankind's failing or of its redemption in laughter. The paradox of
our dual nature, at once tragic and comic, is confirmed in Shakespeare's dramatic device of the play within a play.

The tragic side of the human condition is portrayed in Hamlet's
famous "Mousetrap" scene, in which the prince stages the murder of
his father by his uncle so as to "catch the conscience of the king."
Claudius sees himself in the figure pouring poison into the sleeping

actor king's ear and reacts violently to the sight, evidence enough in Hamlet's mind to confirm his guilt. Shakespeare thus illustrates the power of the stage, an artifice that can "catch the conscience" of an audience who may see themselves in the actors playing parts and, like Claudius, call for light to end the painful revelation.

But then, Shakespeare reminds us, illusion has its lighter side, as in the opening scenes of *The Taming of the Shrew,* an episode he calls an "induction." In the episode a simple tinker, Christopher Sly, falls into a drunken sleep in a tavern and is discovered there by a visiting lord and his servants. The mischievous lord, seizing an opportunity for some amusement, directs his servants to put the tinker to bed and when he awakes persuade him that he is a lord who has been in a coma for fifteen years and miraculously has only just recovered his senses. When a troupe of traveling players arrives at the tavern, at the lord's request they perform a comedy for Sly's entertainment, one that turns out to be the story of Petruchio's rough wooing of Kate.

This "induction" is puzzling, since it seems to have little to do with the central plot and, except for a few lines at the end of opening scene of the play within the play, is never alluded to again. Scholars conjecture that early editors of Shakespeare's works somehow misplaced a concluding episode in which Sly perhaps drinks himself into another stupor and awakens convinced that it was all a dream. Some productions omit the "induction" entirely as an amusing but unnecessary adjunct to the main action, which is amusing enough in itself. But these few scenes are important in what they tell us about Shakespeare's concept of the stage. The theater audience watches actors put on a play about actors who put on a play. And within this play within a play, various characters disguise themselves as personages they are not. The rich young man Lucentio becomes a tutor so that he can woo the beauteous Bianca, and in turn his servant Tranio assumes the identity of the rich young man. Hortensio disguises himself as a music teacher for the same purpose, and a visiting Mantuan is persuaded to impersonate Lucentio's father. Petruchio himself, we suspect, plays the part of an abusive, quarrelsome husband and master only as a device to tame the shrewish Kate.

The plot, in brief, comes down to this: actors put on a play for us about a tinker who thinks himself a lord, who watches actors put on a play for him, one in which characters assume false identities— illusions within an illusion within yet another illusion. If Shakespeare's "induction" is omitted from a performance, an entire layer of fantasy is stripped away and we miss his delicious whimsy about the nature of the stage. Nothing is what it seems, he tells us; none of this is real, neither Kate's anger nor Petruchio's rough wooing. It is all, in Prospero's words, nothing more than an "insubstantial pageant."

Shakespeare includes such episodes in other plays as well, and each instance reveals something about the theater and the power of illusion. The poet includes a play within a play in *A Midsummer Night's Dream*, here perhaps as a gentle satire on his audience, a subtle reminder that they have a role in this flight of fancy. Bottom's bungling "mechanicals" rehearse a play, *Pyramus and Thisbe,* which they hope to present during the celebration of the nuptials of Duke Theseus and Hippolyta, the Amazon queen. And they are anxious about the effect their performance will have on the courtly audience. First they worry that it will be too realistic, and then they worry that it will not be real enough. Fearful that the appearance of a lion will frighten the ladies in their audience, they decide to include a speech assuring them that it's not really a lion, only Snug the joiner playing the part. At the same time they question whether the audience will be able to imagine the set and lighting. To be on the safe side, they assign Snout the tinker to impersonate a wall and another of their number to represent the moon. Thus Shakespeare lightheartedly comments on his audience, some of whom, forgetting that any play is a fantasy, may react unfavorably to his occasional portrayal of the violent or tragic side of human nature. Other viewers, he says, will lack the imagination to reconcile themselves to the bare boards and confined space of the Elizabethan stage, unable, in the words of *Henry V's* Chorus, to "piece out our imperfections with your thoughts." There are those in the audience, the playwright regrets whimsically, who will insist on a moon to be convinced that a scene is bathed in moonshine.

# Masks

Shakespeare was fond of masks, traditionally worn during times of revelry. Some figures wear full-face disguises while others simply cover their eyes, and we are asked to suspend our disbelief and accept the fiction that they cannot be recognized for who they are. The effect is always the same, however; masks offer the illusion of anonymity, and those who wear them are able to drop their inhibitions and act out fantasies. A mask is a license to say and do things that in normal social discourse would be frowned upon. In *Romeo and Juliet,* the romantic hero and his fellow Montagues attend the Capulet festivities as "masquers" (Tybalt recognizes Romeo by his voice). When Romeo spies Juliet, he is immediately smitten, and on approaching her, a complete stranger, the first thing he does is ask for a kiss. She coyly agrees to one, and then to yet another, behavior normally deemed most improper for well-brought-up young people of their social class. But he is masked and customary reticence can be relaxed, for after all what harm could come of a playful kiss?[1]

In a sense, then, illusion can be liberating. The same relaxation of reserve applies even when the characters are aware of one another's identity. In the masked ball of *Much Ado About Nothing,* the confusion of identities assumes dizzying proportions. The comic effect arises when the couples pair off and we are aware of who knows whom and who does not. The avuncular Don Pedro, at the head of

---

1. One assumes that he removes the mask to kiss, otherwise we will have to believe that she falls in love with a voice.

the army returning to Messina after his campaigns, notes that his young officer Claudio has fallen in love with Hero, the daughter of the city's governor. Since Claudio, though a fearless soldier, seems to be terrified at the prospect of courting her personally, Don Pedro proposes that he woo her for him at the masked ball to be held that night. Hero learns of Don Pedro's intentions but is under the impression that he will be speaking for himself. During the encounter each, though masked, is aware of the other's identity, and Hero seems to blossom under the protection of her supposed anonymity. Though she has been all but silent thus far in the play, she is able to shed her customary modesty and respond to Don Pedro's advances with seductive wit.

The comic effect is achieved when the audience is aware that in an encounter each of the masked figures knows the other's identity, but by assuming the guise, again, of supposed anonymity, they can pretend not to. The dialogue between Beatrice and Benedick illustrates the delightful complications that can arise from such a theatrical device. The two were drawn to one another, it seems, during a former visit on the army's outward march, and Benedick apparently left her somewhat scarred by the encounter. On his return, they enter into a "merry war" of words as each insults the other, a posture adopted, according to their friends, so as to hide their mutual affection and avoid rejection once again. They come together at the ball, maintaining the fiction that they are unaware of each other's identity, and Beatrice, pretending that she speaks to a stranger, heaps insults on Benedick, calling him among other things "the Prince's jester, a dull fool." He knows who she is but must hide his indignation because he is masked and thinks she doesn't know who he is. But in a twist to the pattern, apparently she does. She maintains the fiction and at the end of their exchange remarks to this supposed stranger that Benedick is somewhere among the dancers—"in the fleet," as she puts it—and concludes wistfully, "I would that he had boarded me." This oblique admission of her affection is clearly meant for his ears, but he misses its meaning entirely because he is still smarting from her derisive remark that he is "the Prince's jester." This somewhat tedious explication of their exchange illustrates, once again, the futility of explaining a joke and in fact may be entirely unnecessary, since in performance they are masked and it all makes perfect comic sense.

In another instance, the King of Navarre and his three lords pay court to the Princess of France and her three ladies-in-waiting in *Love's Labor's Lost.* The men send small gifts, or "favors," a jewel or a necklace, to each of the ladies with the request that they display them during the evening's masked ball so as to identify themselves. The lords enter disguised as Russians, and each pairs off with the lady wearing his favor; but unknown to the men, the ladies have mischievously exchanged the gifts among themselves, so that the lords waste their honeyed words on the wrong ones. The king woos Rosaline, for example, who is Berowne's choice, while he in turn pours out his heart to the princess, whom the king has his eye on. Masking here brings the lords low when the ladies later reveal the deception and question the sincerity of their vows of devotion, which, as it happens, is a major theme of the play.

## Disguises

Shakespeare's favorite disguise, of course, is a young woman in male attire, easily arranged since female parts in his time were played by boys anyway. Many of these characters assume a masculine identity because they must undertake a voyage that would be dangerous for an unescorted young woman. And they remain in disguise, at times until the very end of the play, for a variety of reasons, not the least of which is Shakespeare's desire to make the most of the comic invention. Rosalind, the heroine of *As You Like It,* for example, becomes Ganymede when she is banished from the court of Duke Frederick and seeks refuge in the Forest of Arden with her exiled father, Duke Senior. On arrival she encounters her lover, Orlando, and maintains the disguise in order to put him through a series of trials to test his devotion. Viola finds herself in a particularly perilous situation in *Twelfth Night.* Shipwrecked on a foreign shore in Illyria, she adopts the role of a young page, Cesario, so as to enter the safe service of Duke Orsino. She promptly falls in love with the duke, who to her distress is devoted to his lovely but unresponsive neighbor, Olivia; and she keeps her male identity because she is unwilling to leave his service.

Other characters follow the same pattern. In *The Two Gentlemen of Verona,* Julia disguises herself as Sebastian when she pursues her lover, Proteus, and remains in the role when she discovers that he has been unfaithful to her. Imogen becomes Fidele in *Cymbeline* when she ventures into the wilderness of Wales in search of her feckless husband Posthumus, and must keep her male identity when she comes under the protection of a Roman general who is leading an invasion of Britain.

Portia has other reasons for donning the robes of a learned doctor of laws, Balthasar, in *The Merchant of Venice.* She appears in the duke's court to rescue Antonio, the generous friend of her husband Bassanio, from the vengeful Jew Shylock. She must maintain the identity to enforce her judgment against Shylock; but she does so also to play a trick on Bassanio, instructing him as to where his true devotion should lie. Bassanio presses Balthasar to accept payment for her services. She at first refuses, but in the end she asks him for a ring he is wearing as a token of his appreciation. It is a gift she had given him prior to their marriage, one which he had solemnly vowed would never leave his finger. Urged on by Antonio, he finally agrees, setting up a situation ripe with comic possibilities when they meet again in the final act.

In each case we are asked to accept the fact that the disguises are entirely successful, even when these figures encounter close relatives and remain unrecognized. Portia, for example, engages her husband in conversation at the end of the trial; Julia performs duties for Proteus; and both Rosalind and Imogen have extended exchanges with their fathers and lovers without revealing their identities. Viola, on the other hand, encounters no one from her former life until the end of the play when she comes face to face with her twin brother, Sebastian. We happily accept the fiction of their hidden identity, however, since the device results in comic encounters, surprising turns of plot, and a buildup of dramatic irony as we await the inevitable disclosure. All of these women are ultimately united or reunited with their husbands or lovers, in keeping with Shakespeare's persistent theme (in the comedies at any rate) that the so-called weaker sex is the more constant, clever, resourceful, and resolute of the two.

The only instance that comes to mind of a man dressing as a woman—a staple of modern farce and college musical reviews—appears in *The Merry Wives of Windsor*. Falstaff presses his amorous attention on Mistress Ford and finds himself trapped in her house when her madly jealous husband appears unexpectedly at the door. In a desperate effort to avoid his wrath, Falstaff dons a disguise as the witch of Brainford, little knowing that Master Ford despises her as much as he does the fat knight himself. Falstaff manages to escape unrecognized, but not before he suffers a beating by Ford, who drums him out of his house.[2]

Characters assume same-sex disguises for several reasons in a number of plays, pretending they are someone they are not. *The Taming of the Shrew,* as mentioned, is full of such impersonations. Lucentio, the rich young man from Pisa, and Hortensio, a local man-about-town, competing for the hand of Bianca, present themselves to her father, Baptista, as tutors for his daughters. The one disguised as a teacher of literature, and the other as a music instructor, they maneuver for her attention. Lucentio wins out in the end by reading to her from Ovid's *Art of Love*. Meanwhile Lucentio's servant Tranio, in the guise of his master, barters for Bianca's hand as well, convincing Baptista that he has sufficient wealth to support her in grand

2. And in the last scene, two boys dress as women to deceive Anne Page's unwanted suitors.

style. The father, impressed by Tranio's perhaps exaggerated account of Lucentio's riches, agrees to his suit but insists that the young man's father, Vincentio, substantiate the claims. This leads to the resourceful Tranio's scheme to persuade a visiting Mantuan to impersonate Vincentio. Everything works out well in the end, since Lucentio has already won the heart of Bianca and dashes off to marry her secretly.

Disguises can occasionally play a role on more serious occasions. On the night before the battle of Agincourt, Henry V borrows a cloak to conceal his identity and wanders through his army's encampment to assess the morale of his soldiers. The disguise embroils him in a potentially embarrassing situation, however, when he exchanges heated words with the common soldier Williams, who expresses doubts that the king will honor his pledge not to be taken prisoner in the impending battle. The two almost come to blows but are persuaded to postpone their quarrel until after the battle. They exchange gloves and agree to wear them in their caps if they survive so as to recognize each other. The victory won, Henry has to employ a rather unkind trick on Williams to avoid the embarrassing spectacle of a king engaged in a quarrel with one of his common subjects.

Richard III is a character who, while not adopting a disguise, consistently presents himself as something he is not. He protests that he is at peace with the world—"I do not know that Englishman alive / With whom my soul is any jot at odds"—and is indignant that anyone should think him otherwise: "Cannot a plain man live and think no harm?" Many see through his protestations of goodwill and loyalty, especially Queen Elizabeth and her family; and even the common citizens take his measure, one remarking, "O, full of danger is the Duke of Gloucester."[3] But with others he is remarkably successful in his subterfuge, deceiving his brother Clarence, the guileless Lord Chamberlain, Hastings, and an impressionable Anne,

3. Richard's title before he is crowned.

whom he persuades to marry him despite the fact that he has murdered both her husband and her father-in-law. The innocent princes are taken in by his avuncular concern, but they are obviously uneasy in his company and fearful when told that, for their protection, they will reside in the Tower. During the course of the play Richard disposes of them all at a time when it suits his purpose.

Richard III's most audacious performance is his appearance before the citizens of London who have come to persuade him to assume the throne. The entire charade is stage-managed by the Duke of Buckingham, who pleads with him to accept the crown. Richard appears on a balcony flanked by two bishops, having answered the summons with great reluctance, he complains, since he is "divinely bent on meditation" and was interrupted in his prayers. He humbly rejects Buckingham's offer, pleading that he is "unfit for state and majesty." The duke turns away in mock disgust, and Richard calls him back to accept the offer of the crown, still complaining, however: "Will you enforce me to a world of cares?" It is a brilliant impersonation of a man with no worldly ambitions, this from one who has schemed and murdered for years to gain the crown. And he succeeds!

Another master of deception is, of course, *Othello*'s "honest, honest Iago." Unlike Richard, he convinces everyone, including his wife who should know better, that he is the soul of integrity. Trading on his reputation as a man of "exceeding honesty," Iago embarks on a campaign of lies and innuendos to persuade Othello that his wife Desdemona is engaged in an illicit affair with his handsome lieutenant Cassio. The fruit of this deception is the wounding of Cassio and the death of both husband and wife.

## Mistaken Identities

A character may deliberately impersonate another or be taken by mistake for someone else, but whichever the case the result can be comic confusion. As a theatrical device, the introduction of mistaken identities creates a unique instance of dramatic irony, since audience members are aware of the true identities and await with mounting expectation the dramatic moment of disclosure. It is an agreeable sensation to watch the look of surprise or consternation on the faces of those who experience a sudden revelation of something we have known all along.

An example of impersonation by conscious design is the time-honored "bed trick." Shakespeare uses it twice, in *Measure for Measure* and *All's Well That Ends Well.* Although we examine the device in greater detail elsewhere,[4] something may be said here of its use as a means of deception. A man lusts for a woman, who is impervious to his charms. A second woman, who for some reason wants to engage the man's affections, persuades the first to arrange an assignation with him on the condition that he come at night, stay but an hour, and remain silent the entire time. The second woman then secretly takes her place without the man's knowledge. The assumption of the bed trick is that the man is so inflamed with desire that he remains oblivious to who it is he is bedding, a condition that calls for a considerable suspension of disbelief on the part of the audience—but it is not wildly improbable.

More often in Shakespeare, however, characters are mistaken for others without their knowledge, which can result in a bewildering sequence of misconceptions. The action often revolves around similarities in appearance of identical twins, and such is the case in Shakespeare's early work, *The Comedy of Errors.* The play is a farce, by which is meant that it contains a great deal of foolery and not much substance. We should not expect profound thought from such a work, but it cannot be dismissed simply because it lacks profundity. *The Comedy of Errors* is, in fact, highly popular in the various Shakespeare festivals throughout the world, where audiences are well advised to check their expectation of meaning and insight in the

4. See pp. 19–20 and 189.

cloakroom and sit back to enjoy a rollicking good comedy. If the play has a theme, it is that physical resemblance is an illusion, concealing the true nature of humans, but it would be unwise to dwell at any length on the thought.

Briefly, the play is an account of two sets of identical twins, one of which is the sons of Egeon, a wealthy merchant of Syracuse, the other the sons of a poor woman whom Egeon had generously adopted to be brought up as servants to his own. The family became separated in a storm at sea: Egeon's wife was carried off with one child from each set, and he was rescued with the other two. Time passes and the children grow to manhood, until Egeon's son, who has been raised in Syracuse, decides to travel, accompanied by his servant, in search of his brother, and the merchant follows him. As the play opens, they land in Ephesus, which is by chance the home of the other brother and his servant, and the fun begins. Productions traditionally dress the twins in similar costumes, and the situation is further complicated by the fact that each set of them has the same name. The merchant's sons are Antipholus of Syracuse and Antipholus of Ephesus, the servants Dromio of Syracuse and Dromio of Ephesus (identified as S. Antipholus, E. Antipholus, S. Dromio, and E. Dromio in the text of the play). The coincidences make for hilarious scenes of misunderstandings, as each Dromio is puzzled by the behavior of the man he believes to be his master, and each Antipholus is enraged by the apparent stupidity of his supposed servant.

One example of the comic effect of mistaken identities will serve to illustrate Shakespeare's skillful use of the device. At one point E. Antipholus instructs E. Dromio to "buy a rope, and bring it home to me." Meanwhile S. Antipholus tells S. Dromio to engage a ship so that they may leave Ephesus. S. Dromio mistakes E. Antipholus for his master and reports that he has secured a ship as ordered, only to be rebuked angrily because he had been sent for a rope, not a ship. Later E. Antipholus mistakes S. Dromio for his servant and instructs him to secure a sum of money for him so that he can pay a debt. E. Dromio finally finds his real master and upon being asked for the money insists that he "was sent for nothing but a rope." Meanwhile S. Dromio delivers the money to his puzzled master, who has no idea where it has come from but accepts it anyway. Shakespeare adroitly keeps the plot rolling from one mistaken identity to another, not allowing the twins to confront one another until the final scene.

Another instance of this comic device is in *Twelfth Night*. Here Viola and her twin brother Sebastian are shipwrecked and separated, each thinking the other drowned. They both converge on the court of Duke Orsino. Again, they are dressed in similar costumes, as Viola assumes the identity of the duke's page, Cesario; and again Shakespeare keeps them apart until the final scene. This confusion of identities results in a number of comic encounters, two of which stand out. In the first, Orsino is madly in love with Olivia, a wealthy neighboring woman, but since she wants nothing to do with him, he sends Viola/Cesario to woo her on his behalf. Olivia is unimpressed with the duke's message but promptly falls in love with his messenger. Viola manages to fend her off, but complications arise when Sebastian wanders innocently into the lady's presence. Olivia mistakes him for Cesario and persuades him to marry her, which, it seems, he is only too happy to do.

A second episode in the play involves the riotous Sir Toby Belch and Sir Andrew Aguecheek, a ridiculous fop who has aspirations, encouraged by Sir Toby, to marry the wealthy Olivia himself. Aguecheek is upset because she pays more attention to Orsino's page than she does to him. On a whim, Sir Toby persuades Aguecheek to challenge Viola/Cesario to a duel, insisting that if he does, Olivia will admire his prowess. The result is a ludicrous scene in which Viola and Aguecheek are compelled to engage in the duel, each having been persuaded that the other is a fierce and accomplished swordsman. They confront one another with drawn swords, but each fearfully attempts to avoid the other. The twin element comes into play when Sir Toby and Aguecheek come upon Sebastian and, thinking him the singularly unwarlike Viola, challenge him, only to find that he is unexpectedly more than able in a fight. The two end up with battered heads, still wondering what happened.

Somewhat less amusing is the mistaken identity in *Cymbeline*. Imogen, the daughter of the king, adopts the disguise of a young man and sets out to find her husband, Posthumus. The king's stepson, Cloten (rhymes with "rotten"), had wanted her for himself and been rudely rebuffed. Seeking vengeance for the rejection, he secures a suit of Posthumus's clothes and pursues Imogen with the intention of ravishing her while dressed as her husband. In her wandering, she comes upon three men, one elderly, the others youths, who pursue a rustic existence, living by the hunt and sheltered in a cave. They develop an immediate liking for her (actually the young men turn out to be her brothers) and take her under their protection. She feels sickly one day and takes a potion she has been told is medicine for her ailment, but which is in fact a powerful drug that reduces her to a deathlike sleep.

Meanwhile Cloten, still wearing the clothes of Posthumus, encounters the three men and is arrogantly abusive, challenging one of the youths to a duel. They exit to engage each other, and the outcome of the fight becomes evident when the youth returns proudly displaying Cloten's head. He scornfully tosses it into a nearby stream, and the men lay the body out for burial. They then discover the unconscious Imogen, whom they believe to be dead as well, so they lay her body next to the corpse of Cloten and move off to prepare the graves. She comes out of her trance and, finding a headless body lying next to her dressed in her husband's garments, sorrowfully concludes that it is he. She subsequently comes under the protection of a paternal Roman general and, still in disguise, finds herself ultimately back in her father's court, where she discovers that Posthumus is alive and well.

*Cymbeline* is a play into which Shakespeare introduces every trick of plot he has learned in two decades of composition: a woman disguised as a man, a Roman invasion of Britain with scenes of combat, a wicked queen and her thoroughly unpleasant son, a father angry that his daughter marries against his will, lost sons returned to their father, a madly jealous husband determined to kill his innocent wife, ghosts of his dead relatives, a *deus ex machina* appearance of Jupiter, a potion that produces the appearance of death, and, as mentioned, a headless corpse. At the end of this crowded spectacle, however, all are reconciled, except for the queen and her son, who are dead—evil is overcome and virtue triumphs.

Mistaken identities may also prove fatal: A mob of Roman citizens, enraged at the murder of Julius Caesar, storm into the streets in search of his assassins. They encounter Cinna, the poet, whom they take for a conspirator of the same name. The poet insists that they have the wrong man and that he had nothing to do with the assassination, but the mob kills him anyway—because his name is Cinna.

## *"Strange Shapes"*

No examination of Shakespeare's illusion would be complete without some mention of the various identities assumed by the spirit world. Supernatural figures, it was thought, can present themselves to human beings in any shape they choose, and will do so perniciously if they are agents of darkness. Hamlet, for example, questions the origins of his father's ghost, "the spirit that I have seen / May be the devil, and the devil hath power / T' assume a pleasing shape."

In *The Tempest,* Prospero has many spirits at his command, and they appear in various guises, some pleasing, some less so. They enter as "strange Shapes" to set a sumptuous table for the shipwrecked lords of Italy, Alonso, the king of Naples, and Sebastian, Prospero's treacherous brother, who had conspired to depose him as Duke of Milan. Later, as goddesses of the ancient world, the spirits perform an entertaining masque to celebrate the betrothal of Ferdinand and Miranda, and still later as vicious hounds they terrify Caliban and his companions, who are plotting Prospero's death. The dutiful spirit Ariel, who serves Prospero, appears for the most part as himself; but he can also change shape, depending on the task assigned him. He confronts the lords of Italy as a fearsome harpy and condemns Alonso to a life of "ling'ring perdition" for his part in overthrowing Prospero. On other occasions he is no more than a voice or the source of enchanting music that leads a charmed Ferdinand to his meeting with Miranda and misleads the comic conspirators into a stinking bog. And at times he comforts Caliban with "sounds and sweet airs, that give delight and hurt not."

Puck is also himself throughout *A Midsummer Night's Dream*, but he admits to assuming bizarre shapes as "that shrewd and knavish sprite / Call'd Robin Goodfellow" to play tricks on humans. He can take the form of a crabapple in an old woman's drink, he says, startling her into spilling it, and he can appear as a "three-foot stool" so that when a woman attempts to sit on it, "then slip I from her bum, down topples she."

Even stranger manifestations of the spirit world are the specters that arise from the witches' cauldron to foretell Macbeth's future with delphic obscurity. The first is an "armed head" that warns him to "beware Macduff," a foreshadowing of his death. The second is "a bloody child" (presumably newborn) assuring him that "none of woman born / Shall harm Macbeth." The third is another child "crowned, with a tree in his hand," who predicts, cryptically, that Macbeth cannot be defeated until "Great Birnam wood to high Dunsinane hill / Shall come against him." The last two oracles fill Macbeth with confidence in his invulnerability—misplaced, as it happens, since Birnam Wood does indeed come to Dunsinane. When finally confronted by Macduff, Macbeth is stunned to hear that his adversary was not "of woman born" but was "from his mother's womb / Untimely ripped." Macbeth learns too late to be wary of "the fiend / That lies like truth" to those singled out for destruction.

Another figure who can conjure spirits from the underworld—

at least according to the English—is Joan la Pucelle (Joan of Arc), as she is portrayed in *Henry VI, Part 1*. She inspires the disheartened French to drive the occupying English forces from their native soil, a highly successful campaign until the battle of Angiers. There her army is routed and she calls upon her demonic forces for aid:

> Now help, ye charming spells and periapts,[5]
> And ye choice spirits that admonish me
> And give me signs of future accidents.

They come at her bidding in the appearance of "fiends," her "familiar spirits, that are cull'd / Out of the powerful regions under earth." But they silently abandon her to the English, who insist she is a witch parading as a "holy maid" and lead her off to be burned at the stake.

Thus in Shakespeare the spirit world has infinite resources to affect mankind, sometimes for good, sometimes for ill, sometimes, like Puck, just for mischief.

Philosophers, theologians, and scientists will continue to ponder this enduring question of mankind's perception of reality. Statesmen will pore over diplomatic dispatches to determine if they say what they seem to say. Television ads will assault us with happy, dancing figures apparently ecstatic over a bubbling glass of sugared water. Men and women will present themselves to us masked or disguised as other than who and what they are. The natural world will offer an image of lush greenery one day, only to transform itself on another into a specter of grey fields and dead branches. And the devil will appear as a smiling benefactor who bears the gift of a small bag of white powder.

And playwrights will continue to place before us figures who embody this enigma, making full use of a medium that is itself the essence of illusion, at the same time warning us to be wary of the

5. A magic jewel or stone, often worn as a necklace.

very deception they practice. Shakespeare returns to this theme time and again with characters who express their distress and bewilderment that things are not what they seem. A thoroughly confused Feste in *Twelfth Night,* mistaking Sebastian for the duke's page Cesario, observes that "nothing that is so is so." Gonzalo, dazed by the sudden appearance of Prospero, exclaims, "whether this be / Or be not, I'll not swear." And Macbeth, shaken by the predictions of the witches, mutters to himself that "nothing is / But what is not." The world, Shakespeare tells us, may be as much an illusion as the stage, and the stage itself, of course, is no more than a fantasy. Indeed, the human race itself may exist only in the imagination of some transcendent playwright.

In Shakespeare, then, illusion may be at times the source of sorrow, but it can also yield delight. The poet puts the petty annoyances of our daily round into a benign perspective. Life may indeed be but a part we play, but if we enact it with grace, all may be well. Whether the role be large or small, it has its place, Shakespeare seems to say, in the chronicle of human history, and it can be either tragic or comic, depending on the illusion we choose to embrace.

# UNIVERSAL ORDER

SHAKESPEARE'S PLAYS contain frequent and at times cryptic passages reflecting articles of belief which were strongly held at the time but which have since passed out of Western culture. Central to the Renaissance concept of the universe was the conviction that since God is one, that is, indivisible, so also is all his creation one, a vast unit in which his grand design can be detected at every level of existence. Shakespeare's contemporaries were anxious to see order and purpose in their discordant world (though perhaps no more so than distracted citizens of our own day), and they looked for signs of a divine pattern to the immensely varied spectacle that nature, the heavens, and mankind presented to the eye. It was a comfortable universe, one the mind could grasp. The stars circled the earth embedded in a sphere with heaven everywhere above it, and learned theologians debated how distant it was from earth. God was up there above the stars, just beyond our reach and comprehension but close enough to be a presence in human affairs, and mankind stood at the very center of it all.[1] Astronomers of the sixteenth and scientists of the seventeenth centuries cast the whole elaborate structure in doubt, however, and some mourned its passing. As early as 1611,

1. The most accessible study of this system of belief is E. M. W. Tillyard's *The Elizabethan World Picture* (London: Chatto & Windus, 1943). It is a short book, barely a hundred pages long, but comprehensive in its coverage. I should mention at the outset that the applicability of Tillyard's analysis to the plays is questioned by modern scholars. Although the book is somewhat out of favor, it is a helpful guide for playgoers to some of Shakespeare's puzzling imagery.

when Shakespeare first staged *The Tempest,* the poet John Donne complained that science had rendered the system of belief "all in pieces, all coherence gone," leaving behind a race of sickly humans and a world in decay.[2]

The imagery of universal order is everywhere in Shakespeare, a recurring theme that finds in the structure of human society or the chronicle of human history a pattern that matches one to be seen in the heavens or the natural world. The most extended definition of the concept in the plays appears in *Troilus and Cressida.* There Ulysses is cautioning the disgruntled Greeks, who after seven long and fruitless years of war on Troy are challenging the generalship of Agamemnon. In his often cited speech on "degree," Ulysses compares their dissent to a violation of the structure of the universe:

> The heavens themselves, the planets, and this centre
> Observe degree, priority, and place,
> Insisture, course, proportion, season, form,
> Office, and custom, in all line of order.

And he warns,

> O, when degree is shak'd,
> Which is the ladder of all high designs,
> The enterprise is sick.
> . . . . . . . . . . . . . . . . . . . . . . . . . . . . . .
> Take but degree away, untune that string,
> And hark what discord follows.

Ulysses compares the image of universal order to the structure of human society, to "communities, / Degrees in school, and brotherhood in cities, / Peaceful commerce"; and he then addresses the immediate concern, the challenge to Agamemnon's leadership. He cautions that "the neglection of degree" among the Greeks threatens their cause, predicting that once "the general's disdain'd," anyone

2. In "The First Anniversary."

up and down the ranks of the army "that is sick / Of his superior" will refuse to obey him, compromising the entire command structure. Troy, he concludes, "in our weakness stands, not in her strength."

In Shakespeare's time this concept of universal order was imagined as a great Chain of Being attached at one end to the throne of God and stretching downward through the ranks of angels and lesser spirits to mankind, nature, and the lowest level of the material world, the inanimate stone, thus encompassing all creation. Mankind's position in the Chain is unique, it was said, in that humans are both physical in their bodies and spiritual in their souls. The image was subjected to elaborate refinement over the centuries, resulting in a complex, though still cohesive, body of belief.

A chain was an effective image of that body of belief, since it is an entity, a "one," if you will, and at the same time an interlocking string of individual links, each of which could be imagined as representing a different level of existence. There are two elements of this system that most frequently appear in Shakespeare's plays. The first is a condition in which events at any one level, or link in the Chain, are reflected in all the others. This is a logical conclusion to draw from the image, since tension on any part of a chain is felt throughout. The second element is equally reasonable: individual links, which again represent separate levels of existence, resemble the entire Chain, and, moreover, one another, as anyone who looks at a chain will confirm. It does not strain belief to conclude that, since God created it all, evidence of his grand design will be found wherever one may seek it. His handprint, in brief, could be seen everywhere.

## The Chain as One

To consider the first element: Shakespeare frequently describes the manner in which events at one level of existence are reflected or foreshadowed up and down the Chain of Being, in the heavens, nature, mankind's social and political world, and within the human spirit. These allusions cannot be dismissed as mere scene-setting; they were, rather, genuine articles of belief at the time. Modern commentators, understandably skeptical of medieval superstition, may suspect that Shakespeare was simply exploiting his audiences' naiveté for dramatic purpose, but there is no evidence that he thought other than they, denied as he was the scientific discoveries of later times.

Several characters in the plays, practical men of the world who seem to doubt the system, come to a bad end. In *Henry IV, Part 1,* Hotspur, the son of the Earl of Northumberland, leads a coalition of Scots, Welsh, and northern English barons in a rebellion against the king. The Welsh were highly regarded for their warlike prowess at the time, but the English generally thought of them as a primitive people, given to ancient ritual and superstitious beliefs. The Welsh leader, Owen Glendower, tries Hotspur's patience with tedious accounts of the miraculous manifestations in heaven and on earth that accompanied his birth—signs, he insists, of his future greatness. The notoriously short-tempered Hotspur risks alienating an important ally by voicing his contempt for Glendower's beliefs: "Why, so would it have done / At the same season if your mother's cat had / But kitten'd, though yourself had never been born."

Again, in *King Lear,* the bastard Edmund succeeds in convincing his father, the Earl of Gloucester, that his legitimate son Edgar is plotting to kill him so as to inherit the title. Gloucester, already shaken by Lear's angry dismissal of his favorite daughter Cordelia, ponders the discord in the kingdom, finding that "these late eclipses of the sun and moon portend no good to us." Edgar's supposed treachery, he concludes, "comes under the prediction; there's son against father"; and in like manner, "the king falls from bias of nature; there's father against child." Gloucester instructs Edmund to "find out this villain" and leaves him alone to contemplate his father's beliefs. Edmund scornfully dismisses such superstitions: "This is the excellent foppery of the world," he scoffs, "that when we are sick in fortune—often the surfeits of our own behavior—we make guilty of our disasters the sun, the moon, and the stars."

Both Hotspur and Edmund, then, express contempt for the notion that the fortunes of mankind are reflected in natural phenomena, that the heavens and the earth are somehow linked. In both plays, it cannot escape notice, both of these thoroughly modern young men are doomed, not as a consequence of their skepticism certainly, but doomed nonetheless. Hotspur is killed by Prince Hal at the battle of Shrewsbury, and in the end Edmund falls to Edgar.

In *Julius Caesar* the conspirator Cassius is yet another skeptic. In his effort to persuade Brutus of the threat that Caesar poses to Rome, he insists that if their liberties are endangered, the blame lies solely on the Romans themselves: "The fault, dear Brutus, is not in our stars, / But in ourselves, that we are underlings." Later he is defiant of the strange events in heaven and on earth on the night before the assassination. An apprehensive Casca remarks on the fierce tempest that assaults Rome and informs Cassius of a slave whose hand burst into flames with no harm done to it, of a lion in the Capitol, and of a report that "men all in fire walk up and down the streets," all signs, he fears, of "portentous things" to come. Cassius declares himself unfazed by the raging elements. He has, he says, "walk'd about the streets, / Submitting me unto the perilous night," and when lightning struck, "I did present myself / Even in the aim and very flash of it." As for the various apparitions, he preys upon Casca's superstition by interpreting the phenomena to suit his purpose, justifying the conspiracy against Caesar. They are, he says, a "warning / Unto some monstrous state," a veiled reference to the fate of Rome should Caesar be declared king and entrusted with despotic power. Casca's fears are closer to the truth, however, for the death of Caesar on the following day ushers in fifteen years of civil strife in the empire, wars and massacres that do not end until Octavius Caesar defeats Mark Antony, as dramatized in the closing acts of *Antony and Cleopatra.* And Cassius dies at the battle of Philippi.

Can we conclude from the deaths of such skeptics as Hotspur, Edmund, and Cassius that Shakespeare was wedded to the old system of beliefs? Surely not, nor can we say he rejected it. We cannot know. We may conclude, however, that he employed the theme of universal order pervasively as a powerful metaphor in his plays, and that he saw it for what it was, a means of stirring the imagination of audiences who accepted the belief as a credible rationale for the inexplicable vagaries of their lives.

Thus dire human events resonate throughout the Chain of Being. The animal world was thought to be closely attuned to the affairs of mankind. At the same time that Casca is voicing his anxiety to Cassius, Caesar's wife, Calphurnia, attempts to dissuade her husband from going to the Senate by giving a fearful account of her dream, in which "a lioness whelped in the streets, / And graves yawn'd and yielded up their dead." Caesar scoffs at her fears; but, just to be sure, he orders the priests to examine the entrails of a sacrificial animal for any signs of trouble. Word comes back that the animal was found to have no heart, an ominous sign; and, though later he is to change his mind again, Caesar decides not to attend the Senate that day. The behavior of birds was especially significant in the ancient world, where their flight was thought to be a message from the gods. In *Julius Caesar,* as the armies are on the march to Philippi, Cassius tells Brutus that the eagles who had been accompanying them have flown off, replaced by unsavory "ravens, crows, and kites." The belief was still alive in Shakespeare's England. On the night Macbeth murders King Duncan, aside from other disturbing events, "it was the owl that shriek'd," an uncommon call for a bird that customarily hoots.

In *Macbeth,* in fact, all of nature responds to the murder of the king. The night is stormy, as if "the heavens as troubled with man's act, / Threatens his bloody stage." Lennox reports that at the same time there were "lamentations heard i' th' air, strange screams of death . . . and some say the earth / Was feverish and did shake." It is further reported as a time when owls unaccountably killed falcons and horses ate one another. The entire universe is uneasy because of the crime. Again, when King Lear is shut out by his "ingrateful daughters" and wanders over the heath in a raging storm, it is not only the heavens that are in disarray. The storm reflects "the tempest" in Lear's mind and at another level disorder in the families of the kingdom—brother against brother, sister against sister, daughters against father, son against father, father against son, and wife against husband. England itself is distressed—the dukes are at odds, a servant kills his master, the king is left to die in the wasteland, and invasion threatens from France. Nothing has gone right since Lear split up his kingdom, and the consequences of his decision are felt at all levels of existence. Thus his distemper and eventual madness are reflected in disorder throughout the Chain, within his mind, the family, the kingdom, and the heavens themselves.

Yet another example of the interconnectedness of different levels of existence is the intrusion of ghosts and other supernatural manifestations of the spirit world into human affairs. Shakespeare's contemporaries had no doubt that the spirits of the dead could walk the earth for various reasons, most frequently to seek vengeance for their death, and we may assume that he shared their belief. Once Macbeth mounts the throne of Scotland, he frets over the witches' prediction that Banquo's heirs will be kings, which if true, he complains, has "plac'd a fruitless crown" on his head and "a barren scepter" in his hand. To remove the threat, he orders Banquo murdered, and on the night he holds a state dinner in the company of his thanes, receives confirmation that he is dead. As the feast begins, the bloody ghost of Banquo enters, taking what was his seat at the table. Seen only by Macbeth, the ghost glares at the king and perhaps points an accusing finger at him. Macbeth is distraught, and his thanes amazed, as he rages at the ghost: "Hence, horrible shadow! / Unreal mock'ry, hence!" It disappears and Macbeth recovers himself, but since the evening is obviously in ruins, Lady Macbeth dismisses their guests.

Again, the appearance of the ghost of Hamlet's father on the battlements of Elsinore leads Horatio to fear "some strange eruption to our state" and Marcellus that "there's something rotten in the state of Denmark." Horatio's fear of "eruption" is indeed prescient, for the specter's visit precipitates events that end in the death of, among others, the royal family of Denmark. In Shakespeare, then, as in popular belief, a ghostly visitation bodies ill for those who see it—these are not benign apparitions.[3]

The witches of *Macbeth* hover between the physical and spiritual realms in that they seem substantial enough but possess the mysterious ability to make a man "dwindle, peak, and pine." They also have knowledge of the future, which they use to tempt Macbeth into fulfilling the destiny foretold him. The fact that their predictions cause Scotland untold miseries is of no consequence to them, since they give every appearance of acting as agents of a malevolent power.

A variation on this theme of unity was the belief that any one link contains all the elements of the entire Chain: the earth is a microcosm of the universe, the human body of the earth, as in the words of the poet John Donne: "I am a little world made cunningly / Of elements, and an angelic sprite."[4] And colonies of insects and animals were said to constitute small replicas of human society. As Henry V prepares to invade France, he is concerned that the troublesome Scots will take advantage of his absence to invade England. The Archbishop of Canterbury advises him to campaign with an army large enough "to make all Gallia shake" and leave the bulk of his forces at home to guard the country's borders. Separate elements of a society play different roles in the state, he goes on, some venture abroad, some protect the homeland, some engage in crafts and commerce. He illustrates the point by comparing England to a beehive,

3. In other instances, Caesar's ghost promises Brutus cryptically that he will see him "at Philippi," a veiled premonition of defeat in the battle and of retribution for his murder. And Richard III is visited by the apparitions of his many victims on the night before his defeat and death at the battle of Bosworth Field. They all curse him: "Despair and die!"

4. In his Holy Sonnet, "I am a little world."

where the many levels of the swarm have distinct functions, the queen, the drones, the gatherers, all working together for the benefit of the community: "So work the honey-bees, / Creatures that by rule of nature teach / The act of order to a peopled kingdom."

In *Richard II* the garden is a microcosm of the state. The king, preoccupied with the splendor of his court, takes no notice of the growing resentment among the nobility because of his arbitrary taxes and unlawful confiscation of their estates. Henry Bolingbroke, the Duke of Lancaster, taps into their discontent and unseats Richard, replacing him on the throne as Henry IV. It is the Duke of York's gardener who takes the full measure of the deposed king, reflecting the sentiments of his subjects when they hear of quarrels among the great. He instructs his workers in terms that call to mind the managing of a kingdom: they are to bind up "yon dangling apricocks," provide support for "bending twigs," and "like an executioner / Cut off the heads of too fast growing sprays / That look too lofty in our commonwealth." They labor thus, he says, so that all the trees will "be even in our government," standing in a tidy line ornamental to the land. He compares Richard's neglect of England to those who allow their gardens to grow untended. Though sympathetic to the overthrown king, he sees his fault clearly: "O, what a pity is it / That he had not so trimm'd and dress'd his land / As we this garden." Like trees, he says, proud men must be pruned: "Superfluous branches / We lop away, that bearing boughs may live"; and if the king had "done so to great and growing men, / They might have liv'd to bear and he to taste / Their fruits of duty." It was because of his "waste of idle hours," he concludes, that Richard has lost his crown.

## *The Chain as Links*

The influence of turmoil at one level of existence upon all creation is but one of the elements of the image of universal order that Shakespeare made use of. Also prominent in the plays is the belief that the different levels resemble one another in significant respects. Logically, since God created everything, all levels are stamped with his signature; or in terms of the Chain of Being, any one link is much like another. Thus human society can be compared to the orbiting of heavenly bodies or a community of bees. Our emotions are at times like calm seas, at others a raging tempest; and we resemble on the one hand saints who preside over celestial spheres and on the other beasts that roam the wild. Existence may greet the eye with an infinite variety of things—peaks and valleys, creatures in myriad shapes and sizes, flowers in a rich profusion of colors, trees both stately and stunted, endless deserts, barren coasts, and fertile fields. But in the medieval system of belief, it's all one, and the human body has much in common with the worm.

The manner in which God's design could be perceived at all levels of existence was ingeniously demonstrated in numerology. The figure seven had religious significance—seven sacraments, seven corporal works of mercy, and the seven days of creation, on the last of which God rested. The material world reflected its union with the spiritual in such parallels as the seven days of the week, the seven celestial bodies that could be observed, it was thought, circling the earth, and the seven openings in the human head. It would not have been thought insignificant in those times that, as was later discovered, there are seven seas and a like number of continents.

The figure four was also important, particularly in the belief that the elemental essences of the material world are earth, air, fire, and water. Cleopatra, as she is dying, rejoices. "Husband I come!" she exclaims, "I am fire and air; my other elements [earth, water] I give to baser life." A mysterious "quintessence" was said to be the end result of a merging of the four elements, reducing them to one pure substance, the desired outcome of experiments by medieval alchemists. The elements were matched by another four, the humors of the human body, identified as blood, phlegm, and black and yellow bile, the last two sometimes referred to as melancholy and choler. It was believed that Adam and Eve were endowed with an immortality attributed to the even balance of humors in the body, but that fallen humanity is plagued with an uneven distribution determined by the confluence of the stars at birth. All humans come into the world with this imbalance, it was said, a legacy of the first couple's sin, and continued health depends on maintaining the distribution they are born with. It was this belief that led to the barbarous remedies of the time for any illness or injury—bleeding, purging, leeching, and cupping.[5] In Shakespeare's *Henry IV, Part 1,* Bardolph has a serious complexion problem, a condition, he says, caused by an excess of choler in his system. In *Henry IV, Part 2* and *The Merry Wives of Windsor,* Nym ends every remark with "that's the humor of it," by which he means, "that's the way it is," or "this is how I am." Further, it was said that any sort of excessive behavior, anger, melancholy, or hatred, arose from the same cause. Duke Frederick's courtier, Le Beau, warns Orlando in *As You Like It* that he would be well advised to flee for his life because "the Duke is humorous" and has taken a strong dislike to the young man.

This pattern of resemblance between the various links in the Chain of Being is repeated in the expression of human emotions, where pride, self-control, love, and resolve are identified with levels of existence above and below humanity. Julius Caesar, presented with appeals for clemency for a banished Roman citizen, refuses, declaring that his will is "as constant as the northern star," the only fixed body in the night sky. Gazing up at a lighted window, Romeo declares that "it is the east, and Juliet is the sun." Contemplating

---

5. These remedies were practiced until the nineteenth century. Dr. Benjamin Rush, who courageously remained in Philadelphia to care for the sick during the yellow fever plague of 1792, prescribed a cure of "purge and bleed." In more modern times, Anthony Quinn in the film *Zorba the Greek* undergoes a "cupping," in which heated goblets are applied to his back to draw out the venomous "humors" that cause his illness.

"two of the fairest stars in all the heaven," he asks, "what if her eyes were there, they in her head?"[6] In *Henry V,* a nervous French envoy asks the king if he can deliver the dauphin's insulting message without incurring his wrath, and Henry assures him that his passions are as subject to his will as are the "wretches fett'red in our prisons." The dauphin's mocking gift of tennis balls, a symbol of Henry's misspent youth, proves a serious challenge to his resolve, however. The French envoy may have escaped unharmed, but a similar bearer of bad news to Cleopatra is less fortunate. When he informs her of Antony's marriage to Octavia, she beats him, raging that the news has made Egypt for her "a cistern of scal'd snakes." As King Lear enters in the final scene bearing the body of Cordelia, he demands of his followers not that they pray, or weep, or mourn, but that they respond to the sight with an animal cry: "Howl! Howl! Howl!" And Henry V urges his soldiers to show their bravery and "imitate the actions of a tiger" as they enter battle.

The concept that all levels of existence resemble one another is prominent in Shakespeare's portrayal of social relationships. Integral to the system was the provision that each level has a dominant figure. As God rules over all creation, it was said, so the sun rules the heavens, the lion beasts, the eagle birds, the whale fish, and within the realm of inanimate objects the diamond is prominent among stones. The report on Macbeth and Banquo in the battle to repel the Norwegian invasion is that the one was as an eagle among sparrows, the other a lion among hares. In the human sphere, generals command armies, fathers preside over families, and, as is frequently noted in the plays, the king rules over his subjects. It is all part of that grand design shaped by the hand of God, one in which, as we have seen in the counsel of Ulysses, "degree" is the cement that binds the whole social structure together.

This imagery of hierarchy surfaces throughout the plays, espe-

6. Shakespeare invokes a long tradition of love poetry here with imagery that survives to our present day in popular lyrics, though stripped of its metaphysical significance.

cially in the authority of a father over his family. His right to choose husbands for his daughters receives its most unambiguous expression by Hermia's father, Egeus, in A *Midsummer Night's Dream*.[7] When she rejects Demetrius, her father's choice as a husband, in favor of Lysander, Egeus accuses her lover of turning his daughter's "obedience, which is due to me, / To stubborn harshness." "As she is mine," he insists, "I may dispose of her," and he repeats the image of ownership: "She is mine, and all my right to her / I do estate unto Demetrius." He is overruled in the end, of course—this *is* a comedy—but his claims graphically illustrate the preeminent role of the father in the family.

The pattern is repeated in the accepted authority of husband over wife, a dominance buttressed by scriptural authority, God's punishment of Eve: "Thy desire shall be to thy husband, and he shall rule over thee."[8] In *The Merchant of Venice*, young Bassanio pays court to the beautiful and wealthy Portia. To win her hand, however, he must agree to the conditions imposed by her dead father. Three closed caskets are placed before him, one each of gold, silver, and lead, and he must select the one that holds her portrait. He finds it successfully in the lead one, and a delighted Portia commits herself to him as "her lord, her governor, her king." It was customary at the time for the husband to inherit his wife's wealth, so she happily confirms that "myself, and what is mine, to you and yours / Is now converted."

The wife, like the daughter, was often described as a legal possession of her husband, a tradition that receives its most brazen expression in *The Taming of the Shrew*. Petruchio, having married the ungovernable Kate, announces that they will leave immediately for his estate in Verona, despite entreaties that he at least remain for the bridal dinner. She refuses to accompany him and he insists, asserting his right to command her in highly provocative terms:

7. See "Love and Hatred," pp. 16–17 and 102.
8. Genesis 3:16.

I will be master of what is my own.
She is my goods, my chattels, she is my house,
My household stuff, my field, my barn,
My horse, my ox, my ass, my any thing.

In the closing scene of the play, Kate, to all appearances tamed, chides the other wives for their failure to accept their husbands as "thy lord, thy life, thy keeper, / Thy head, thy sovereign" whom "they are bound to serve, love, and obey." The language of Portia and Petruchio falls harshly on modern ears and was perhaps a bit extreme even in Shakespeare's time; but, again, in a world ordered by "degree" it was thought that a dominant figure presided over every level of nature and human society, including the family. Besides, we need not take their words too seriously, reminding ourselves that these are, after all, comedies.

## Political Order

There are so many kings, emperors, princes, dukes, earls, and governors in Shakespeare's plays that the imagery of dominance is most prominently displayed in the political sphere. That imagery portrays the king as ruler by divine right. Subjects who challenge that right are said to endanger the welfare not only of themselves but of an entire nation for generations to come. Nowhere do the role of God in the rule of a nation and the imagery of resemblance between different levels of existence appear more pervasively than in *Richard II*. When confronted by a coalition of rebellious nobles led by Henry Bolingbroke, the Duke of Lancaster, the king wavers between defiance and submission. He challenges their presumption in questioning his right to reign. It was customary then, as it is now, for the priests to anoint English kings with holy oils at their coronation as a symbol of divine sanction; and Richard proclaims as much: "Not all the waters of the rough rude sea / Can wash the balm off from an anointed king." Deserted by his own forces and cornered at Flint Castle in Wales, Richard nonetheless defies the rebels, citing his divine right: "Show us the hand of God / That hath dismiss'd us from our stewardship, / For well we know that no hand of blood and bone / Can gripe the sacred handle of our sceptre."

When the king shows signs of weakness, he is reminded by the loyal Bishop of Carlisle that "the Power that made you king / Hath power to keep you king in spite of all." With renewed resolve, Richard launches into an impassioned exposition on the analogy between the sun's domination of the heavens and the king's rule over his subjects: traitors and murderers thrive in the night when the king is absent, but they hide once the sun rises and he returns. And he concludes with a soaring assertion of his faith in divine favor: "God for his Richard hath in heavenly pay / A glorious angel; then if angels fight, / Weak men must fall, for heaven still guards the right." Bolingbroke invokes the same analogy. Seeing Richard on the battlements of Flint Castle, he compares him to "the blushing discontented sun" struggling through "envious clouds" that seek "to dim his glory." The helpless but still loyal Duke of York, gazing on the same scene, employs a different image from the Chain of Being: "Yet looks he like a king! Behold his eye, / As bright as is the eagle's, lightens forth / Controlling majesty."

The sun-king analogy surfaces with some frequency in other plays as well. In *Henry IV, Part 1,* Prince Hal soliloquizes on his youthful indiscretions, carousing with the disreputable Falstaff and his band of thieves and wastrels in the Boar's Head Tavern. When he assumes his destined role in the kingdom, he predicts, his subjects will wonder at the transformation. He will be like the sun "breaking through the foul and ugly mists / Of vapors that did seem to strangle him," and he will therefore shine the more brightly once he has emerged from behind "the base contagious clouds." This parallel between a king's rule and celestial order is developed in other terms elsewhere in the play. When King Henry attempts to persuade the rebellious nobles to lay down their arms, he promises them amnesty if they will resume their proper role as planets orbiting about the sun/throne, where "you did give a fair and natural light" rather than acting as meteors, the "portend / Of broached mischief to the unborn times." Again, the analogy lies behind Hamlet's pun in his opening lines in the play. His stepfather, King Claudius, asks the brooding prince why "the clouds still hang" on him, and he replies with biting wit, "not so, my lord, I am too much in the sun." Having been denied succession to the throne when Claudius married his widowed mother, Hamlet, still the son, must continue to live in the reflected glory of his king-father.

The notion that the king is ordained by God to rule and that his crown is therefore inviolable was encouraged by monarchs in Shakespeare's time and thereafter. One advocate of divine right later in the seventeenth century went so far as to say that "we are not to *speak Evil of the Ruler of the People*: not only for *Gods* sake, whose *Vicegerent* he is, but for his own."[9] Another insisted that should the king prove tyrannical, corrupt, or even mad, the only recourse his subjects have for relief from his oppression is "Prayers and Teares."[1] If they attempted to depose him, so went the belief, they were tampering with the deity's sacred design; and if they succeeded, not only the rebels themselves but the entire nation would suffer retribution for the impious act of disrupting that design. John of Gaunt is aware of Richard II's iniquities, but he insists that it is "God's quarrel" and he can take no action against "God's substitute, / His deputy anointed in his sight." "Let heaven revenge," he concludes, "for I must never lift / An angry arm against His minister."

When Bolingbroke deposes Richard II to become Henry IV, the loyal Bishop of Carlisle angrily denounces him, prophesying the terrors that will follow; "The blood of English shall manure the ground," he warns, "and future generations groan for this foul act." Richard had said as much when he defied Bolingbroke at Flint Cas-

9. John Turner, *The Souldiers Catechisme*, London, 1684, p. 12.
1. Thomas Swadlin, *The Souldiers Catechisme*, Oxford, 1645, p. 3.

tle: God "is mustering in his clouds on our behalf / Armies of pestilence, and they shall strike / Your children yet unborn and unbegot." And when he lies dying under an assassin's knife, he predicts the same: "Exton, thy fierce hand / Hath with the King's blood stain'd the King's own land." King Henry, on hearing of the murder and perhaps with Carlisle's curse echoing in his conscience, vows to "make a voyage to the Holy Land, / To wash this blood from off my guilty hand."

Shakespeare's dramatization of the next eighty years of English history seems to confirm these prophecies. The reign of Bolingbroke, as staged in *Henry IV, Parts 1 and 2,* was a time of almost incessant civil strife, as the northern nobles, York and the Percies of Northumberland, in alliance with the Scots and Welsh, conspire to overthrow a king who had overthrown a king, confirming Ulysses warning against the violation of "degree": "Untune that string, / And hark what discord follows."[2] Dissension at home abates for a time as Henry V unites his subjects in a campaign to conquer France, but their unity is short-lived. *Henry VI, Parts 1, 2, and 3* chronicle the years of the devastating War of the Roses, when proud nobles contend for the crown, confirming Carlisle's prophecy that "the blood of English shall manure the ground" as a consequence of Bolingbroke's sacrilege.[3]

That crime—the deposition and murder of an anointed king— is never far from the consciences of Richard II's successors. When Henry IV rebukes his son, Prince Hal, for his irresponsible behavior, he sounds like a modern, exasperated father who asks, "What have I done to deserve this?" He wonders whether God "for some displeasing service I have done, / That in his secret doom, out of my blood / He'll breed revengement and a scourge for me." As the king lies on

2. In some productions Henry is shown to be suffering from a slowly wasting disease, one that finally takes his life in *Part 2.*

3. Shakespeare, as mentioned earlier, wrote the Henry VI plays years before he undertook to dramatize the history of Henry IV. Apparently the theme of divine retribution came late to his pen.

his deathbed in *Henry IV, Part 2,* he freely admits to his son "by what by-paths and indirect crook'd ways / I met this crown," and laments "how troublesome it sat upon my head." And later, as Henry V, Hal kneels to pray in the early morning hours of the day at Agincourt. He pleads with God to relent and withhold his vengeful hand from the battle to come: "Not to-day, O lord / O, not to-day, think not upon the fault / My father made in compassing the crown!" He lists all the pious acts he has performed in penance for the crime—so many gifts to the poor, so many chapels built, so many holy masses recited—so that God will "pardon blood."

It is of interest to note that in Shakespeare's plays set in the ancient world, the ruling figures do not claim the right by divine sanction. It would be anachronistic, of course, to call upon the Christian God in plays set in pagan times, but the various figures seldom refer to the "gods" as determining human affairs. In ancient Greek literature from Homer to Euripides, the various deities constantly meddle in the lives of mortals, harrying heroes, both tragic and comic, this way and that because of jealousies aroused by seemingly petty disagreements among the Olympians. But in Shakespeare's portrayal of ancient Rome, the gods are conspicuous by their absence. Both Caesar and Coriolanus claim their right to public office not because they are endorsed by some divinity but because of what they have done and who they are. Caesar's unalterable will, as "constant as the northern star," he proclaims, is reason enough for him to preside over Rome. He goes to the Senate expecting to be made king, and so he plays the part, insisting he is not as other men, but he does not claim the right according to some cosmic design. Coriolanus infuriates the Roman people with his arrogant insistence that he does not need their approval for elevation to the office of Consul, insisting that it is just reward for his lifelong service to the city and his wartime achievements.

In the practical world of ancient Rome, the imperial crown passes to the man with the most legions at his back, even in the case of Titus Andronicus, who refuses the role and lives to regret it. Allusions to a divinity in the plays come off the tongue of the speaker as curses—"The gods condemn thee"—prayers—"The gods protect thee"—or exclamations—"O ye gods." There is little sense that they have a role in human affairs. *Troilus and Cressida,* for example, is based on Homer's *Iliad.* But while the Olympians are a constant presence in the epic poem, manipulating the outcome of battles— Zeus hurling thunderbolts and Apollo assaulting Patrocles—they are entirely absent from the play. In Shakespeare's Greece and Rome, humans are left to fight it out among themselves. The only episode that comes anywhere close to the Elizabethan pattern is in *Antony and Cleopatra,* when Hercules is said to abandon Antony before his final battle with Octavius Caesar; but this is the only indication in the play that a godlike figure has any influence in human events, and we only learn of it when he washes his hands of the affair and leaves Antony to his fate.

In Shakespeare, however, the patterns of universal order are not always associated with dynastic struggles or hierarchical preroga- tive. In *The Tempest* he offers an image of the Chain of Being that projects a more benign influence on human affairs. The magic island of the play is a miniature of the known and unknown universe, a microcosm of all creation. Prospero stands at the top of the Chain. The "good god o' th' island" employs his "so potent art" to order events so that evil is held in check, love can flourish, and innocence is preserved. When he holds his enemies in his power, he relents and, in an image of divine mercy prevailing over justice, releases them, for, as he says, "the rarer action is / In virtue than in vengeance." Further down the Chain, creatures of the spirit world serve him as they would some reigning metaphysical deity—the du- tiful Ariel and those who appear from time to time to set a table or dance in a masque.

Below the spirit world is the company of humans, some good (Ferdinand, Gonzalo), some wicked (Antonio, Sebastian), some ridiculous (Trinculo, Stephano), and some innocent (Miranda). At the next level is the ambivalent Caliban, who serves as a link between mankind and the animal world. As a human he is endowed with thought and language, and can plot murder. As an animal he lusts unashamedly for the innocent Miranda. He finds nothing wrong with his instinctive desire to ravish her, admitting gleefully that had he not been prevented he would have "peopled else / The isle with Calibans." Prospero nurtured his human side, teaching him to how to talk and "name the bigger light, and how the less"; but because of his lower instincts he must be kept in check, assigned to duties proper to his station, hauling wood and trimming the cave. Next is the vegetable world that Gonzalo sees about him, "every thing advantageous to life." And at the lowest level of this grand design is a cave that serves as home for Prospero and Miranda and the "hard rock" where Caliban keeps himself.

Thus the play traces the links in the Chain of Being from the God of justice and mercy who presides over the whole down to the lowly, inanimate stone. And all creation serves this "god o' th' is-land"—the spirits that do his bidding, the humans who must sub-mit to his will, the reluctant Caliban, the natural world that provides him sustenance, and the rocky cave that offers him shelter. It seems a shame he must leave it and return to a dissension-riddled Italy.

This, then, is the universe Shakespeare portrays in his plays, a place of apparent disorder but containing evidence of design throughout. Confidence in that design was soon to crumble, how-ever. In the early decades of the seventeenth century, Galileo peered through his telescope to see not a circling sphere of stars but the endless expanse of space; and Thomas Harvey discovered the circula-tion of blood in animals, calling into question the theory of "vital spirits," itself derived from belief in the four humors. At the end of the century Newton demonstrated that the universe operated on immutable laws. It spins like the movement of a perpetually wound clock, not at the command of some celestial force imposed by an im-manent deity that kept all things in motion, from the orbiting of the moon to the pulse of the human heart. The discredited body of beliefs nonetheless remained a force in the minds of ordinary people and continued to feed the imagination of poets into the eighteenth century. Alexander Pope wrote of "the Great Chain of Being" in which mankind occupied "this isthmus of a middle state," a vital link between the spiritual and material segments of the Chain;[4] and he imagined that the invisible world was as richly populated as the visible. In "The Rape of the Lock" a "thousand bright inhabitants of air" and squadrons of Sylphs, "the light infantry of the lower sky," rally to protect Belinda from the Baron. The poet portrayed the apparent discord of the universe as divine order hidden from human eyes, and he concluded: "Whatever is, is right."

In fact, poets of all ages have depended on the concept of the unity of all creation for the language of their vision. Alfred Lord Tennyson imagined that "a flower in a crannied wall" held all the secrets of "what God and man is." William Butler Yeats found the dissolution of social order in his time comparable to a figure of nature, a falcon escaping the voice of his falconer, and more ominously a threatening "vast image out of *Spiritus Mundi,*" the spirit of the earth or universe.[5] Dylan Thomas wrote that "the force that drives the water through the rocks / Drives my red blood," and but a few lines later, "I am dumb to tell a weather's wind / How time has ticked a heaven round the stars."[6]

The notion of the essential unity of all existence is not as archaically quaint as it may appear at first glance. Indeed, modern scientists are as driven as were their medieval predecessors by a "rage for order," in the words of the poet Wallace Stevens.[7] Biologists tell us that one human cell is a microcosm of the entire body, containing all the genetic material of the whole, and, moreover, that all life at the cell level looks pretty much the same. They have shown that the

4. In his "Essay on Man."
5. In "The Second Coming."
6. In "The Force That Through the Green Fuse Drives the Flower."
7. In "The Idea of Order at Key West."

genetic code of a chimpanzee matches that of a human being in 99 percent of its elements.

It is said that when Galileo first looked through his telescope and detected four moons around Jupiter, his associates urged him to look again—there had to be seven to match the number of observable planets in the universe. In the same way modern astronomers scan the skies in search of some common thread on which to string the stars. They peer into distant galaxies hoping to find worlds like our own with orderly planets circling a burning star, and they are puzzled and disappointed to discover that other planets circling other stars bear little resemblance to our own. Ecologists urge that the human species is an integral part of nature, not its master, and that mankind participates in the life of the globe we inhabit, a beneficiary with other creatures of its forests and streams, and the blessed air we breathe. Our quantum and astrophysicists are determined to find a "unified theory" to all things. They are persuaded that all matter and energy was "one" before space and time came into being with the "Big Bang," which shattered that first entity into the four (again) basic forms of energy that define the material universe, presently described as gravity, magnetism, and the weak and strong nuclear forces.

Thus the passion for unity is as strong today as it was hundreds of years ago, as is, apparently, the fascination of the figure four. This construct of universal order, then, does not demand an extraordinary stretch of the imagination for modern playgoers. They can easily enter the mind of a sixteenth-century patron of an Elizabethan theater who hears that a king is like the sun and a man may be a lion or an eagle. We may not accept the analogy as an article of belief, but the idea that all creation is one is not alien to us.

# THE SUPERNATURAL

❧

THE PRECEDING CHAPTER on "Universal Order" gives some
sense of the system of belief that prevailed during medieval and Renaissance times. It was said that the universe had been created by
God and that his influence could be detected in the patterns of nature and the chronicle of human history. The material and the spiritual worlds were thought to be very close, indeed they were joined
in mankind, possessed as we are with a mortal body and an immortal soul. The two worlds were indeed so close that spirits could cross
the divide between them in the form of ghosts of the dead that appeared to the living, and of unearthly beings lurking deep in forests,
as well as harmless fairies, gnomes, and leprechauns who could be
seen dancing in woodland glades.

Some beings lived at the very edge of that divide—witches in
human form endowed with knowledge of the future and power to
influence events. Others were mortals steeped in ancient arts, who
could conjure spirits to serve them by weaving arcane spells and
reciting mysterious incantations. Our concern here is with those
who stand astride or cross that line between the spiritual and material worlds, who for good or evil affect the lives of ordinary humans
and shape the course of history.

What, then, was Shakespeare's vision of the supernatural? His
works offer a mixed message. They feature a variety of visitations
from the spirit world, but these appearances on the whole intend
more harm than good for mankind. The supernatural does not in

fact play a significant role in his works, which attribute human suffering largely to human failings. With some exceptions, when otherworldly beings intrude, they are more likely to be prophetic than manipulative. This does not prevent his distracted humans from attributing their fate to spiritual powers, or calling on them for comfort, or raging at them when justice is wanting. Shakespeare's contemporaries, and presumably himself, were believing Christians, convinced, as has been noted, that God shaped human destiny; but they were often bewildered when that destiny seemed to defy their perception of right and wrong. Why, they ask, do the wicked prosper and the virtuous suffer? It is an age-old question of humanity, never satisfactorily answered by the pious sentiment that "God works in mysterious ways, his wonders to perform." Shakespeare poses the question time and again in the plays, most dramatically in the histories and the tragedies.

## *Ghosts*

Shakespeare's plays include several instances of spectral appearances of the dead and at least one parade of those not yet born. His contemporaries, and presumably he himself, believed that only a thin veil separated the here from the hereafter, and that those who have passed on to the unknown can return to plague or comfort the living. The best known of these apparitions is Hamlet's father, who materializes on the battlements of Elsinore and again in his widow's bedchamber. He comes in search of vengeance for his murder, and it is a curious message he brings, a contradictory mixture of pagan and Christian religions, for he seems to suffer the torments of the afterlife ordained by both. Like the spirits of the unburied dead of ancient myth, he is "doom'd for a certain time to walk the night" and at the same time is "for the day confin'd to fast in fire," enduring the purgatorial punishment of Christian sinners.

The mythology of the ancient world taught that if the mortal remains of the dead were not interred with proper ceremony, their spirits were left to wander the earth endlessly, denied the eternal rest they all longed for. The warriors of Homer's *Iliad* are often seen fighting over the body of a fallen comrade to prevent the enemy from leaving the corpse for birds and beasts to consume, thus denying its spirit peace in the afterlife. Shakespeare's Titus Andronicus insists on the sacrifice of the captive son of the Goth's queen, Tamora, so that the spirits of his own sons, slain in the wars, need not "hover on the dreadful shore of Styx."[1] The young man's death is demanded "t' appease their groaning shadows that are gone."

The ghost of Hamlet's father is condemned to "walk the night" not because he was denied proper burial but because of the way he died; and here Christian belief enters the mix with pagan myth. He must "fast in fire" because he was murdered, as he says, "with all my imperfections on my head," that is, unshriven, without the benefit of confession and absolution that church doctrine offered the faithful as a means to ensure salvation. The contradiction at the heart of the ghost's mandate to Hamlet to avenge his death is that no tenet of Christian faith provides that a sinner's sentence in Purgatory will be shortened by the death of his murderer; indeed, the Almighty's injunction is unequivocal; "Thou shalt not kill." The ghost implies, though it is left unspoken, that the death of the murderer will somehow end his wandering and relieve his suffering.

Hamlet vows to obey his father's spirit, but later, when the opportunity presents itself, he holds his sword, unwilling to kill a Claudius apparently deep in penitent prayer. To dispatch him at such a moment, Hamlet reasons, might ensure his immediate transport to paradise while his father's spirit continues to suffer purgatorial torments. That would not be proper vengeance, he concludes, and, leaving the king to his prayers, he passes on.

Other doubts trouble the prince. It was believed that agents of evil could appear in any guise, tempting humans to death and damnation. Hamlet's companions attempt to prevent him from ac-

---

1. According to the myth, the grim boatman Charon ferried souls across the Styx, the river of forgetting, to their final rest.

companying the ghost, fearing that it will "assume some other horrible form / Which might deprive your sovereignty of reason, / And draw you into madness." And later he feels the need to confirm the apparition's account of the murder, since "the spirit that I have seen / May be a devil, and the devil hath power / T' assume a pleasing shape." He arranges for the performance of a play, *The Murder of Gonzago,* to "catch the conscience of the king" and compel him to demonstrate his guilt, thereby confirming that the ghost is what it says it is. Shakespeare leaves the issue clouded. Claudius is indeed guilty, but the intrusion of the ghost leads ultimately to the destruction of the entire court—the king, the queen, the prince, the long-winded courtier Polonius, his two children Laertes and Ophelia, and two hapless outsiders, Rosencrantz and Guildenstern, who wander innocently onto the scene. Was this indeed the spirit of the dead king, or, in light of the ruin that followed upon its appearance, the devil in a "pleasing shape," come to prey upon Hamlet's melancholy and destroy the royal court of Denmark?

Other ghostly appearances are less ambiguous. An additional element of medieval lore held that the spirits of the dead can render themselves visible only to those whom they choose. When Hamlet confronts his mother in her bedchamber, the ghost reappears to him, come, as he says, "to whet thy almost blunted purpose." But it is not visible to Gertrude, who is doubly distraught to see her son talking to an apparently empty space. Again, when the ghost of Julius Caesar appears to his assassin, Brutus, on the eve of a crucial battle, none of his attendants see or hear it. The ghost promises cryptically, "thou shalt see me at Philippi," and at Philippi, of course, Brutus suffers a crushing defeat and takes his own life. Shortly before his death, Brutus views the body of the suicide Cassius, his fellow assassin, and acknowledges, "O Julius Caesar, thou art mighty yet!"[2]

2. The phenomenon is repeated at Macbeth's feast where the bloodied apparition of Banquo materializes and takes a seat in the midst of his guests but reveals itself to the king alone.

Rather than walk the earth, some ghosts appear in dreams. In *Richard III,* Clarence, on the night before his murder, has a dream in which he is visited by the spirits of Henry VI and his son Edward, whom he had betrayed by deserting them at the battle of Tewkesbury. And the sleep of Richard himself is plagued on the night before the battle of Bosworth Field. Shakespeare's setting of the scene is initially somewhat disconcerting. Both Richard and his foe, the Lancastrian Earl of Richmond, set up their tents on opposite sides of the stage, and the audience is meant to imagine that they are in fact hundreds of yards distant from each other. Both retire, and both are visited in their sleep by a long precession of the spirits of Richard's many victims, among them Henry VI, his son, the king's brother Clarence, his wife Anne, and the young princes. As the ghosts comes down stage center, each intones a curse on the king—"Despair and die!"—and turn to Richmond with words of encouragement—"Live and flourish!" Their appearance foreshadows Richard's defeat and death in the battle to come.

Broadly speaking, these spirits of the dead do not mean well for those they appear to. Indeed, the only instance that comes to mind of a benign appearance of ghosts is in *Cymbeline.* There the hero, Posthumus, imprisoned and awaiting execution, is visited in his sleep by the spirits of his father, mother, and brothers, who mourn his plight and challenge the justice of Jupiter, questioning why he allows a virtuous man to die. The god descends and angrily warns them to mind their own business, assuring them that he has everything under control and all will be well.

## Witches and Soothsayers

The witches of the world, predominantly women, are said to have special powers, chiefly the ability to communicate with "the other side." In early times that "side" was said to be demonic, and they were condemned as beings possessed by the devil to act as his agent in the destruction of souls. Such was the claim at the persecution of young women in the infamous Salem witch trials of colonial America's history. Witches have become more respectable recently, however, even to forming a labor union in England.

In Shakespeare's time they were said to be creatures who lived on the border between the material and spiritual worlds, human in appearance and speech but gifted with otherworldly powers. The best-known example in the plays is, of course, the "weird sisters" on the heath in *Macbeth,* certainly the most dramatic of those figures that bear messages from the other world to mankind. Their motives are indecipherable, but one of them relates a short account of an incident that incurred her displeasure, one that may give some indication why they intercept Macbeth upon the heath. She once approached a woman who was eating chestnuts, she tells her sisters, and asked her for one. On being rudely refused, she vowed revenge for the affront by plaguing the woman's sailor husband, who was on a sea voyage to Aleppo. A witch, it appears, is denied the power to inflict direct bodily harm on a human, but she can deprive him of sleep, causing him to "dwindle, peak and pine"; and though she cannot sink his ship, she can raise a storm that will render it "tempest-tost." So the witches' reason for tempting Macbeth might have arisen from any trivial affront by him or someone close to him, or perhaps from a general resentment toward the human race for the rough treatment witches suffer at the hands of society.

Whatever their motives, the appearance and powers of Macbeth's witches identify them as creatures who inhabit both the here and the hereafter. They have a human form, though to Banquo they "look not like th' inhabitants o' th' earth." They are clairvoyant, however, and at the first meeting with Macbeth predict that he shall be the Thane of Cawdor and "king hereafter." They do not lie, though at their second meeting, called at Macbeth's command, their message of warning and promise is delivered in more obscure terms. They raise apparitions from their boiling cauldron that advise him to "beware Macduff," but go on to assure him that "none of woman born / Shall harm Macbeth" and that he will not be overcome until "Birnum Wood to high Dunsinane hill / Shall come against" him. They see the future and report it, though in delphic messages that fill him with a false sense of security.

The intriguing question of the play is the influence of the witches on Macbeth's actions. On the one hand, they are clearly agents of a darker power, in league with Hecate, the goddess of the underworld, and their purpose is to foment "toil and trouble" for mankind.[3] They prey upon Macbeth's weakness; having detected a small, secret flame of ambition in him, they feed it with their predictions until it becomes a consuming conflagration. Once he becomes king, his complaints to his wife about their sleepless nights call to mind the witches' ability to plague the woman's sailor husband. The affliction causes Macbeth to "dwindle, peak, and pine," and his worries about Banquo render Scotland "tempest-tost." Distraught by the appearance of the ghost at his feast, Macbeth returns to the witches, demanding to know if their prediction that his heirs will inherit the throne is still true. They reply with a procession of crowned specters followed by the ghost of Banquo, who smiles at Macbeth and points mockingly at them, driving him into a fit of helpless rage. The witches' demonic powers seem to pervade the play, leading him on to despair and death.

On the other hand, a moment's reflection might have suggested to Macbeth a possible connection between the warning about Macduff and the assurance of his own invulnerability to anyone "not of woman born." The thought would have recommended an inquiry into the thane's birth rather than the impulsive decision to massacre his family. But in his obsessive state of mind, Macbeth is not given to moments of reflection: "This deed I'll do before this purpose cool." It is not the witches who kill King Duncan, though they

3. The sections where Hecate appears are not thought to be Shakespeare's but a later addition to the play by Thomas Middleton, who included them presumably because the audience delighted in supernatural apparitions, so the more the better.

clearly foresee the act, nor do they arrange for the death of Banquo, or impose a reign of terror on Scotland, or direct the brutal murder of Macduff's innocent wife and son. And "the affliction of these terrible dreams / That shake us nightly" could just as well be evidence of a guilty conscience.

We are left with the inescapable conclusion that Macbeth brings about his own destruction. Having murdered to attain the crown, he fears that all around him are capable of the same treachery. He keeps spies in the houses of all his powerful subjects and disposes of those he suspects of disloyalty until, as Macduff reports to Malcolm, "each new morn / New widows howl, new orphans cry, new sorrows / Shake heaven on the face." Macbeth's destiny is of his own making, not a fate conjured by otherworldly forces. Although the powers of darkness surely set him on the path to his destruction, he follows it of his own volition.

Another of Shakespeare's witches is more substantial. Joan la Pucelle (Joan of Arc) claims in *Henry VI, Part 1* that a vision of "God's mother" has revealed the future to her. Prophesying victory, she rallies the defeated French, retakes Orleans, and goes on to further victories. Shakespeare puts a distinctly English spin on the tale, however, describing her as inspired not by the queen of Heaven but by a group of "fiends." Joan's fortune changes when the French are routed at Angiers and the fiends desert her, leaving her to the mercy of the English, who burn her at the stake.

Some of Shakespeare's women seem witchlike in their ability to foretell the future, but they do not appear to be aided by supernatural powers. Margaret, the widowed queen of Henry VI, returns to England in *Richard III* to predict the fate of the house of York at the hands of the devious Duke of Gloucester. She prophesies that none of Queen Elizabeth's children will survive and that, like herself, she will "die neither mother, wife, nor England's queen." She warns the Duke of Buckingham to be wary of Richard, to "take heed of yonder dog. / Look when he fawns, he bites"; and taking her leave, she promises that events will prove "poor Margaret was a prophetess." Her prophecies are all confirmed in the course of the play. When she later encounters Elizabeth in mourning for the death of her two young sons, Margaret gloats over her sorrow. In lines resembling a demonic incantation, she insists that their deaths are just retribution for the losses she has suffered. She compares the death of her husband, Henry VI, and Edward, her son, to Elizabeth's loss of her sons, Edward and Richard, all murdered by Richard III.

> I had an Edward, till a Richard kill'd him;
> I had a Harry, till a Richard kill'd him:
> Thou hadst an Edward, till a Richard kill'd him;
> Thou hadst a Richard, till a Richard kill'd him.

Perhaps the most famous prophetess in all literature is Priam's mad daughter Cassandra. The myth has it that Apollo fell in love with her and endowed her with the gift of clairvoyance; but when she rejected him, the god decreed that no one would ever believe her prophecies. She makes brief appearances in *Troilus and Cressida,* predicting that unless the Trojans "let Helen go," the city will burn, and later warning Hector to avoid a confrontation with Achilles. The play is an intriguing instance of Shakespeare's revision of his sources. It is based, of course, on Homer's *Iliad,* whose lines record the frequent meddling of the gods in human affairs. In the epic, Zeus tips the scales in favor of the Trojans; Hera seduces him so that she can turn the tide of battle to benefit the Greeks; and Apollo revives Hector and immobilizes Patrocles so that the Trojan can kill him—to mention but a few such instances. But Shakespeare excludes the supernatural from the play, save only for the prophecies of Cassandra, which no one pays attention to anyway. In this omission Shakespeare seems to say that the human race is solely responsible for its destiny and must suffer the consequences of its own iniquities.

The plays have their share of soothsayers who, though not witches, possess their prophetic knowledge. These figures never reveal the source of their power, but it is limited to prophecy, as one of them admits: "I make not, but foresee." The most famous of these seers is, of course, the one who warns Julius Caesar to "beware the ides of March." Caesar dismisses him haughtily: "He's a dreamer. Let us leave him." The soothsayer confronts him once again on his way to the Senate, and his death. Caesar taunts him—"The Ides of March are come"—to which he replies, "Ay, Caesar, but not gone." Another appears on two occasions in *Antony and Cleopatra.* He reads the palm of Charmian, the queen's handmaid, and predicts darkly, and cryptically: "You have seen and prov'd a fairer form of fortune / Than that which is to approach." In the end, Charmian joins Cleopatra in death by accepting, like her, the sting of the asp. Later he warns Antony less ambiguously to avoid competition with Octavius Caesar, since "if thou dost play with him at any game, / Thou art sure to lose." And, of course, lose he does. Shakespeare inserts these figures briefly into the plays perhaps only to enhance the dramatic irony of the action, since their predictions always prove true but their warnings, like Cassandra's, are invariably disregarded.

# Clerics

"Men of the cloth" are neither witches nor soothsayers, but in Shakespeare's time they were endowed with special powers enabling them to administer the holy sacraments to the faithful, deemed essential to salvation, and they were regarded as possessing heightened insight into matters of the spirit. In *Richard II* it is the Bishop of Carlisle who most eloquently and ominously predicts the consequences of deposing an anointed king. When Henry Bolingbroke forces Richard to surrender the crown, Carlisle warns the usurper that a vengeful God will visit terror upon England if he persists in his impious intent: "The blood of English shall manure the ground, / And future generations groan for this foul act," he prophesies, and "disorder, horror, fear and mutiny / Shall here inhabit, and this land be call'd / The field of Golgotha, and dead men's skulls." And his prophecies are borne out in the carnage of War of the Roses.

In *Henry V* the king turns to the Archbishop of Canterbury for confirmation that his claim to the French throne is just in the eyes of God. Although Canterbury may have secular motives for advising war, the fact remains that Henry could not pursue his ambition without the sanction of the church. If God is not on his side, he firmly believes, the enterprise is doomed, so the approval of one who is said to have an intimate knowledge of divine justice is crucial to his cause.

While on the subject of clerics, it is worth noting that although they are men entrusted with spiritual powers essential to the salvation of their flock, they do not fare well in Shakespeare. His contemporaries saw no distinction between state and church. Since the universe was ruled by divine order and an immanent God presided over human affairs, politics and religion were not seen as separate, conflicting concerns, as they are in some modern cultures. Indeed, a vestige of that worldview survives today in Britain, where the monarch is still head of the Church of England. Medieval clerics could exercise their spiritual powers to political ends by excommunicating stubborn monarchs, depriving them of access to the sacraments, the loss of which, it was feared, would deny them salvation. In *King John* the papal legate Pandulph excommunicates the king for his failure to appoint Rome's choice for Archbishop of Canterbury, and he then foments war between England and France by absolving King Philip from his political alliance with John, once his adversary has been cast out of the church. John finally relents, surrenders his crown to Pandulph as a gesture of submission, and receives it back again as a symbol of papal power; but by then it is too late, since Philip has already invaded England.

Pandulph, who has achieved all he intended as far as John is concerned, attempts to dissuade the French from continuing the war, but they will not be deterred. The war does in fact end, not, however, because of Pandulph's mediation, but as a consequence of two natural disasters. The French supply fleet is shipwrecked by a storm at sea, and the English army is demolished by a flood in the

Lincolnshire lowlands. It would be a mistake, perhaps, to make too much of the fact that the forces of nature achieve what papal persuasion fails to do, but the coincidence is striking.

High-ranking churchmen in the pre-Reformation era of Shakespeare's history plays filled important public offices as chancellors, chief ministers, and members of Parliament; and although they never achieved the dominance in public affairs enjoyed, for example, by the mullahs of modern Iran, they exercised important political power. They did so, however, under the pressure of divided loyalties, since they owed allegiance both to their kingdom and to Rome. In *Henry VIII* the king's Lord Chancellor and Archbishop of Canterbury, Cardinal Wolsey, at first urges his divorce from Queen Katharine, who has failed to produce a male heir. But when the king shows signs of replacing her with Protestant Anne Boleyn rather than Wolsey's choice, a Catholic princess, he advises the Pope to withhold approval.

In their public role, churchmen all too often subordinated the pastoral and spiritual obligations of their calling to an entirely secular ambition for power and wealth. Cardinal Wolsey, for example, is toppled when it is revealed that he has imposed onerous taxes on the English people and kept the revenues to increase his own private fortune. Henry dismisses him from his office as lord chancellor and replaces him with a layman, Sir Thomas More, though Shakespeare is ambiguous about whether the king does so because of the cardinal's opposition to the divorce or as punishment for his mercenary greed. In the *Henry VI* plays, England is torn by rival factions competing for influence, one of which is dominated by the powerful Cardinal Beaufort, Bishop of Winchester. He orchestrates the murder of his adversary, the Duke of Gloucester, the loyal lord protector of the realm during the minority of Henry VI and until his death one of the king's most trusted advisers.[4]

4. In another instance the quarrelsome Archbishop of York in *Henry IV, Part 2* resents what he sees as the king's high-handed treatment of his former allies and leads a rebellion against the crown.

The lower orders of the clergy do not fare much better in Shakespeare. Many are subjected to the poet's gently satirical pen—those such as the Welsh parson Sir Hugh Evans, who delights audiences with his outlandish accent and overblown language in *The Merry Wives of Windsor,* and Sir Oliver Martext in *As You Like It,* whose name reflects his inadequacy. Friar Francis in *Much Ado About Nothing* seems to be compassionate and resourceful. Young Claudio, having been deceived by Don John's plot, accuses Hero of unchastity, or, as he puts it, of knowing "the heat of a luxurious bed," causing her to fall into a faint. The friar counsels that she should be reported dead so as to change Claudio's "slander to remorse" and allow for the truth to be told. Of course, the plan may not work, in which event his only solution is that, because of her "wounded reputation," she must resign herself to "some reclusive and religious life." Friar Laurence, in *Romeo and Juliet,* however well-meaning, badly bungles the rescue of the lovers, and at the end, fearing discovery, he abandons Juliet to her fate in the crypt.

Shakespeare, it would appear, thought of clerics as comic, or inept, or, contrary to the vows of their sacred office, far too worldly and unscrupulous in their desire for gain. Indeed, the Bishop of Carlisle may be the only churchman in all the plays who appears to be faithful to his priestly calling, and he is forced to retire to confinement in a monastery for his resistance to Henry IV.

# Deus ex Machina

In the plays of ancient Greece, it often proved necessary for gods to descend from Olympus and exercise their supernatural powers in order to resolve the complex situations in which humans entangled themselves. The actors in the roles of these deities were lowered to the stage at the end of a rope suspended from a derricklike piece of stage equipment and so became literally the "god out of the machine." The phrase *deus ex machina* is used today by theater critics to find fault with a play whose plot is so convoluted that it requires some miraculous intrusion to unravel it, a sudden flood that drowns lurking villains or the death of a previously unmentioned wealthy uncle whose legacy saves a virtuous heroine from a life of shame. Shakespeare is not above such last-minute intercessions. In *As You Like It*, the wicked Oliver is intent upon seizing his brother Orlando and dragging him back to court for punishment. As it happens, Oliver falls asleep in the forest and is threatened by a lurking lion. Orlando rescues him by chasing the beast off, suffering in the process a slight wound, and the two are reconciled. Later the vindictive Duke Frederick leads an armed force into the forest, determined to do away with his brother, Duke Senior, and his fellow exiles. On the way, however, he encounters "an old religious man" who converts him "both from his enterprise and from the world," and he returns the dukedom to his brother, whom he had deposed. So a lion and a guru sort things out. Good things happen in the forest.

Shakespeare's gods occasionally join the company of humans, but they seem to have little influence on the outcome of his plays. In *As You Like It*, Hymen, the god of marriage, appears in the final scene, but he is purely a ceremonial figure, come to preside over the various unions that Rosalind has already arranged. Hecate, the goddess of the underworld, appears to the witches in *Macbeth*.[5] She scolds the weird sisters for acting without her authority but joins them to prepare for Macbeth's next visit, her role being to recruit the apparitions that will rise from their cauldron. They will, she claims, give him a false sense of confidence in his future, since, as "you all know, security / Is mortal's chiefest enemy." As a result of their messages, she predicts, "he shall spurn fate, scorn death, and bear / His hopes 'bove wisdom, grace, and fear." But none of these occult figures, as we have seen, directly affect the tyrant's fate. It is not a false sense of security that brings about his downfall, but his determination to intensify his reign of terror, ordering the murder of Macduff's wife and children, an act that suggests heightened fear

5. As mentioned, it is doubtful that Shakespeare wrote the scene.

rather than security. And he falls when his disaffected thanes flee his service to join forces with the invading army of Malcolm and Macduff.[6]

When the gods do make an appearance, it is often in a dream rather than in person. In *Cymbeline*, Posthumus is sleeping when he sees the ghosts of his family and an angry Jupiter, but again all the god does is deposit a mysterious tablet containing a cryptic message which confirms the justice of a resolution that the humans will eventually work out for themselves. The only instance in which a god plays a significant role in human affairs, and is thus a *deus ex machina* in the classic sense, is in *Pericles*. The prince is happily reunited with his daughter, Marina, whom he had thought dead. The goddess Diana appears to him in a dream, instructing him to worship at her shrine in Ephesus and to give her "maiden priests" there a full account of his life, including the loss of his wife Thaisa at sea. Pericles obeys and finds Thaisa, who had survived and served for the intervening years at the temple of Diana.

Thus when the gods do appear in Shakespeare, they are for the most part ornamental, exerting little influence on the outcome of events. Mankind bears responsibility for human actions, the poet tells us repeatedly. We cannot blame our troubles on some interfering deity.

## Magicians and Fairies

Not all beings who cross the line between the spirit and material worlds do so to create discord and despair for mankind. Medieval doctrine distinguished between white and black magic. The white,

6. In other examples of the gods' ornamental but inconsequential appearance, Prospero's celebratory masque in *The Tempest* features Juno, Ceres, and Iris, but their only role is to bless the betrothal of Ferdinand and Miranda; and besides, they are spirits playing parts in a display of Prospero's "so potent art." Again, the godlike Hercules is said to champion Antony in his wars, but we learn of him only when he abandons the emperor on the eve of his final battle with Octavius Caesar.

a gift from Heaven, accounted for the miracles of healing and the protection of virtue recorded in the annals of the church, the black for instances of collusion with the forces of evil for power or gain. Our Lady of Lourdes could cure illness, but Dr. Faustus strikes a bargain with the devil, bartering his soul for supernatural skills.

The appearance of Joan la Pucelle's "fiends" and the mysterious apparition raised by the witches of Macbeth are examples of black magic; Prospero's is of the white variety. It is true that he can be a fearsome master. He threatens Ariel to "rend an oak / and peg thee in his knotty entrails" if he doesn't behave, and Caliban that he will "rack thee with old cramps, / Fill up thy bones with aches" if he shirks his duties. But he uses his magic to protect the innocent, plague the guilty, encourage love, and bring about reconciliation. Prospero's powers are not delegated to him by some superior being, as was claimed by some kings in Shakespeare's time. Rather, like Faustus, he learns his art from books. When he was deposed by his wicked bother Antonio and cast adrift with Miranda, the good Gonzalo supplied him with his volumes, and he gained his command over the spirits of the island from the knowledge of their pages. In the end, as he is about to return to Milan, he abandons his powers, breaking his staff and drowning his book "deeper than did ever plummet sound." He has had enough of magic and no longer wants to be a god. His only desire now is to complete his life as a mere mortal, one whose "every third thought shall be" of his grave.

In *A Midsummer Night's Dream*, dissension among the mighty in the fairy kingdom can have devastating consequences for mankind. The quarrel between Oberon and Titania over possession of "a little changeling boy" has disrupted the order of nature. Titania describes how the wind has "suck'd up from the sea / Contagious clouds," later drenching the land so that rivers overflow their banks, causing crops to rot in the fields and "rheumatic diseases" to spread among humans. The seasons alter, with spring and summer so afflicted by winter frosts until no one can tell "which is which," all, she says, because of "our debate." On the whole, however, they look upon their human counterparts with sympathetic, if somewhat condescending, concern. Puck shakes his head at their antics—"Lord, what fools these mortals be!"—but Oberon attempts to remedy the lovers' conflicts with the juice of "a little western flower." And at the end, the fairy king dispatches his subjects about the palace to ward off evil forces and ensure that the offspring of the lovers' marriage beds will be born without blemish.

In a comic twist on the belief in woodland creatures, Mistress Page and Mistress Ford play a trick on Falstaff in *The Merry Wives of Windsor.* The fat knight believes he has seduced them with his manly charms, and they lure him into the forest with false promises of an assignation. But they have prepared a surprise for him. He appears, only to be assaulted by a horde of Windsor folk disguised as satyrs, fairies, and hobgoblins, who fill him with terror since he is convinced that "he that speaks to them shall die" and "no man their works must eye." They dance about him and sing a taunting song: "Lust is but a bloody fire, / Kindled with unchaste desire." In the end they unmask and the ladies good-naturedly invite him, chastened but still a jovial guest, to dinner, where they will "laugh this sport o'er by a country fire."

Shakespeare raises the question of the role of the supernatural in human affairs, and, as we have come to expect of him, it is a mixed message. Some indeed are benevolent, the woodland fairies of *A Midsummer Night's Dream*, the spirits of *The Tempest,* and the various deities, Jupiter, Diana, and Hymen, who appear in dreams or in person. The magician Prospero wields his mysterious power to protect innocence and hold evil in check; and the solemn soothsayers offer prophecies which, if heeded, would avoid tragedy.

On the whole, however, creatures of the spirit world and those who hover on its edges in Shakespeare's plays are more malignant than benign. The Christian God is anything but benevolent. The fields of England run red with blood for generations because a presumptuous Bolingbroke thrust Richard II, "His minister," from the

throne. If Henry V was victorious at Agincourt, it may be only because God heard the king's prayer and withheld his vengeful hand
during the battle. When otherworldly beings meddle in mankind's
affairs, they are more likely to prey on human weakness, as do Macbeth's witches and perhaps even King Hamlet's ghost. Even
Oberon, the sympathetic fairy king in A Midsummer Night's Dream,
as well-meaning as he is, makes a hash of the lovers' affections, and
poor Bottom awakens from his dream thoroughly bewildered: "The
eye of man hath not heard, the ear of man hath not seen . . . what
my dream is."

Shakespeare's human characters often seek the intercession of
their deities. Battered by the storm, Lear rages, "let the great gods, /
That keep this dreadful pudder o'er our heads / Find out their enemies now"; and Macbeth calls up the "weird sisters," only to curse
them later as "the fiend / That lies like truth" when he learns that
Birnum Wood has indeed come to Dunsinane. But the gods appear
to be either deaf to pleas or, as the blind Gloucester laments in King
Lear, they answer only to plague the living: "We are to the gods as
flies to wanton boys. / They kill us for their sport." Or like Antony's
Hercules and Joan of Arc's "fiends," they desert us just when we
need them most. In the final analysis, we're on our own, and since
we seem to be able to make enough trouble for ourselves as it is,
we're better off without them. Prospero was probably wise to drown
his book.

# EVIL (AND GOOD)

❦

SHAKESPEARE'S CONTEMPORARIES attributed the ills of the world to the work of the forces of darkness. Looking about them, they could see that the great majority of people lived lives that were "solitary, poor, nasty, brutish, and short," in the words of the seventeenth-century philosopher Thomas Hobbes, and they sensed that mankind need not be so debased. Of course, there were plenty of human agents to blame for such misery—tyrannical kings, rapacious landlords, corrupt magistrates, military adventurers, and the haughty nobility—but the common people of the era believed that more powerful, occult forces were responsible for evil in their world. Satan and his minions, fiends, witches, and assorted unseen spirits, it was said, plagued the earth, tempting vulnerable humans to wickedness to ensure the damnation of their souls. Indeed, Protestant pulpits rang with the warning that the devil had even usurped the power of Rome and ensnared the Pope in his web of iniquity. To reformers, the Pontiff was the Antichrist.

As we have seen, Shakespeare populated his plays with spirits— those same fiends, witches, and ghosts, along with grizzly apparitions like the bloody child and dancing dagger of *Macbeth*, forest fairies in *A Midsummer Night's Dream*, a fearsome harpy in *The Tempest,* and even an occasional visit from divinities of the ancient world, Jupiter in *Cymbeline* and Diana in *Pericles*.[1] But for Shake-

1. See p. 173.

speare the true source of misery in the world was mankind itself, scheming villains or men and women twisted by hatred, jealousy, thwarted desire, or just plain meanness. The ghost of Hamlet's father may precipitate a series of events that lead to the extinction of the Danish royal family, and witches may inflame an ambition that has lain harmlessly dormant in Macbeth's secret thoughts; but the tragedies that follow the appearance of these unearthly figures are all man-made.

Mark Antony opens his famous speech over the body of Julius Caesar with the observation that "the evil that men do lives after them, / The good is oft interred with their bones." It is true, perhaps, that evil "lives after them" because vice is so much more interesting than virtue, as a glance at modern media will confirm. A significant contribution to Shakespeare's popularity over the centuries was his ability to offer theater audiences fascinatingly wicked men and women. Richard III, certainly his most entertaining villain, captivates viewers in part because he is matched with a cast of improbably gullible and colorless characters, but principally because he is so unapologetically evil. An audience will find itself awaiting his entrance to enliven an otherwise staid scene.

Shakespeare's villains come in many guises. Some, like *Othello*'s Iago, pursue their wicked designs simply because it is their nature to do so. Some have goals in mind which in their judgment justify any means, however malevolent, to attain—such as Richard III, who sets his sights on the crown of England and never wavers in his intent. Others are initially virtuous or noble figures who embark on a career of destruction because of some fatal weakness in character, the consuming ambition of Macbeth, for example.

Among Shakespeare's characters are several who, in a fit of jealousy or anger, engage in uncharacteristically cruel behavior. King Leontes, in *The Winter's Tale,* for example, becomes insanely jealous because he finds his wife, Hermione, overattentive to his visiting friend, King Polixenes. Leontes puts her on trial for adultery and has her newly born daughter abandoned on a desolate seacoast because he believes her to be the child of Polixenes. He acknowledges his error, however, and, thinking both mother and daughter dead, mourns the loss for sixteen years until they are miraculously returned to him. And any number of Shakespeare's fathers, enraged when their daughters marry against their wishes, are cruelly harsh to them, only to repent their anger in the end. The figures in this latter group serve the playwright's purpose well in creating conflict within a plot, but they are normally benign human beings who are only temporarily overwrought, not wicked, and so may be set aside in this consideration of Shakespeare's theme of evil.

## Evil by Nature

Villainy may be defined as a conscious intent to do others harm, for whatever motive. Some of Shakespeare's villains inflict suffering upon their victims for no apparent reason, or they cause injury to a degree that seems far in excess of the grievances they profess to harbor. But Shakespeare wastes little time justifying their actions; he is no more interested in explaining why his characters are evil than he is why they fall in love. They simply are, and they do. It's the way we humans are, endowed with the gift of reason that we can employ for either good or evil. He introduces a character who is determined to do harm to others and lets it go at that—to get on with the play.

*Titus Andronicus* is crowded with villains. The empress Tamora's two sons, Chiron and Demetrius, are irredeemably wicked, the bad seed of their vengeful mother. They develop a passion for Titus's daughter Lavinia, and almost come to blows over who will have her. Tamora's evil lover, Aaron, urges them to stop their wrangling, advising that there is nothing to prevent them both from enjoying her. The idea pleases. Coming upon Lavinia and her betrothed, Bassianus, in the forest, they murder him, toss his body into a pit, and drag her off to have their pleasure. Having violated her, they cut off her hands and tear out her tongue to prevent her from identifying them as her assailants. In the end Titus imposes a rough justice on this pernicious pair by killing them both and serving their sliced-up carcasses to their mother in a pie.

But *Othello's* Iago is Shakespeare's quintessential villain. He hates the Moor, he says, because he selected Michael Cassio as his lieutenant, ignoring Iago's years of faithful service. He also suspects that Othello is sleeping with his wife, Emilia, though there is certainly no evidence of it in the play. He suspects Cassio of the same offense—indeed, he seems to think the entire army is sharing her bed! None of these grievances, taken singly or as a whole, satisfactorily explains the depth of his hatred for the two men or justifies "the tragic loading of this bed," the lifeless bodies of Othello, Desdemona, and Emilia in the final scene. When the full story of Iago's deception becomes known, Othello asks what induced him to work such evil. He replies defiantly, "from this time forth I never will speak word"—and he never does.

Iago's animosity toward Cassio suggests some darker sources of his wickedness, however. He resents the lieutenant, he says, because "he hath a daily beauty in his life / That makes me ugly." Shakespeare attributes a similar sentiment to other figures who harbor hatred toward their intended victims. In *Much Ado About Nothing,* the devious Don John, who has been defeated in a rebellion against his brother, Don Pedro, schemes to disturb the impending marriage between Claudio and Hero because the young man "has all the glory of my overthrow." In like manner, Oliver plots the death of his younger brother Orlando, in *As You Like It,* because he is so "enchantingly belov'd . . . that I am altogether mispris'd." When confronted by a person who is more attractive, more successful, more loved, or more admired, the villain seethes with envy. More to the point, he is possessed by a compulsion to destroy the paragon.

Shakespeare alludes to a teaching of the church in staging such figures. Medieval mystery plays portrayed Satan as an archangel who was expelled from heaven and condemned to hell for his rebellion against God. Ever since his fall, it was said, he has been plagued by the memory of the bliss he has lost, and any reminder of his former joy is torment to him. As a result, any evidence of beauty, love, happiness, or simple goodness fills him with anguish, and he is compelled to destroy anything on earth that bears resemblance to the joyous existence now forever denied him. We catch a glimpse of this legend when Othello finally accepts the full horror of what he has done and confronts Iago, whom he imagines for a moment as demonic, the hideous, horned, cloven-hoofed fiend of popular conception. He rages at his tormentor, "I look down towards his feet. . . . If that thou be'st a devil, I cannot kill thee," and wounds him with a thrust of his sword. But, he says, "that's a fable"; and so it is for Shakespeare as well, who insists that the source of evil in the world is a twisted human spirit, not some tormented supernatural being.[2]

In a lighter vein, we may add to the number of figures who seem to be evil by their very nature the treacherous pair in *The Tempest*—Antonio, who has usurped the dukedom of Milan from his brother Prospero, and his accomplice Sebastian, the younger brother of the King of Naples. Antonio persuades Sebastian to kill the king and seize the throne, and they are thwarted in their design only by the timely intercession of the spirit Ariel. The comic irony of their scheme is that all three of them are marooned on a desert isle with no apparent prospect of rescue. Hence the murder of the king would serve only to earn Sebastian a throne he has little hope of enjoying. Antonio and Sebastian nonetheless conspire to gain a crown, it would appear, simply because treachery comes to them naturally; it is just the way they are, possessed of an instinctive, inborn bent toward evil, whatever the circumstances. Their abortive plot is matched in absurdity by Caliban's design to kill Prospero, a proposal enthusiastically embraced by Stephano, the king's drunken steward, and Trinculo, his jester, who seem pleased with the

2. It cannot escape notice, however, that Othello does in fact fail to kill Iago.

prospect of ruling a kingdom with a population of four people. These Italian princes, Shakespeare seems to say, and their servants as well, are not only congenitally wicked but also unconscionably stupid.

## Villains for Cause

Some of Shakespeare's villains tread a path of crime for familiar motives. Richard, Duke of Gloucester, has but one goal in mind, to reign over England as Richard III, and he sets about to attain that goal with single-minded ruthlessness. A number of obstacles stand in his path to the throne, including an older brother, Clarence, who is in line to become lord protector on the death of the failing king, Edward IV, and Queen Elizabeth, who is the head of a powerful court faction. She is the mother of two young boys, heirs to their father's crown, and can count on the support of a brother and grown sons from her first marriage. The court of the dying king is bristling with wrangling men and women poised for a struggle over succession to the power of the throne, a scene of hostility that provides ample room, as Richard remarks gleefully, "for me to bustle in!"

In his opening soliloquy, Richard regrets this "winter of my discontent," a "weak piping time of peace" during which his prowess as a warrior has little place and his misshapen body cuts an unattractive figure. The only alternative for him, he concludes, is "to prove a villain." Richard is utterly remorseless in his pursuit of the crown—and vastly entertaining. Before the king's death he has his brother Clarence murdered so that he may assume the role of lord protector during the minority of the young heir, Edward V. Exercising the authority of that office, he assumes control of the young princes, age twelve and nine, and has the queen's older relatives put to death. Along the way he marries the daughter of a powerful family, Anne of Warwick, and later disposes of her; and then he does away with members of the court who show reluctance to accept his claim to the throne. As king he commits his final outrage, ordering the murder of the two princes.

We watch him tread this path of blood with a mixture of fascination, admiration at his ingenuity, and dismay at the scope of his iniquity. He is the villain we love to hate, an engaging and compassionless murderer who shows no sign of guilt in his climb to the throne. He does have a brief moment of self-pity after a dream in which the ghosts of his many victims parade before him, each condemning him to "despair and die." "There is no creature loves me, / And if I die, no soul will pity me," he laments—but then quickly regains his composure to rally his army for the impending battle.

Macbeth, like Richard III, has a clearly defined motivation for his villainy, to secure and retain the crown of Scotland. He murders the king and on mounting the throne has his friend and comrade-in-arms Banquo killed. He then imposes a reign of terror on the kingdom until, as Malcolm reports, "each new morn / new widows howl, new orphans cry, new sorrows / Strike heaven in the face." When Macduff deserts to England, in hope of raising an army to depose the tyrant, Macbeth has his wife and children brutally murdered. Like Richard, he is killed in the end, and his successors hail a new era of peace and harmony.

Unlike Richard however, who is villainous from beginning to end, Macbeth is seen initially as a noble figure, loyal to King Duncan and in battle a lion among hares. He is, in his wife's words, "too full o' th' milk of human kindness / To catch the nearest way." He does, however, take that "nearest way" by murdering the king; but, again unlike Richard, he suffers thereafter from the distress of guilt. His sleep is afflicted with "terrible dreams"; and, having committed murder to attain the throne, he suspects all about him of the same treacherous intent. He is obsessed with the witches' prediction that Banquo will beget kings and rages that, should their prophecy prove true, "upon my head they have plac'd a fruitless crown, / and put a barren scepter in my gripe." His response to the threat differs from Richard's carefully calculated devilry. The witches answer his demand to know the fate of his crown by evoking a ghostly parade of Banquo's royal heirs, and in an irrational reaction he impulsively orders the massacre of Macduff's family.

At the end in Dunsinane Castle, as he awaits the approaching English forces, Macbeth swings back and forth emotionally between heroic defiance, anger, and sour regret. Shakespeare composed *Macbeth* a decade after *Richard III*; and no better appreciation of his maturing art as a playwright can be found than the contrast between Richard III's "there is no creature loves me" and Macbeth's final expression of regret:

> My way of life
> Is fallen into the sear, the yellow leaf,
> And that which should accompany old age,
> As honor, love, obedience, troops of friends,
> I must not look to have.

Thus while Iago, Oliver, and Don John seem to act out of an almost demonic compulsion to destroy, driven by a congenital hatred of anything good or beautiful, Richard III and Macbeth are motivated by a recognizable human failing: "vaulting ambition." Macbeth differs from the others, however, in that while they are evil from the outset of the play and remain so to the end, he is transformed from an initially admirable figure into a monster. We watch as he sinks to lower and lower depths of infamy, finally ordering the murder of innocent women and children, a crime whose horror is amplified by the fact that we are witness to it. Evil leads on to further evil, Shakespeare tells us, or as Macbeth voices the theme, "I am in blood / Stepp'd in so far that, should I wade no more, / Returning were as tedious as go o'er."

Mention should be made of villainous characters who play somewhat less than a major role in a tragedy but whose menace is essential to the plot. Edmund in *King Lear* and Claudius in *Hamlet* do not appear to be evil by nature, but they devise murderous schemes that, however nefarious the means, are designed to attain understandable ends. The bastard Edmund does not seem to harbor animosity toward his half-brother Edgar or his father Gloucester. There is nothing in him of Macbeth's obsessive malice toward Macduff or of Iago's "I hate the Moor." Indeed, Edmund is rather engaging in his matter-of-fact recital of his ambitions. He simply wants to replace his brother as heir to his father's title: "Well then, / Legitimate Edgar, I must have your land." Later, when he discovers that his father has been in secret communication with the invading French, he decides that he might as well have "no less than all"—that is, betray him and succeed as Earl of Gloucester. It is only natural, he observes philosophically, that "the younger rises when the old doth fall."

Claudius is certainly treacherous, having murdered King Hamlet to acquire his wife and his throne; but in the play he appears to be genuinely fond of Queen Gertrude and gives every evidence of competence in his management of state affairs—for example, successfully averting a war with Norway. He is intelligent and resourceful. Once he suspects that Hamlet has designs on his life, he promptly devises an ingenious scheme to remove the threat, sending the prince off to England accompanied by letters commanding his death. When that plot fails, he alertly conceives another, persuading Laertes to kill Hamlet in what is announced as a friendly dueling match. He is the villain of the play, surely, but he does not give the impression of one who is inherently evil.

# Shylock

In the fourth act of *The Merchant of Venice,* Shylock the Jew prepares to carve a pound of flesh from the body of the Christian merchant Antonio, and there can be no doubt that he fully intends to do so, inflicting wounds that must inevitably prove fatal. Is Shylock therefore a villain? To review briefly the events leading up to this chilling scene: Antonio secures a loan from Shylock to assist his young friend

Bassanio in his design to woo the wealthy Portia. But since Antonio's assets are temporarily committed to cargoes at sea, he signs a
bond promising to repay the loan in three months. Shylock suggests, "in a merry sport," as he puts it, that Antonio pledge a pound
of his flesh as security for the loan, and the merchant agrees in the
belief that it is unthinkable the Jew would collect such a penalty in
the event of default. It is quite possible that Shylock intends no
harm at the time; but later events remind him of the long history of
Christian persecution of the Jews, and when Antonio is unable to
repay the loan, he demands his pound of flesh.

The court of Venice, constrained by its laws, is forced to award
Shylock his bond; but the clever Portia, disguised as a learned doctor of laws, finds additional Venetian statutes that prevent him from
collecting his bond and, moreover, impose severe penalties on a Jew
who threatens the life of a Christian. Shylock retires in defeat, forced
to pay a heavy fine and convert to Christianity.

Several figures in the play refer to Shylock contemptuously as
"the devil," and it is safe to say that Shakespeare's contemporaries
saw him in one way or another as evil incarnate. Steeped in a tradition of fear and mistrust, Christian audiences of the time considered
the Jew an alien presence in their midst, a race defiled for all time
by complicity in the death of Jesus Christ and reviled for their devious pursuit of material gain.[3] For a century and a half after he first
appeared on stage, Shylock was enacted as a comic villain or as the
embodiment of evil, the caricature of the hand-wringing, hunch-
shouldered, beak-nosed Jew, scheming to ensnare honest, unwary
Christians. In the mid-eighteenth century, however, English actors
began to portray a very different figure entirely: the noble Jew
courageously defying a tradition of mindless intolerance, seeking
retribution for countless acts of oppression. Shylock has been played
more or less in that manner ever since.

3. In the year 2000 the Catholic church finally repudiated the charge of
Christ-killing and apologized for the persecution that Jews have suffered in its
name. The accusation survives, however, in the Muslim world.

Shakespeare allows room for either interpretation, leaving modern audiences torn between revulsion at his murderous hatred of Antonio and sympathy for the centuries of persecution that engendered it. The image of the Jew gleefully sharpening his knife in anticipation of his revenge is replaced moments later by a Shylock who is humiliated once again, stripped of his wealth and compelled to repudiate his faith. In our own time, audiences, with the horrors of the Holocaust engraved indelibly in memory, find him the most troubling of Shakespeare's characters.

## Evil Women

The plays contain their share of women villains, prominent among them King Lear's daughters Goneril and Regan. Their inhumanity arises from no stated cause. They seem to harbor resentment against their father and jealousy at his preference for their younger sister Cordelia. But Shakespeare does not pause to analyze their motives. He presents them as naturally wicked whatever the cause, with confidence in his audience's awareness that in the history of the human race such daughters do appear from time to time. They quite clearly detest their father, whom they seem to enjoy humiliating as they deprive him of his retinue of a hundred knights; and Regan gains a cruel satisfaction in barring the castle doors to him, leaving the old man to wander the heath at the mercy of a raging storm. Their inherent wickedness is all the more evident when they both fall in love with Gloucester's bastard son Edmund, an obsession that incites Goneril to poison her sister and later kill herself when her plot to do away with her husband is discovered. We do not waste the slightest scrap of sympathy on this rapacious pair.

Others have good reason for their devilry. When Titus Andronicus returns in triumph to Rome from his war with the Goths, he brings with him several captives, including their queen, Tamora, and her sons. Despite her anguished pleas, he has one of them killed in a ritual sacrifice to ensure that the spirits of his own sons killed in the wars, "the groaning shadows that are gone," may rest in peace. Tamora catches the eye of the lascivious emperor, Saturninus, and when he takes her as his empress, she is in a position to fulfill her vow of vengeance against Titus. And Cymbeline's queen attempts to poison the king's daughter, Imogen, because she rejects Cloten, her unpleasant son by a former marriage, choosing instead the common gentleman Posthumus for her husband. In *Henry VI, Part 3,* Queen Margaret takes delight in taunting the captive Duke of York before joining others in stabbing him. But she has every reason to hate the house of York. These are the men who slaughtered her helpless young son and later add to their iniquity by murdering her imprisoned husband.[4]

Hence it may be said that, with the exception of Goneril and Regan, the treachery of Shakespeare's women villains, though surely reprehensible, is understandably motivated by a concern for the welfare of their sons and husbands, or by a desire to avenge harm done them.

## Comic Villains

Shakespeare sprinkled his comedies with an assortment of villains to spice his plots, figures who during the course of the play either see the error of their ways or come to a bad end. In *As You Like It,* Duke Frederick and Oliver, who both hate their brothers, force the principal characters of the play to seek refuge in the Forest of Arden. Indeed, this seems to be the only reason for their inclusion in the cast, since they have little to do with the delightful antics of the exiles once there, and both eventually repent of their iniquity.

Other objectionable figures loom larger in the plots. In *Measure*

---

4. And, of course, Lady Macbeth is ambitious for her husband, shaming him into the murder of Duncan when he shows signs of reluctance.

*for Measure*, the Duke of Vienna deputizes Angelo to restore respect for the law in the city while he absents himself on unspecified travels. Angelo takes his task seriously. His first acts are to close the city's brothels and arrest a young man, Claudio, for impregnating his betrothed before their marriage. It seems that one of the laws of Vienna forbids fornication, the penalty for which is death. *Measure for Measure* is not a tale of love triumphant. It features a parade of madams, pimps, and posturing frauds who display the underside of love in characters who are either consumed by lust or pursue the trade that caters to their appetites. They are all amusing in their way, except perhaps for Angelo, but on the whole a bit distasteful.

Claudio's sister Isabella, an aspirant in a local convent, pleads with Angelo for her brother's life, and the uncompromising deputy at first refuses. But during the interview he is suddenly possessed by an overwhelming physical desire for the virtuous Isabella and offers to spare Claudio's life if she will submit to his passion. She appears to agree, but unbeknownst to Angelo, it is arranged for another woman, Mariana, to take her place in his bed. Mariana is willing since she seems to love the unpleasant Angelo, who had callously broken off their intended marriage some years earlier when a shipwreck deprived her of a dowry. To add to Angelo's iniquity, even though he believes he has had his way with Isabella, he treacherously orders Claudio's execution to be carried out anyway. The duke reappears to sort out the various entanglements, eventually compelling Angelo to marry Mariana, which we may assume he does with an ill will.

Cymbeline's thoroughly distasteful stepson, Cloten, is comic in his villainy. The king, angry at his daughter Imogen for marrying Posthumus against his wishes, banishes him and confines her. In the absence of Posthumus, Cloten presses his attentions on Imogen, only to be rudely rebuffed. Her husband's "mean'st garment," she replies contemptuously, "is dearer / In my respect than all the hairs above thee."

In time Imogen, disguised as a young man, goes in search of

Posthumus in the wilderness of Wales, where she comes under the protection of three friendly rustics. The ill-tempered Cloten, smarting from her dismissal, especially the remark about her husband's "mean'st garment," decides to follow her. He secures a suit of Posthumus's clothes, scheming inanely to punish Imogen for her insult by ravishing her while he is dressed as her husband. He encounters one of the rustics, whom he berates as a renegade and rashly challenges to a fight, with the result that he loses his head.

A few additional malicious figures are scattered among Shakespeare's comedies—an irate Egeus in *A Midsummer Night's Dream,* who demands that his daughter be severely punished for rejecting his choice for her husband, and Queen Dionyza in *Pericles,* who plots the death of the virtuous Marina because she outshines her own daughter. But these are minor figures who create tension in the plot without playing a significant role in events.

Many of the comedies, though they may contain some distasteful characters, entertain without the aid of an outright villain. *Troilus and Cressida* is a biting satire on love and war, but the various characters in the play are more ridiculous than wicked. Thersites rails bitterly at the Greek warriors, but he does them no harm. Achilles never rises to a level of malice that would dignify him as a villain. He is distinctly unheroic, of course, when he rallies his Myrmidons to slaughter Hector rather than engage him in single combat, but he is more cowardly than evil. Pandarus encourages the affair between Troilus and Cressida and arranges a tryst enabling them to consummate their love; but again, he does no harm. Indeed, in his closing speech he laments the fact that his labors on their behalf are underappreciated. "Thus is the poor agent despis'd," he complains, asking "why should our endeavor be so lov'd and the performance so loath'd?" Several of the comedies feature some unattractive characters—Malvolio in *Twelfth Night,* Bertram in *All's Well That Ends Well,* and the two-faced Proteus in *Two Gentlemen of Verona*—but we find no one in such plays who is unreservedly evil. None of these figures can approach the infamy of a Cloten or an Angelo. Even the best-intentioned and best-natured human beings, Shakespeare tells us, are fully capable of making trouble for themselves. We don't always need the wicked to bedevil us.

While we are on the subject, it is of interest to note that many of Shakespeare's tragedies as well contain no villains. Tragic events are often caused not by the malice of wicked men and women but by other factors entirely. Whom would we call evil in *Julius Caesar?* Caesar himself, though dangerously overimpressed with his own worth, is not a wicked man. Cassius is an obvious candidate, but he plots the assassination of Caesar out of fear, not unwarranted, that he will assume dictatorial powers; and the cause is endorsed by Brutus, a paragon of honor and integrity. When Cassius and Brutus take their own lives after their defeat at the battle of Philippi, we are struck with a sense of tragic loss rather than satisfaction that justice has been done. And no scheming villains haunt the palaces of Rome and Alexandria in *Antony and Cleopatra,* only strong men and women vying for control of an empire. Coriolanus, though arrogant and vile-tempered, is not evil, nor is anyone else in the play. He is incensed that, despite a lifetime of honorable service to Rome, the people choose to humiliate him by demanding his banishment. He's not wicked, he's just angry, and with some justification. Were we to name a villain in the Roman plays, it would have to be Rome itself, its wealth and power grown so vast and its people so decadent that ambitious men find room "to bustle in" it, as does Richard III in the court of England.[5]

*Othello* has its Iago, *King Lear* its Edmund, and *Hamlet* its Claudius, but there is no one evil in *Romeo and Juliet.* Tybalt is an impulsive, hotheaded youth, but only marginally more so than Romeo himself or his volatile friend Mercutio, both of whom challenge the Capulet to a duel. If there is anything wicked in the play, it is the city of Verona where, in the words of the Chorus, "civil

5. *Titus Andronicus,* of course, has more than its share of irredeemably evil characters: the scheming Tamora; her lecherous sons, who rape and mutilate Titus's daughter Lavinia; and Tamora's lover Aaron, who urges them to it.

blood makes civil hands unclean." It houses a culture that for generations has condoned the violent excesses of rival families locked in fatal feuds over grievances long forgotten, wrongs committed beyond the memory of any of their vengeful fathers and sons. In this tale they hate simply because they hate. And while *Timon of Athens* offers a group of minor characters despicable for their greed and hypocrisy, none of them is conspicuously wicked. Nor is Timon himself. After his fall he becomes a sour misanthrope who just wants to be left alone.

# The Good

Tolstoy wrote that unhappy families are unhappy each in their own way while happy families are all alike. Goodness is simply not as interesting as evil; but it does deserve consideration in a medium like the theater, which professes to portray the human condition in all its dimensions. It is difficult to conceive of good without contrasting it with evil, to contemplate virtue unless we have some notion of vice, or to lie unless the truth is known. In the words of the poet John Milton, "the knowledge of good and evil, as two twins cleaving together, leaped forth into the world," and we can only know "good by evil."[6] Innocence is touching, as any doting grandfather will bear witness as he watches his daughter's toddlers, but it cannot be praised as good since it has yet to be tested by life's temptations.

Shakespeare offers characters with some complexity to them, villains with marks of goodness who succumb to the evil propensities that mankind is heir to. A few, it is true, seem completely empty of humanity, those such as Iago, Richard III, and Cymbeline's ridiculously churlish stepson Cloten. But most, though far from good, exhibit some redeeming qualities. When we first hear of

6. In his *Areopagetica*.

Macbeth, we learn that he is a man of great skill and courage, entirely loyal to his king. He is horrified at what he has done in murdering Duncan and appears to be sincerely devoted to his wife. Indeed, his only fault seems to be "vaulting ambition," which leads to his later crimes. Even the venomous Moor Aaron in *Titus Andronicus* has room to feel affection for his infant son, the fruit of his adulterous union with the empress Tamora. The baby is dark-skinned, as is Aaron, and her attendants insist that it be put to death to avoid scandal. Aaron saves his son by killing everyone who was present at the birth, except for the mother, of course; but at least it can be said that he is devoted to something other than himself. As we have seen, in *Hamlet,* Claudius is an able statesman and seems genuinely fond of his queen Gertrude; and Angelo, in the opening scenes of *Measure for Measure,* is a loyal servant of the Duke of Vienna, obedient to his master's wish that he assume responsibility for improving the moral climate of the city. With a few exceptions, then, Shakespeare's villains do show a sliver of humanity.

The good people in these plays are continually under siege, particularly in the case of virtuous maidens who fall victim to ambitious villains. In *Richard III,* Anne of Warwick accepts the Duke of Gloucester in marriage. He weds her to gain political advantage, and once he ascends the throne has her done away with when he decides to strengthen his hold on the crown by marrying Elizabeth of York. In *King Lear,* Cordelia rescues her father from the sisters who wish him dead, but then is herself killed on the orders of the bastard Edmund. And Desdemona dies as a result of Iago's poisonous insinuations that she has been unfaithful to Othello.

If good and evil are comprehensible only when contrasted with each other, virtuous characters in a play lend emphasis to the infamy of the wicked, and vice versa. In *Macbeth,* for example, King Duncan is a fatherly figure, generous in his praise and quick to reward loyal service. His brief entry in the early scenes places before us the image of an ideal monarch, establishing a standard of royal behavior against which we can measure the tyrant's cruelty once he mounts the throne.[7] The line between good and evil is clearly drawn in *King Lear*—the virtuous champion the king, the wicked seek his death. Cordelia's loving care of her father accentuates her sisters' malice toward him, and Edgar's devotion to his blind father lends emphasis to the depth of Edmund's iniquity in betraying him.

In *Othello,* Desdemona is, of course, innocent of her husband's accusation that she has been unfaithful to him; but despite her pleas, he refuses to reveal the reason for his suspicion. He dismisses her with a curt command to prepare for bed, and she obediently complies. Before their fatal encounter, Shakespeare inserts a brief, poignant scene in Desdemona's bedchamber, in which he reaffirms her innocence. She asks her worldly handmaid Emilia if "there be women [who] do abuse their husbands / In such gross kind," and Emilia assures her that "there be some such, no question." Desdemona finds the idea repellant: "I do not think there is any such woman." Her innocence stands in sharp contrast to Iago's malevolence, and her devotion to Othello is a vivid contradiction of the ancient's cynical insistence that love "is merely a lust of the blood and a permission of the will."

There is little room for goodness in Shakespeare's history plays, where unscrupulous barons engage in endless conspiracies and open warfare to enhance their power. Henry VI is an almost saintly king who wants only peace for England, but he is no more than a pawn in the game of stronger, more resolute men determined to have their way.

In the tragedies, goodness cannot survive in a wicked world. In *Hamlet,* Polonius is killed, guilty of little more than incessant prying; Ophelia is driven to her grave by sorrow over her losses; and Rosencrantz and Guildenstern die, having come unwittingly "between the pass and fell-incensed points / Of mighty opposites." In

7. In the play, the ability of Edward The Confessor to cure his subject's illnesses with "the king's evil" stands in sharp contrast to Macbeth's reign of terror, which sickens his.

the final scene the stage is littered with dead—the good, the bad, and the blameless. And *Othello* ends with "the tragic loading of this bed," the Moor, Desdemona, and Emilia, all undeserving of their fate, victims of a malicious Iago. Evil invariably receives its just reward in the end, but the good perish as well.

In the comedies, on the other hand, virtue triumphs, and in *Pericles* Shakespeare attributes uncommon powers to it. Marina incurs the envious anger of Queen Dionyza, who arranges for her murder; but pirates interrupt the deed and carry her off. Miraculously, while she is in their custody, she retains her chastity, and we soon discover why. The pirates sell her to a brothel in Mytilene, where Bawd and Pandar anticipate they can get a good price for her services and spread word that they have a virgin available. But to their dismay, she preaches to their customers, shaming them into repenting of their ways. Lysimachus, the governor of Mytilene, visits the brothel to have his pleasure but is dissuaded by her virtue: "Had I brought hither a corrupted mind, / Thy speech had altered it." This is, of course, bad for business, and Pandar's servant Boult proposes to ravish Marina so as to make her more serviceable. But he too falls under her spell and helps find her more honorable employment.

So good triumphs over evil, and predatory males, confronted with a vision of spotless virtue, turn from their wicked ways—in the comedies, at least. Actually, in *Measure for Measure*, virtue has precisely the opposite effect. Isabella is an aspirant in a convent, where she hopes to escape the corrupted world; but she is persuaded to emerge from her sanctuary and plead for her brother's life with the puritanical Angelo, who has condemned him to death for fornication. He is so struck by her eloquence, grace, and virtue that he develops a consuming passion for her, much to his consternation. "Dost thou desire her foully," he asks himself, "for those things / That make her good?" Virtue prevails in the end, after scenes involving disguises, a bed trick, a severed head, and the timely reappearance of the Duke of Vienna. But Angelo seems destined to an unpromising future as a result of his encounter with virtue.

Innocence is another matter, it seems. It raises the question as to whether one who has no experience with evil can be praised as virtuous. Can Adam and Eve be considered good before the serpent invades the Garden? Prospero's daughter Miranda is Shakespeare's most appealing portrait of innocence. She has been raised on an isolated island without knowledge of the corrupt world, and when her father finally decides to enlighten her, she seems inattentive to his tale of the villainous princes of Italy. Her eyes are constantly drawn to the spectacle of what appears to her as "a brave vessel, / Who had, no doubt, some noble creature in her, / Dash'd all to pieces." She is distracted by pity for the distress of those on board, ironically, even as her father is attempting to explain to her just how treacherous those "noble" creatures on the ship truly are. When she first sees Ferdinand, she imagines him "a thing divine, for nothing natural / I ever saw so noble." Although he seems a nice enough young man, he is but one of a company of unsavory characters who have violated the pristine sanctuary of the island, albeit against their will. Later, when she finally sees this gang of cutthroats, she is innocently elated: "How beauteous mankind is! O brave new world, / That has such people in 't!" Prospero can only mutter sadly, "'tis new to thee."

The instinctive response of an audience to the image of innocence is a sense of delight mixed with pity and regret that it must in time come to an end. The loss of innocence is a persistent theme of the stage—the coming of age of young men and women who have thrust upon them the sudden realization that the world is not the welcoming place they thought it to be. We are spared that revelation with Miranda, who has gained love but is as yet without experience. Once Prospero regains his dukedom, the play ends in happy anticipation of the return voyage to Milan, but the theatergoer's mind inevitably drifts toward thoughts of what awaits Miranda there. Her once-attentive father will retire to his books and, as he says, his "every third thought shall be of [his] grave," leaving her on her own to face the realities of this "brave new world." The unrepen-

tant Antonio and Sebastian, who had conspired to kill Alonso, will
return to their natural element and conspire again, and her devoted
Ferdinand may in time play her false.

Shakespeare's vision of evil, then, includes the possibility that it
may be inherent in mankind, as in a Iago or a Richard III. Again, he
sets no store in the notion that the villain acts under the influence of
supernatural powers. These otherworldly figures may taunt human
beings with dreams and apparitions, as they do Macbeth, but the
villain must already harbor the thought of evil for them to be successful. No, in Shakespeare's plays mankind creates its own misery.
The wicked in effect corrupt normal human qualities. When the ordinary aspirations of the human spirit rise to the level of a ruling
passion, then betrayal, rape, and murder seem justified, and in time
necessary. Ambition, desire, and the need for security are common
to the race, but when pursued in excess they become obsessions,
leading to suspicion, greed, jealousy, and hatred. Wickedness is self-
perpetuating in Shakespeare's vision—evil leads on to other evils:
persecution and injustice arouse anger, thwarted love sparks
vengeance, and hate breeds hate. Some of his characters are able to
break out of the cycle of despair into a healing time of hope and reconciliation—Duke Frederick and Oliver in *As You Like It,* for example, King Leontes in *The Winter's Tale,* and perhaps it may be hoped
of the Montagues and Capulets, stunned into recognition of their
folly by the loss of the two "star-cross'd lovers." Others are destined
to end their lives untouched by goodness, as do Iago, Richard III,
and the comic Cloten, while some survive to scheme again, those
such as the unrepentant Sebastian and Antonio in *The Tempest.* And
it is difficult to hold out much hope for a change of heart in *Measure
for Measure*'s Angelo.

Goodness prevails in Shakespeare's comedies, of course, which
all end in reconciliation and rejoicing. But that happiness is often
hard won, the reward of many trials testing virtue and constancy,
trials that Miranda has yet to face. The tragedies can end on a hope-

ful note—*Macbeth* for example; but most of them close upon a circle of stunned survivors, good men and women all, who are left to pick up the pieces of a world shattered by evil, hoping that all may yet be well.

# THE HERO

᪾

THE WORD "HERO" is so misused, and overused, in the modern media that a brief definition of the term as it applies to Shakespeare's plays will prove helpful at the outset. The heroic, as a theme, may be said to apply to three groups of Shakespeare's characters: the martial, the tragic, and the comic. The martial hero or heroine fits the traditional definition of the word, a person who displays exceptional valor in the performance of deeds that are dangerous, often quite audacious, and in the service of a worthy cause. In this sense a soldier in the ranks may be called heroic if he places his life in jeopardy above and beyond the call of duty to destroy a malignant enemy or rescue a wounded comrade, a firefighter if he enters a burning building to save a life, a policeman if he places himself in harm's way to protect a citizen or community from criminal violence, or an ordinary citizen if he performs some extraordinary act of sacrifice to preserve a life or right a grievous wrong. Thus a common element of acts that are recognized as heroic is the risk of death or severe bodily harm.[1]

This being said, there are few heroic commoners in Shakespeare's plays, and where they do appear they are more likely to be comic. His chronicles of England's wars record the conflicts between kings and barons, leaving little room for the exploits of ordinary sol-

---

1. In this sense the courageous police and firemen who, without regard for their own safety, rushed to the aid of those trapped in the World Trade Center on the morning of September 11, 2001, more than meet these standards.

diers. Those we do see to any extent have little taste for battle—the group of volunteers from the Boar's Head Tavern in *Henry V,* for example, who shun the breach in Harfleur's city walls when the king urges them to assault it "once more," and Falstaff's reluctant recruits in *Henry IV, Part 2*—Feeble, Wart, and Shadow—who are singularly unfit for military service. There are no firefighters in the plays, and Shakespeare's police are more often than not addled comics like Dogberry and his inept watch in *Much Ado About Nothing* and the constables Elbow in *Measure for Measure* and Dull in *Love's Labor's Lost,* all of whom are much given to malaprops. When commoners appear in a scene, like the gardeners in *Richard II* and the three citizens in *Richard III,* they are properly submissive to their social betters or fatalistically uneasy about the wrangling of the kingdom's nobility. Shakespeare often endows them with uncommon insight into the affairs of the mighty, however, casting them as choruslike figures. Or they may be absurdly simpleminded, like the peasants drawn to Jack Cade's rebellion in *Henry VI, Part 2,* who want to "kill all the lawyers" and hang a man because he can read and write. There are no heroes in such groups, only ordinary men and women who react to events over which they have no control, as would any workaday shopkeeper or farmer.

Shakespeare's heroes and heroines are nobly born, of kings or barons, legitimately or otherwise. He wrote of an age when eager youths of noble birth aspired to make their name in battle and reap the rewards of martial valor—fame, wealth, adulation, and the gratitude of royalty. It is not surprising, then, that the traditional heroes of his plays are highborn warriors skilled in the martial arts and ready to risk their lives on the field of battle, figures such as Henry V, the noble Talbot in *Henry VI, Part 1,* and the bastard Faulconbridge in *King John.*

The theater's tragic and comic heroes call for an entirely different definition of the word. "Hero" in this sense may mean only the chief character of a work. A tragic hero may be a villain like Macbeth, an irascible old monarch like Lear, or a contemplative Hamlet uncertain of his cause. A comic hero may be the antithesis of the traditional martial figure, a Sir John Falstaff, for example, who is overly solicitous of his own skin and unsheathes his sword only for personal gain. Such characters are certainly entertaining, but they arouse little admiration in an audience.[2]

## The Martial Hero

The traditional hero of Shakespeare's plays is a soldier. He is characterized by his personal valor, a nobility of purpose, and a willingness to risk death for his cause. Admittedly, some of Shakespeare's villainous or comic figures are equally adept—Richard III, Macbeth, and even the callous Bertram in *All's Well That Ends Well*—but they are seen as men intent only on personal glory while the martial hero seems larger than life because he is devoted to a larger cause. Literature and history preserve the names of those whose skill and sacrifice save a people's heritage or battle against malignant forces intent upon enslaving them, those such as the Spartan Leonidas, who with a small band of warriors held off the vast Persian armies at the "hot gates" of Thermopylae, and Charlemagne, who stemmed the advance of the Moors into Europe. George Washington challenged the mighty British Empire with a ragged army of resolute patriots; Wellington defeated Napoleon at Waterloo; and countless valiant men and women shattered Adolf Hitler's dream of a triumphant Third Reich.

In Shakespeare's time, Henry V was a figure of comparable, almost mythic proportions for the English people. For a short time in the early fifteenth century, after an arduous five-year campaign, he united the crowns of England and France, the pinnacle of his country's fortunes until the emergence of the British Empire some three hundred years later. Shakespeare celebrated the life of this "star of

2. These figures are examined in the chapter to follow, "The Comic Muse."

England" from his unpromising youth to his final triumph, a year before his life was cut short while campaigning in France.

When we first see him as Prince Hal in *Henry IV, Part 1,* he is an irresponsible playboy who frequents the taverns of London's Eastcheap and engages in frivolous pranks with the common people of the Boar's Head, chief among them the unruly Sir John Falstaff— hardly suitable companions for the Prince of Wales. We follow his career as he emerges from his reckless youth to accept the obligations of an heir to the throne, joining and then leading his father's armies to subdue dangerous rebellions by disaffected nobles. *Henry V* chronicles the deeds that raise Hal to heroic stature. He assumes the throne and unites his contentious country in "a well-hallow'd cause" to assert the English king's long-standing claim to the French crown. The play records his invasion and seizure of the French seaport at Harfleur, his resounding victory at Agincourt over an army vastly superior to his own, and the final capitulation of the King of France.

As mentioned earlier in these pages, modern critics are divided in their judgment of Henry V, some praising him as the embodiment of the sturdy English spirit prevailing in the face of daunting odds, others condemning him as a soulless military adventurer, intent only upon personal glorification.[3] Both sides neglect the human drama of the figure, whom Shakespeare endows with qualities that place him within the scope of anyone who has set aside the heedless joys of youth to confront the obligations of maturity. He wins the admiration of both friend and foe by his conduct on the battlefield and demonstrates martial skill and physical courage by subduing the formidable Hotspur in single combat. But he is drawn time and again to the company of Falstaff, whose irrepressible gaiety and irreverent parody of civic virtues stand in sharp contrast to the public burdens imposed on the prince by royal birth. It is only when Hal mounts the throne that he banishes the fat knight from his

3. See p. 52.

presence, as he must a figure who represents a cynical disregard for everything a Christian king is expected to uphold—honor, sacrifice, honesty, valor, and respect for the law. It may be assumed that he does so with a certain regret as he closes out his carefree youth to assume the obligations of the crown.

In *Henry V,* Shakespeare defines the heroic. The king endangers his life in leading an assault through a breach in the walls of Harfleur. He shows wisdom and restraint when he forbids looting during the army's march through Normandy, reasoning sensibly that "when lenity and cruelty play for a kingdom, the gentler gamester is the soonest winner." And he enforces the order, even at the cost of the lives of Bardolph and Nym, two companions from his Boar's Head days. He lifts the spirits of his soldiers, who are faced with fearsome odds, challenging them to "dishonor not your mothers; now attest / That those whom you call'd fathers did beget you," and appealing to them as "we few, we happy few, we band of brothers." He enjoys the loyalty, even the affection, of his soldiers, from his royal brothers down to the lowest man-at-arms. And he deploys his army skillfully to repulse the attack of the superior French to win a resounding victory at Agincourt.

At the same time Shakespeare fleshes out the heroic figure with touches of humanity. His King Henry is no mythic superman but a figure who displays many of the virtues and failings of any human being. On the night before battle he hides his identity and sits comfortably by a campfire with a group of common soldiers talking of life and death, but he flares angrily when one of them questions the king's oath to refuse capture and ransom. And after the battle, in a device reminiscent of Falstaff, he plays a cruel trick on that same soldier to cover his chagrin at having challenged one of his own men in a moment of heat. Finally, in a charming scene after the war, King Henry woos the French princess Katherine, though he has no need to since her hand in marriage is one of the demands he has imposed on her father. Somewhat disingenuously he pleads, "I speak to thee plain soldier. If thou canst love me for this, take me," although those of us who have followed his career know there is a great deal more to him than the "plain soldier" he claims to be. In his youth, then, Henry V enjoys the unrestrained gaiety of irresponsible companions; and as king he responds heatedly to a personal affront and courts his future wife with charming guile. Shakespeare portrays a complete human being, not some stilted icon.

Lord Talbot, in *Henry VI, Part 1,* is another of Shakespeare's heroic figures, though he is more in the tradition of the chivalric hero, "the knight without fear and without reproach." As commander of the English army in France after the death of Henry V, to Talbot falls the task of maintaining control over the rebellious French who resent the occupying forces. They continue to resist, inspired by Joan la Pucelle, championing the cause of the son and heir of Charles VI, the Dauphin Charles who was disinherited by the treaty between the two kingdoms. Talbot is a fierce and able warrior, much feared as "the terror of the French" and "the scourge of France," so much so that English soldiers rush into battle crying "A Talbot! A Talbot!" sufficient, it seems, to send the French into terrified retreat.

Talbot's chivalry is shown when he accepts an invitation from the Countess of Auvergne. She plots to imprison him but is thwarted when he calls in soldiers whom he has taken the precaution to have nearby. True to his code as a knight, he does not retaliate against the lady, assuring her gallantly that he is not offended by her treachery, and asks only that they may dine together.

The noble Talbot is unconditionally loyal to the young King Henry VI, taking no part in the growing discord between jealous factions within the royal court, the most dangerous of them the animosity between Henry Beaufort, the powerful Bishop of Winchester, and the Duke of Gloucester, who serves as lord protector of England during the minority of the king. In *Henry VI, Part 1,* Shakespeare dramatizes another of the dynastic divisions that plague the kingdom in the contentious scene between Richard Plantagenet, Duke of York, and the Duke of Somerset, when they pluck the white rose and the red, sowing the seed for the War of the Roses. Talbot eventually falls victim to these feuding lords when he is surrounded by superior French forces before Bordeaux, and both York and Somerset neglect to come to his aid, each blaming the other for the failure. So Talbot is slain, "the Frenchmen's only scourge, / [Their] kingdom's terror and black Nemesis," and England loses France.

The engaging Philip Faulconbridge, called simply the "Bastard" throughout Shakespeare's *King John,* has marks of the martial hero about him. He bears such a striking resemblance to the late King of England, Richard Cordelion (*Coeur-de-Lion*), that Queen Elinor, Richard's mother, takes the young man into her service. As it turns out, King Richard was indeed Faulconbridge's father as a result of a momentary dalliance with the young man's mother. Because the path to fame and fortune in medieval times lay through the battlefield, the Bastard is determined to make a name for himself, as well perhaps as to live up to the reputation of his warlike father.

Faulconbridge accompanies King John as he leads an army to confront the French. The Bastard is eager for battle and is scornful of the two kings when they arrive at a peaceful resolution of their differences. He rants privately against "that smooth-fac'd gentleman, tickling commodity," by which he means their expedient willingness to forgo "a resolved and honorable war" in favor of "a most base and vile-concluded peace" because they will profit from it. He voices the soldier's complaint against the merchant's inclination to place self-interest ("commodity") above national honor. In the end, the peace proves to be short-lived, and France invades England, successfully occupying London. King John is so disconsolate that the Bastard has to rouse him from his lethargy—"Let us, my liege, to arms!"—and appointed by the king to command the English forces, he leads them against the French, who eventually withdraw.

Shakespeare has his share of female martial heroes as well, prominent among them Joan of Arc, called "la Pucelle" in *Henry VI, Part 1,* and Queen Margaret in *Part 3.* They are both French, for whatever one may wish to make of the fact. Did Shakespeare feel that it was unseemly for the ladies of England to appear in warlike guise? Joan enters as the legendary maid of Orleans, inspired, she announces, by a vision of "God's mother" to revive the French cause. She is skilled in single combat, proving her prowess in a duel with the dauphin and holding her own against the mighty Talbot. And she is adept politically as well, eloquently persuading the Duke of Burgundy to renounce his allegiance to the English and join his native France to oppose the occupation. Under her command the French relieve Orleans by force and take Rouen by cunning, and they rout the English before Bordeaux, where Talbot, deserted by York and Somerset, finally falls.

This is an English play, of course, and to them Joan is the "foul fiend of France" and "accursed minister of hell." York and Somerset finally join forces and defeat her at Angiers, where, as Shakespeare portrays her, she is not the saintly virgin of Orleans inspired by the mother of God, but a wanton abetted in her exploits by a company of underworld fiends. They desert her, however, and she is captured, to suffer humiliation when, in an effort to escape the stake, she reveals that she is pregnant. Whatever her end, she proves a formidable warrior.

Henry VI's queen, the fiery Margaret of Anjou, is not called upon to demonstrate physical prowess in single combat, but in *Henry VI, Part 3,* Shakespeare portrays her as a resourceful enemy of the house of York. She assumes command of the Lancastrian forces in the War of the Roses in the place of her ineffectual husband; indeed, at one point the king is asked to leave the battlefield because "the queen hath best success when you are absent." She routs the Lancaster army at Wakefield and St. Albans. Defeated later at York, Margaret escapes to her native France where she persuades the king to embrace her cause. In alliance with powerful English lords, she returns at the head of an army to rescue her husband, who has been captured and imprisoned. She is ultimately defeated at Tewkesbury, forced to watch the slaughter of her son Edward, and sent back to France in exile, closing out an impressive military career.

Mention might be made of King Lear's daughter Cordelia, who invades England at the head of a French army to rescue her father from the hands of her malicious sisters; but the gentle Cordelia has none of the warlike qualities of a Joan or Margaret. Indeed, in all of Shakespeare's plays, no other women can compare with them in a martial prowess that approaches the heroic in scope. Many are as courageous, resolute, loyal, and cunning as they, but none bear arms or lead armies in battle.

Shakespeare's martial heroes, then, are first of all physically courageous. Fears and doubts may possess them before and after battle, but they are resolute in the heat of combat. They remain unreservedly loyal to their lords or kings, and devoted to their country and its cause. They are gallant to a valorous foe or, as in the case of Talbot, to a lady, though the chivalric code was a fading ideal in Shakespeare's time. But they are not the peerless knights of medieval romance. Shakespeare's endows them with recognizable human qualities—a Henry V roused to indiscreet anger by a soldier who doubts the king's veracity, a Talbot reduced to despair, or a Faulconbridge who regrets the wasted opportunity to achieve fame when the two kings, in his mind selfishly committed to "commodity," reach a "base and vile-concluded peace."

# The Antihero

Many of Shakespeare's most appealing comic figures delight us precisely because they are parodies of the traditional hero. Falstaff, for example, certainly the theater's most engaging scoundrel, scoffs at the qualities that are usually associated with the ideal warrior of history and legend. In *Henry IV, Part 1,* he dismisses honor as a "mere scutcheon": "What is honor? Air. A trim reckoning! Who hath it?

He that died a' Wednesday. Doth he feel it? No. 'Tis insensible then? Yea, to the dead." He is a self-indulgent thief, loyal to no one but himself, and he betrays the trust placed in him. By his own admission, he misuses "the king's press damnably," accepting bribes from wealthy recruits to release them from military service and conscripting whoever is left, however unfit they may be. Prince Hal, viewing Falstaff's company, is dismayed: "I did never see such pitiful rascals." Falstaff is also cowardly. He and his companions take to their heels, leaving their loot behind, on the night that Hal and his friend Poins surprise them after the robbery at Gadshill, an occasion for great hilarity among them afterward. And he feigns death when he encounters the fiery Scot Douglas during the battle of Shrewsbury.

Shakespeare offers examples of the *miles gloriosus,* the false or braggart soldier, who embellishes his martial prowess and bristles belligerently at the slightest hint of a challenge to his honor, but quickly backs down in the face of danger. Parolles in *All's Well That Ends Well* and *Henry V*'s Pistol are such figures. The former is insufferably militant but crumbles when placed in jeopardy. His fellow soldiers, tiring of his bluster, disguise themselves as the enemy and pretend to capture Parolles, threatening him with death unless he reveals details of his army's strength. Reduced to trembling fear, he blurts out the names and numbers of its units and is properly humiliated when his tormentors unmask and reveal their identities. Pistol is quick to draw his sword and just as quick to put it away. He is full of high words but slinks from battle, showing his mettle when he urges others "unto the breach" in a mockery of Henry V's stirring speech, and then scurries for cover rather than join the attack.

*Troilus and Cressida* is Shakespeare's consummate satire on love and war. The play transforms Homer's Greek and Trojan warriors into witless thugs and pompous frauds. Hector is a parody of the chivalrous knight, so ridiculously devoted to "fair play" that he spares weaker opponents rather than take advantage of his superior strength and skill; and Achilles is a devious, self-important coward. When the two meet in battle, Hector soon has the advantage. Achilles, explaining that he is a bit out of shape, asks that they pause for a time so that he can catch his breath. Hector, with misplaced gallantry, allows him to retire, which gives him time to call up his Myrmidons and return treacherously to slaughter the disarmed Trojan.

The common soldier Thersites is a scurrilous choric figure in the play, an insubordinate malcontent who heaps scorn on Homer's legendary heroes. To him the mighty Ajax "hast no more brain than I have in my elbow"; he is a thickminded warrior who "wears his wit in his belly, and his guts in his head." Thersites scoffs at Achilles to his face, reviling him as the "idol of idiot-worshippers" whose "wit too lies in your sinews." "I would rather be a tick in a sheep," he rails, "than such a valiant ignorance." Agamemnon "has not so much brain as ear-wax," Menelaus is "the bull, the primitive statue, and oblique memorial of cuckolds." No one escapes the scathing tongue of Thersites: Patroclus is "a masculine whore," Nestor a "stale old mouse-eaten dry cheese," Diomedes a "false-hearted rogue," and Ulysses a "dog-fox." He watches them in battle and finds the spectacle an unseemly brawl: "Now they are all clapper-clawing one another." So much for heroes!

## The Tragic Hero

In Shakespeare's tragedies the central figures do not conform to the model of the martial hero. They do not shirk danger, certainly, but their courage is of another order and their character more complex. The death of Talbot, deserted by his squabbling lords, strikes us as regrettable, but it does not move an audience as do the dying moments of a Hamlet or a Lear. The murders of the imprisoned Henry VI and Richard II are certainly pitiful to watch, but neither has the impact of an Antony dying in the arms of Cleopatra. Richard does rise up in righteous anger against his assailants, but his futile gesture cannot compare with Macbeth's majestic defiance when he challenges his adversary: "Lay on, Macduff, / And damn'd be him who first cries, 'Hold, enough!'" The figure we call a "tragic hero" calls for a different definition entirely.

The insatiably inquisitive Greek philosopher Aristotle turned his attention at one point to the stage. He examined the theater of his time to determine why some plays were successful and others not, that is, why some pleased and others failed to please an audience; and he recorded his conclusions in a short work, *Of Poetics.* As philosophers will do, he starts by creating categories. A tragedy, he tells us, is a play in which the chief character experiences a change from good fortune to bad, and in a comedy, alternately, the change is from bad to good. At first glance this may not seem a particularly profound observation, but it helps explain the medieval use of the word "comedy." Dante called his great poem *La Commedia* not because it was especially amusing but because the pilgrim begins his journey in hell and ends it in heaven. Aristotle's definition, moreover, provides a frame of reference for the appreciation of some of Shakespeare's plays that artfully blend the two broad categories of drama. *The Merchant of Venice,* for example, is a comedy in that as it opens the merchant Antonio is melancholy, the romantic hero Bassanio is bankrupt, and the heroine Portia is "aweary of this great world." At its close Bassanio has won the love of Portia, who is rich, and Antonio has been restored to good humor. The tragic is present as well, however, in the figure of Shylock, who, when we first encounter him, is a prosperous moneylender and when last seen is a man stripped of his dignity, his daughter, his wealth, and his religion.

The Greeks held long theater festivals in which dozens of plays competed for prizes, and in *Of Poetics* Aristotle, it seems, analyzed the winners to determine the features they had in common. He concluded, not surprisingly, that the plot is the most important element of a successful play, but it is his brief analysis of character that can most enhance our appreciation of Shakespeare's tragic heroes. The most compelling tragic figure, Aristotle wrote, is a person of high office, a king or a queen, or of some special accomplishment, a renowned warrior or a human endowed with uncommon occult powers. They are, moreover, figures with whom the audience is already familiar through history or myth passed down from generation to generation, an Oedipus or Agamemnon, a Theseus or Medea. Of equal importance, they are not absolutely good or irredeemably evil but "a man between these extremes." Reasonably, the death of an innocent infant is certainly a sad event, but it cannot be said that the untimely end of a life with no history is tragic, except of course to its parents, who suffer the loss. By the same token, we cannot regret the loss of an absolute villain, whose death seems just retribution for his wickedness. Tragic heroes must be recognizable human beings, endowed with the same virtues and failings as anyone in the audience, who can thereby identify with their dilemmas, rejoice in their triumphs, and share their sorrows.

Aristotle proposed that the most successful tragic heroes are brought low by some personal failing, pride, ambition, or desire for gain, qualities with which any member of the audience is all too familiar but which, when carried to excess, can become a ruling passion, crowding out the virtues that temper them in a balanced human spirit. Heroes fall because of *hamartia* in their makeup. This Greek word is variously interpreted but has been traditionally translated as an "error or frailty" in character, a moral weakness or "tragic flaw."

Scholars disagree over what Aristotle meant by *hamartia,* some insisting that it does not imply a character flaw or moral failing but simply a "significant mistake" on the hero's part. This reading, however, does little to explain the effect of a tragic death upon an audience. If a central character dies only as a consequence of a series of blunders, the death is merely pathetic, the stuff of melodrama, not tragedy. That death is certainly more compelling as theater if it arises from some inner compulsion urged by the very nature of the figure, some human quality common to us all but out of control in the spirit.

Macbeth would seem to violate Aristotle's contention that the tragic hero should not be inherently evil, but this is, after all, the tale of a good man gone wrong. The death of the tyrant is certainly justified, indeed applauded, but at the opening of the play he is an essentially good man, a valorous warrior and a thane loyal to the king, "too full o' th' milk of human kindness" to his wife's regret. His ambition is real enough, but it is only a secret thought, harmless until nourished by the witches' prophecy, and his career of terror is precipitated by the fear that a throne acquired by crime will prove untenable. His death is tragic in that his ambition to gain and retain the crown becomes a consuming passion, leaving him empty of normal human feeling, unable even to mourn the loss of his wife except to mutter sourly that "life's but a walking shadow . . . signifying nothing."

The cause of Hamlet's inaction, which leads ultimately to his death, is a mystery, one, it seems, consciously designed by Shakespeare. At one time or another during the play Hamlet vents his anger and frustration, both verbally and physically, on almost everyone he encounters. He manhandles Ophelia, his mother, and Laertes, and he ridicules Polonius, the king, and the court fop Osric. And we receive every assurance that it is quite unusual for him to be so unsociable and unpleasant to be around. Because of his indecision and delay in killing Claudius, he is responsible, directly or indirectly, for the death of not one person but eight, himself included, most of whom are entirely innocent of any wrong.

What is it in Hamlet's nature that prevents him from gaining swift vengeance on his father's murderer? Shakespeare offers tantalizing clues to the cause of his inaction, beginning with an oblique allusion to the possibility that the answer lies within the prince himself. Awaiting the appearance of the ghost, Hamlet and Horatio privately censure the king for his unseemly custom of carousing into the small hours of the night. Hamlet observes:

So, oft it chances in particular men,
That for some vicious mole of nature in them,
As in their birth—wherein they are not guilty,
Since nature cannot choose her origin—
. . . . . . . . . . . . . . . . . . these men,
Carrying, I say, the stamp of one defect,
. . . . . . . . . . . . . . . . . . . . . . . . . . . .
Shall in the general censure take corruption
From that particular fault.

A single "fault," in brief, may spell doom for anyone. The passage is a poetic expression of Aristotle's theory of the tragic hero's "error or frailty" in character; and though Hamlet is speaking of Claudius here, the allusion clings to him as well.

And what is Hamlet's "fault"? Shakespeare offers an array of answers. It may be an oppressive melancholy that disables him. When we first see him, he is sunk in profound sorrow, and throughout the play his thoughts return time and again to the contemplation of death. It may be that his subconscious desire for his mother prevents him from harming a father figure like Claudius.[4] Or it may be that he is inhibited by a moral reluctance to take another's life. Having seen the ghost and vowed vengeance, he suddenly realizes the enormity of what he must do: "The time is out of joint; O cursed spite, / That ever I was born to set it right!"

Then too, it might be his philosophical habit of mind, a tendency to overintellectualize choices, that drains Hamlet of resolve. Action is demanded of him, but he is by nature contemplative. On the single occasion when he is presented with an opportunity to kill his father's murderer, a thought intrudes: "That would be scann'd." Paradoxically, Hamlet is physically vigorous and fully capable of action, but when he acts he does so without thought, "rashly," as he puts it, "and prais'd be rashness for it." He impulsively runs his

4. For a discussion of the psychological syndrome known as the Oedipus complex, see p. 33.

sword though the wallhangings in his mother's chamber, killing Polonius; he leads the assault on the pirate ship; he leaps into Ophelia's grave; and at the end he kills Laertes in a rage and, driven by desperation, finally does away with Claudius.

Hamlet is well aware that an overly contemplative habit of mind can rob one of the will to act. Indeed, he alludes to the possibility himself on two occasions, the first as he is pondering the obstacles to suicide:

> Thus conscience does make cowards of us all,
> And thus the native hue of resolution
> Is sicklied o'er with the pale cast of thought,
> And enterprises of great pith and moment
> With this regard their currents turn awry,
> And lose the name of action.

Late in the play he flagellates himself for his delay, wondering whether he might be guilty of "some craven scruple / Of thinking too precisely on th' event— / A thought, which, quarter'd, hath but one part wisdom, / And three parts coward." He exclaims in frustration, "I do not know / Why yet I live to say 'This thing's to do,' " and still not do it.

Hamlet doesn't know, and neither do we. Shakespeare endows him with various "flaws," none of which rise to the level of what we might call a human fault, but any one of which might be responsible for his delay in avenging his father's murder until circumstances force the act upon him. Hamlet remains an enigma.

Lear's faults are more accessible. They arise from the imperious arrogance of a monarch whose long unchallenged reign has accustomed him to flattering deference and left him unable to distinguish between those who truly love and honor him and those who do not. His folly is in evidence from the outset when, to feed his vanity, he insists that his daughters voice their affection for him in court ceremony. When Cordelia, his youngest and his favorite, refuses to debase her devotion in this way, explaining, "I cannot heave

/ My heart into my mouth," Lear flies into a rage, disowns her, and banishes the loyal Earl of Kent for taking her part. His further folly lies in the belief that he can divide his kingdom among his heirs, lay down the duties and responsibilities of the crown, and still "retain / The name, and all th' addition to a king."

When his other two daughters, who had flattered him extravagantly, seek to deprive him of his retinue of a hundred knights, which he considers an essential "addition to a king," he is reduced to bartering between them. One suggests that he keep but fifty, her sister that twenty-five will suffice him, so he accepts the first offer, convinced that fifty knights is "twice [the] love" of twenty-five. When they both agree that he need have none, he can bear their presence no longer and in a frantic rage rushes onto the barren heath at the mercy of a violent storm. Lear's life has left him blind to love, which he foolishly measures in terms of honeyed words in a royal court and the number of knights in his train.

It can be said that Othello falls because of an overly passionate nature, but other factors contribute to his downfall, all of which he himself alludes to at one time or another. He is a Moor, and though a highly respected general in the service of the Venetians, he remains an alien presence in their culture. He is, further, a soldier, unfamiliar with their sophisticated society, a man who is more at ease in an army encampment than a drawing room. Add to these circumstances his age—many years older than his bride, Desdemona—and we have the image of a man out of his element in marrying the daughter of a wealthy Venetian merchant, a young woman who has been raised in the protective environment of a respectable household, her experience limited to the city's narrow social world.

Othello is a deeply passionate man. In the opening lines of the play, Roderigo, a suitor for the hand of Desdemona, is upset with his friend Iago: "I take it much unkindly / That thou . . . shouldst know of this." The "this" of his complaint is a scandalously rash act, the secret marriage of Othello and Desdemona, a precipitous union born of mutual passion. Iago incites her father, Brabantio, with news of the marriage, and then attempts to enflame Othello with lies about Brabantio's "scurvy and provoking terms / Against your honor." Soon two groups of armed men are prowling in the night along narrow walkways that border winding Venetian canals, and they suddenly meet at a dark turn. Weapons are drawn and Iago attempts to provoke a brawl; but Othello prevents it, commanding, "put up your bright swords, for the dew will rust them." He addresses Brabantio with courteous reserve: "Good signior, you shall more command with years / Than with your weapons."

Thus reason governs passion in Venice. It is agreed that the issue should be placed before the duke, where, each man is confident, the law will prevail. There Othello explains that he was often invited to Brabantio's house, where Desdemona became enthralled with his tales of "the battles, sieges, fortunes, / That I have pass'd," and their affection grew: "She lov'd me for the dangers I had pass'd, / And I lov'd her that she did pity them." The duke, moved by the account, judges the marriage legal, and Brabantio is compelled to submit. He does so with an ill will, however, refusing to shelter his daughter when her husband is hastily dispatched on a mission against the Turks. She asks to accompany him on the campaign, and Othello seconds her request. With quiet dignity he insists that he does not ask so as "to please the palate of my appetite, / Nor comply with heat," and he assures the duke that he will not permit his love for her to distract him from his mission. Dedication to duty, the rule of reason, will prevail over "appetite," he pledges, and the duke nods his approval.

In Venice, then, Othello is in full control. He prevents bloodshed, thwarting Iago's designs, and shows proper deference to the decorum of the city's highest court. But the mere mention of his "appetite," whose "young effects" he dismisses disingenuously as "defunct" in a man of his age, raises the question of just how close to that dignified and deferential surface his passions lie. Othello assumes command in Cyprus, a distant colony of Venice, close to the menacing Turks; and here, far from the reach of Venetian law, we see a different man emerge. Iago had failed to incite an altercation in Venice, but he succeeds in Cyprus, this one between Othello's lieutenant, Cassio, and the former governor, Montano. Othello comes upon the scene and angrily commands the two to "put by this barbarous brawl," warning them:

> My blood begins my safer guides to rule,
> And passion, having my best judgment collied,
> Assays to lead the way. If I once stir,
> Or lift this arm, the best of you
> Shall sink in my rebuke.

The subtle Iago preys upon Othello's insecurity, citing the differences between him and his young wife, and finally persuades him that Desdemona has betrayed him by engaging in an illicit affair with Cassio. Othello's "appetite" rises to the surface as consuming jealousy, supplanting any vestige of the restraint or reason that had ruled his conduct in Venice, and his "passion" does in the end "lead the way." His anger at Desdemona's supposed infidelity runs as deep as had his love for her, eclipsing his "best judgment." He murders her and, when his folly comes to light, takes his own life.

Shakespeare's comedies feature any number of female figures who perform a central role in the play, those such as Rosalind in *As You Like It*, Portia in *The Merchant of Venice*, Helena in *All's Well That Ends Well*, and Imogen in *Cymbeline*, to mention but a few. But the same cannot be said of the tragedies, where few female characters can be called tragic heroines in the sense that the drama centers on them, as it does a Hamlet or a Lear. Juliet may be one, though she must share the stage and her fate with Romeo against a backdrop of wrangling Montagues and Capulets; and others suffer tragic deaths—Ophelia and Gertrude in *Hamlet*, Cordelia in *King Lear*, and Desdemona in *Othello*. But the one who unquestionably dominates the play, about whom the entire plot revolves, is Cleopatra. She appears prominently in scene after scene, and even when absent she is on the tongue of others. The episodes in Rome, where solemn men talk of war, empire, and dominion, invariably end in inquiries about Egypt and her queen, and she is never far from Antony's thoughts. She dominates the last act, after his death, and the final majestic end of her life is the tragedy of the play.

And yet it is difficult to identify her as one who falls victim to a "tragic flaw," unless it is her indulgence in sensual pleasures. But she deploys her sensuality with conscious intent, like legions in battle array, to capture and retain the love of Antony. Cleopatra's historic and dramatic role bears resemblance to that of Rosencrantz and Guildenstern, whose deaths Hamlet describes unsympathetically as a consequence of their indiscretion at coming "between the pass and fell-incensed points / Of mighty opposites." Cleopatra stands between these "mighty opposites," Caesar and Antony, who contend for the rule of an empire, and she casts her lot with one of them, out of love for him and concern for her kingdom. The tragic irony of her life is that her incomparable allure, her "infinite variety," the source of her power over Antony, is the very quality that disarms him, drains his energy, and distracts him from attention to his vital interests.

Can we fault her for her intrigues? Perhaps she revels too much in her influence over her lover, persuading him, for example, to confront Caesar at sea in the battle of Actium, a decision that leads to his defeat. Shakespeare leaves it an open question as to which she values more, her love for Antony or her devotion to Egypt. He becomes convinced that she betrays him on three separate occasions: the unexplained flight from Actium, her ambiguous interview with Caesar's envoy Thidias, and the final defection of the Egyptian fleet. But he forgives her all three. In the last act she takes her life as much to avoid humiliation in Rome as to affirm her love for Antony. Shakespeare leaves the judgment to us, but there is no denying the tragic impact of her dying words: "Methinks I hear / Antony call; I see him rouse himself / To praise my noble act!" and in answer, "Husband I come! / Now to that name my courage prove my title!" She remains a fascinating figure, four hundred years after

Shakespeare penned her lines and two millennia after her death, confirming the judgment of Enobarbus: "Age cannot wither her, nor custom stale / Her infinite variety."

The tragic hero, then, is a person of high office or renown, one who, though endowed with superior status, intellect, or martial skills, nonetheless shares in the failings of all humans. Any of us, at one time or another, may well find ourselves in the grips of Macbeth's ambition, Hamlet's melancholy, Lear's blindness, Othello's passion, or Cleopatra's sensuality. And this is both a theme of Shakespeare's tragedies (the mighty are much like us) and a source of their enduring appeal (we can see ourselves in them). The only difference is that when such figures fall, great dynasties dissolve, kingdoms crumble, and empires shudder.

Were one to define Shakespeare's tragic theme in the most basic terms, it would be this: the seeds of our destruction lie within us. Our destiny is shaped not by evil otherworldly forces, some unrelenting goddess of Fate, an unfathomable turn of Fortune, the frivolous hand of Chance, or the malevolent designs of hidden villains, but by ourselves alone. Life itself may indeed impart a very different lesson—a sudden fatal accident, the inexplicable onslaught of a deadly disease, the unmerited suffering of the innocent and prosperity of the wicked, the inescapable evidence of injustice in human affairs. But Shakespeare exposes the truth of the matter: it's all our own doing, the legacy of a grim contradiction in the makeup of mankind, our infinite capacity for good coupled with a darker attraction to evil.

Shakespeare's tragic heroes protest the absence of justice in the universe and gain a dignity at the end that ennobles them in our eyes so that we see their death as at once inevitable and unnecessary, reducing us to speechless awe at the spectacle. Macbeth rages at the "fiend that lies like truth" but stands against Macduff, though he knows the thane is "not of woman born" and will destroy him. During the storm, Lear calls upon the "great gods" for justice, and at the end, bowing over the lifeless body of Cordelia, questions why "a dog, a horse, a rat have life, / And thou no breath at all." Hamlet insists that Horatio survive to tell his story, so that the death of so many will somehow appear justified in the eyes of the world. Othello, acknowledging his own guilt, demands of the impenetrable Iago, "why he hath thus ensnar'd my soul and body," but goes to his death unanswered. Reminding the stunned survivors of the carnage that he has "done the state some service," he stabs himself. They all inflict their fate upon themselves, surely, but ask us to question why it need be so, why justice seems to hide its head in human affairs.

The hero, then, is not merely someone who excels in a particular endeavor—in sports, science, or public office; nor a man or woman who has proven resolute in prevailing against great odds—an illness, handicap, or other adversity; nor one who has devoted a lifetime to loyal and dedicated but relatively uneventful service to society. Such figures are surely admirable and well worthy of our respect, but a hero on the stage, whether the world's or Shakespeare's Globe, calls for a different evaluation. If such a figure is martial in nature, the hero must be at the center of great events and perform deeds out of the ordinary, acts of personal valor or inspirational leadership—a Henry V or a Talbot. These men and women are courageous, resourceful, and committed human beings, and if they die in defeat, they leave us with a sense of loss, of a precious life passed.

But the death of a tragic hero leaves us with something more. Such a death may or may not alter the course of human events. The fate of Antony and Cleopatra ushers in a new era in Roman history, to be sure, and Hamlet's dying wish places a Norwegian prince on the throne of Denmark. But Othello's death will have no effect on the future of Venice, and England seems but an empty husk of a nation as Lear breathes his last over the body of Cordelia. Rome will pursue its relentless path to greatness after the death of Coriolanus; and, although it is left rudderless in *Titus Andronicus* after the loss of its emperor, its empress, and its greatest soldier, the empire, we sense, will prevail. The legacy of Shakespeare's tragic heroes leaves

us with something more immediate than their role in history, however—the uneasy awareness that were we faced with the same
choices as they, it is well within our nature to choose the path they
took to destruction. And Shakespeare's antiheroes add bite to that
realization by dwelling on our fragile vulnerability to their fate.

# THE COMIC MUSE

❧

SHAKESPEARE'S COMIC HEROES and heroines are very different from those we call martial or tragic. Comedy is not easy to describe. A joke that requires explanation is seldom amusing, which may explain why literary scholars prefer to dwell on the "dark side" of Shakespeare's comedies, whose humor, in the words of one lugubrious critic, lies "close to sorrow; close at least to heart-ache, sometimes close to heart-break."[1] Of course a joke can be cruel. It is always told at someone's expense and can be resented as an affront to ethnic, gender, age, religious, or cultural sensibilities. Little humor is allowed by modern advocates of equality and diversity, and what there is makes for pretty heavy going. Humor tends to reinforce stereotypes and encourage prejudice, it is said, unjustly humiliating the objects of jokes by presenting them in a less than attractive light: the dim-witted Irishman or Pole or Swede, the bloodless Englishman, the acquisitive Jew, the inscrutable Oriental, the lusty Latin lover, the docile black, the flighty female, and the insensitive male. The only legitimate targets left seem to be the rich and powerful: Hollywood stars, English royalty, political candidates, presidents, and prime ministers.

It was not so in Shakespeare's time, when the theater was young. Despite the threat of government censorship, no one escaped the

---

1. Sir Arthur Quiller-Couch, in his introduction to *Much Ado About Nothing* (Cambridge: Cambridge University Press, 1923), p. xv.

satirical sting of the stage, not monarchs, magistrates, soldiers, men, women, social classes, nor nationalities, the high and the low of the social and political structure. None were exempt from the edge of Shakespeare's wit, though at the same time his humor is sympathetic, with an element of compassion for those he exposes to laughter.

In this "description" of Shakespeare's comic muse, I am compelled to explain jokes and resort to quoting some lengthy exchanges between characters to illustrate the wit of them. I see no other alternative if these pages are to render the humor of the plays accessible to playgoers. Readers will forgive me perhaps if these accounts seem at times to belabor the obvious and at others to appear somewhat heavy-handed, but they may be thankful for a window into Shakespeare's wit the next time they attend a performance. In any event, it is better than dwelling on the "dark side" of the comedies.

## Court Fops and Nincompoops

One of the minor characters that appeared on the Renaissance stage was the effete dandy known as the "court fop," a ridiculous figure adept at courtly manners but little else. He was immediately identified by his elaborate dress, a parody of high fashion with frills of lace at the collar and wrist, a brightly colored velvet doublet, gloves that reached to the elbow, and an enormous hat, which he swept off in an exaggerated bow at the slightest provocation. Perhaps the most devastating description of the figure is that in *Henry IV, Part 1*. The warrior Hotspur, resting wearily after a fierce battle with the Scots, is catching his breath and tending his wounds when a royal courtier approaches him to demand that he surrender his prisoners to the king.

As Hotspur describes him,

Came a certain lord, neat and trimly dress'd,
Fresh as a bridegroom, . . . . . . . . . . . . . . .
He was perfumed like a milliner,
And 'twixt his finger and his thumb he held
A pouncet-box, which ever and anon
He gave his nose and took 't away again.[2]
. . . . . . . . and still he smil'd and talk'd,
And as the soldiers bare dead bodies by
He call'd them untaught knaves, unmannerly
To bring a slovenly unhandsome corse
Betwixt the wind and his nobility.

Particularly galling was his talk of the war. It "made me mad," Hotspur continues,

To see him shine so brisk and smell so sweet
And talk so like a waiting-gentlewoman
Of guns and drums and swords.

He brought Hotspur's anger to a boil when he concluded, with a condescending air, that "but for these vile guns, he would himself have been a soldier."

The fop is so taken up with courtly dress and manners that he is singularly thickheaded about anything else, which renders him a ready object of ridicule by sharper wits, who misuse him with mockery to which he seems oblivious. When Osric issues the king's invitation to Hamlet to engage in a friendly duel with Laertes, the prince toys with him, mocking his courtly manners and flamboyant speech with inflated politeness. After Osric sweeps his hat off in an exaggerated bow, Hamlet bids him to recover, then to take it off again:

2. A "pouncet box" was a small container of perfume carried to ward off unpleasant odors. The fop is also seen with a large, highly scented handkerchief, which he waves about.

*Osric:* I thank your lordship, it is very hot.

*Hamlet:* No, believe me, 'tis very cold, the wind is northerly.

*Osric:* It is indifferent cold, my lord, indeed.

*Hamlet:* But yet methinks it is very sultry and hot for my complexion.

*Osric:* Exceedingly, my lord. It is very sultry—as 'twere.

Hamlet then bids him put his hat on again. Osric is bewildered by Hamlet's recitation of elaborate nonsense but remains properly deferential to a prince of the blood and pretends to understand him, totally unaware, it would seem, that he is being ridiculed.

Though not a court figure, perhaps the most ridiculous of Shakespeare's foppish characters is Sir Andrew Aguecheek in *Twelfth Night*. He dances, sings, and drinks but can do little else, and he is notoriously dim-witted. When Sir Toby Belch introduces him to the maid Maria, he urges him, "accost, Sir Andrew, accost." Thinking it her name, Aguecheek responds politely, "good Mistress Accost, I desire better acquaintance"; and Sir Toby must explain that he means "front her, board her, woo her, assail her." Sir Toby values Aguecheek as a harmless companion in his revels but also as a source of revenue, having already, he says, bilked him for "two thousand strong" with the promise that he may win the hand of his niece, Olivia. When Aguecheek is later persuaded to issue a challenge to Viola, who is disguised as a page and is, he thinks, a rival for Olivia's affections, he writes a letter full of nonsensical contradictions, concluding with "thy friend . . . and thy sworn enemy."[3]

Other characters are not necessary foppish but may be portrayed as such in performance. The courtly Le Beau in *As You Like It* seeks out Rosalind and Celia to invite them to attend a wrestling match, and the two young women, aided by Touchstone, talk rings around him:

3. Roderigo, in *Othello,* is another mindless dupe whom Iago keeps on a string, milking him of his wealth with promises of winning Desdemona.

*Le Beau:* Fair Princess, you have lost much good sport.

*Celia:* Sport? Of what colour?

*Le Beau:* What colour, madam? How shall I answer you?

*Rosalind:* As wit and fortune will.

*Touchstone:* Or as the Destinies decree.[4]

*Celia:* Well said! That was laid on with a trowel.

*Touchstone:* Nay, if I keep not my rank—

*Rosalind:* Thou losest thy old smell.

*Le Beau:* You amaze me, ladies.

When Le Beau can finally get a word in to issue the invitation, Touchstone quips that "it is the first time that ever I heard breaking of ribs was sport for ladies."

The lines given to Goneril's steward, Oswald, in *King Lear,* do not indicate that he is especially slow-witted or effete, but something may be seen in the contrast between him and the earthy, plainspoken Earl of Kent. The disguised earl takes an instant dislike to Oswald, kicking his heels from under him when he shows disrespect to the king. Kent later challenges him to a duel, subjecting him to a tirade of insults, of which Shakespeare seems to have had an inexhaustible supply. Among other things, the earl calls him a "lily-liver'd, action-taking, whoreson, glass-gazing, superserviceable, finicle rogue," "finicle" here meaning "foppish." Again, young Abraham Slender of *The Merry Wives of Windsor,* though not especially courtly, is certainly dim-witted and pitifully inept in the English language. When asked if he can love Anne Page, he admits that he doesn't know her very well, but "if there is no great love in the beginning, yet heaven may decrease it upon better acquaintance." He will agree to the marriage, he says, being "freely dissolv'd and dissolutely."

These are all, as mentioned, minor figures in the plays who provide occasion for the main characters to demonstrate their supe-

4. Or "As fate would have you answer."

rior wit. Although they are, for the most part, uncomprehending innocents, they are good for a laugh in the comedies and a scene of comic relief in the tragedies.

# Fools and Clowns

The court jester, or "fool," was a familiar figure in the higher circles of medieval and Renaissance society. Perhaps the best description of his role in court appears in the famous scene in *Hamlet* where the prince is handed the skull of Yorick, his father's jester, by the gravedigger, who remembers him well: "A pestilence on him for a mad rogue! 'a pour'd a flagon of Rhenish on my head once." Hamlet is taken by surprise: "I knew him, Horatio, a fellow of infinite jest, of most excellent fancy. He hath borne me on his back a thousand times." Contemplating the skull, he asks; "Where are your gibes now? Your gambols, your songs, your flashes of merriment that were wont to set the table on a roar?" This then was the role of the fool, to dance, to sing, to jest, to play tricks on unsuspecting victims, an entertainer in a rough age when entertainment was hard to come by.

The jester was identified by his costume, a suit of multicolored patches called "motley," a hat with drooping ends decorated with bells, and a mock scepter in his hand marking him as a "king of jests." His "gibes" and "flashes of merriment" were often at the expense of powerful members of the court who understandably resented being held up to ridicule, so the fool had to walk a fine line between discretion and entertainment. Opera lovers will recall Verdi's *Rigoletto,* where the jester so infuriates the nobility that they decide to humiliate him in return by seducing his daughter, Gilda. In *King Lear* the Fool comes too close to the bone and the king warns him: "Take heed, sirrah, the whip."

Two of the best-known jesters in Shakespeare are Touchstone in

*As You Like It* and Feste in *Twelfth Night.*[5] Touchstone is a creature of the court, completely out of his element in the natural setting of the Forest of Arden, where there are few comforts and only simple shepherds. Upon arrival he looks about him and quips: "Ay, now am I in Arden, the more fool I." He crosses wits with the old shepherd Corin and attempts to seduce the unsophisticated Audrey, complaining all the while that no one appreciates his jokes. Corin retires good-naturedly, admitting, "you have too courtly a wit for me," and Touchstone later remarks to Audrey, "I wish the gods had made thee more poetical."

Feste is a slightly different matter, since he seems to be as much a traveling minstrel as a court jester. It would appear that he is attached to Olivia's household, since she chides him for his absence, but he turns up in Count Orsino's court, seeking employment wherever there is profit to be had. Feste extracts payment for his talents with disarming wit. After an exchange with Viola, she gives him a coin, which he examines closely and asks, "would not a pair of these have bred?" When the duke does the same, he remarks, "but that it would be double-dealing, sir, I would have you make it another," and having received a second, tries for a third. Feste joins in the carousing of Toby Belch and Andrew Aguecheek and participates in the humiliation of the puritanical Malvolio, here and there entertaining with song, "O mistress mine, where are you roaming?" for his fellow revelers and "Come away, come away, death" for the melancholy duke. And he provides the epilogue to the play with the engaging, "When that I was a little tiny boy."

One the favorite comic devices of Shakespeare's fools is the seemingly outrageous statement, followed by a circuitous chain of reasoning that proves it true. When, for example, Feste returns to Olivia's household, she peremptorily orders an attendant to "take the fool away." Feste quickly turns the tables on her, ordering "take

5. A fool, or jester, is sometimes identified as a "clown" in the cast of characters.

the lady away." Olivia, accustomed to his wit, is intrigued, demanding his explanation for calling her a fool. The clown reminds her that she has taken a vow to mourn her brother's death for seven years, and the following exchange ensues:

*Clown:* Good madonna, why mourn'st thou?
*Olivia:* Good fool, for my brother's death.
*Clown:* I think his soul in hell, madonna.
*Olivia:* I know his soul is in heaven, fool.
*Clown:* The more fool, madonna, to mourn for your brother's soul, being in heaven. Take away the fool, gentlemen.

In another such exchange, Touchstone asks Corin if he has ever been to court; and when the old shepherd answers that he has not, the clown announces, "then thou art damn'd." Corin objects, and Touchstone explains in a torturous train of logic:

Why, if thou never wast at court, thou never saw'st good manners; if thou never saw'st good manners, then thy manners must be wicked, and wickedness is sin, and sin is damnation. Thou art in a parlous state, shepherd.

Another fool's device is the riddle, and Shakespeare often employs the wit of these exchanges to lay bare the absurdities of human nature. King Lear's Fool uses riddles to bring home to his master the folly of splitting up his kingdom. He asks Lear "why one's nose stands I' th' middle on's face" and explains: "Why to keep one's eyes on either side one's nose, that what a man cannot smell, he may spy into." He continues:

*Fool:* Canst tell how an oyster makes his shell?
*Lear:* No.
*Fool:* Nor I neither; but I can tell why a snail has a house.
*Lear:* Why?
*Fool:* Why, to put 's head in, not to give it away to his daughters, and leave his horns without a case.

And finally:

> *Fool:* If thou wert my Fool, nuncle, I'd have thee beaten for being
>   old before thy time.
> *Lear:* How's that?
> *Fool:* Thou shouldst not have been old till thou hadst been wise.

Thus Shakespeare's fools are often full of wisdom. In his brief appearance in *Timon of Athens,* the fool prefers the companionship of
the learned philosopher Apemantus to all others. The seemingly un-
likely pair excites comment. When they are found together, the fool
is asked, "what do you in this wise company?"

# Insults

Shakespeare is said to have the richest vocabulary of insults of any
writer in the English language. A modern reader will need a complete set of footnotes to decipher their meaning, but a theater audience will have no doubt as to their tone and intent and can delight
in the relish of their delivery. Mention has been made in another
context of the Earl of Kent's tirade against Goneril's steward Oswald
in *King Lear*, but his lines are worth repeating in full. The steward,
Kent contends, is:

> A knave, a rascal, an eater of broken meats, a base, proud, shallow,
> beggarly, three-suited, hundred-pound, filthy, worsted-stocking
> knave; a lily-liver'd, action-taking, whoreson, glass-glazing, super-
> serviceable, finicle rogue; one-trunk-inheriting slave; one that
> wouldst be a bawd in a way of good service, and art nothing but
> the composition of a knave, beggar, coward, pandar, and the son
> and heir of a mongrel bitch.

And so forth. But the poet's inventiveness is nowhere so richly displayed as in the exchanges between Prince Hal and Falstaff in *Henry
IV, Part 1.* The fat knight weaves an incredible tale about his

courage and martial prowess during a robbery attempt, describing how many men he has "pepper'd"; and Hal, who was there at the time, challenges his outrageous invention. Again, it is impossible to convey the flavor of these litanies of invective without quoting them in full:

> *Prince:* Why these lies are like their father that begets them, gross as a mountain, open, palpable. Why, thou clay-brain'd guts, thou knotty-pated fool, thou whoreson, obscene, greasy tallow-catch. . . . This sanguine coward, this bed-presser, this horse-back breaker, this huge hill of flesh—.

Falstaff responds in kind, but runs out of breath:

> *Falstaff:* 'S blood, you starvling, you eel-skin, you dried neat's tongue, you bull's pizzle, you stock fish! O for breath to utter what is like thee! You tailor's yard, you sheath, you bowcase, you vile standing tuck—.

Later, in a "play extempore" inspired by Falstaff, they rehearse Hal's anticipated interview with the king, who disapproves of the company his son keeps. Hal plays the role of his father, scolding the prince, who is enacted by Falstaff:

> Thou art violently carried away from grace; there is a devil haunts thee in the likeness of an old fat man, a tun of man is thy companion. Why dost thou converse with that trunk of humors, that bolting-hutch of beastliness, that swoll'n parcel of dropsies, that huge bombard of sack, that stuff'd cloak bag of guts, that roasted Manningtree ox with the pudding in his belly, that reverent Vice, that grey Iniquity, that father ruffian, that vanity in years?

Falstaff, still playing the prince, cleverly defends himself:

> That he is old, the more the pity, his white hairs do witness it, but that he is, saving your reverence, a whoremaster, that I utterly deny. If sack and sugar be a fault, God help the wicked! If to be old

and merry be a sin, then many an old host that I know is damn'd. If to be fat be to be hated, then Pharaoh's lean kine are to be lov'd.

It should not be thought that such exchanges imply animosity between the two, as in the case of Oswald and Kent. Insults are often the language of affection between friends and family members, a mark that they are so close that jests will never be taken amiss. Anyone who has attended a large family gathering will be familiar with the good-natured laughter raised by an oft-repeated account of a much-loved sibling's most embarrassing moment. It is a pattern of behavior perhaps more closely associated with the male of the species, as anyone who has been present at a prenuptial bachelor party will attest. Prince Hal and Falstaff are so solidly entrenched in each other's affection that insults are the language of their bond.

More sophisticated insults fly between Beatrice and Benedick in *Much Ado About Nothing,* and once again it would be a mistake to assume that these two combatants in their "merry war" despise each other. Their friends, at any rate, are convinced that they are in fact very much in love, but that each is reluctant to declare affection for fear of being ridiculed by the other, and so they adopt the protective façade of mutual mockery. The opening exchange between them is illustrative of their abusive banter:

*Beatrice:* I wonder that you will still be talking, Signior Benedick, nobody marks you.

*Benedick:* What my dear Lady Disdain! Are you yet living?

*Beatrice:* Is it possible disdain should die while she hath such meet food to feed it as Signior Benedick? Courtesy itself must convert to disdain, if you come in her presence.

*Benedick:* Then is courtesy a turncoat. But it is certain I am lov'd of all ladies, only you excepted; and I would I could find it in my heart that I had not a hard heart, for truly I love none.

*Beatrice:* A dear happiness to women, they would else have been troubled with a pernicious suitor. I thank God and my cold

blood, I am of your humor for that: I had rather hear my dog
bark at a crow than a man swear he loves me.

*Benedick:* God keep your ladyship still in that mind! so some gentleman or other shall scape a predestinate scratch'd face.

*Beatrice:* Scratching could not make it worse, and 'twere such a face
as yours were.

*Benedick:* Well, you are a rare parrot-teacher.

*Beatrice:* A bird of my tongue is better than a beast of yours.

*Benedick:* I would my horse had the speed of your tongue, and so
good a continuer. But keep your way a' God's name, I have
done.

*Beatrice:* You always end with a jade's trick, I know you of old.

A "jade" is a horse that drops out of a race, so Beatrice accuses him
of quitting the verbal contest. Later, seeing her approach, Benedick
ducks out, exclaiming, "O God, sir, here's a dish I love not, I cannot
endure my Lady Tongue." Beatrice always manages to have the last
word in this "merry war"—until the very end, that is, when
Benedick silences her with a kiss.

It is worth mentioning the abuse a servant must endure from his
master when he is slow-witted or wittily disrespectful. Shakespeare's
servants are more likely to be the latter, sometimes quite mali-
ciously as when the sharp-tongued Thersites of *Troilus and Cressida*
angers Ajax by calling him a "mongrel beef-witted lord," a "stool
for a witch," and a "scurvy valiant ass." "Thou hast no more brain,"
he rages, "than I have in mine elbow," and receives a beating for his
insolence. More often, however, they are sympathetically insightful
about their masters' foibles, as when Launce mocks Valentine's
lovesick condition in *The Two Gentlemen of Verona*.[6]

In *The Taming of the Shrew,* Petruchio abuses his servants for
other reasons entirely. In his campaign to cure Kate's distemper, he

6. See p. 11.

performs a charade of anger at the supposed ineptness of his household staff. Entering his house, he rages at their neglect: "You loggerheaded and unpolish'd grooms! / What? no attendance? no regard? no duty?" Finding his dinner ill-cooked, he hurls abuse, and dishes, at them: "You heedless joltheads and unmanner'd slaves!" Later he dismisses a tailor with insults appropriate to his trade:

O monstrous arrogance! Thou liest, thou thread, thou thimble,
Thou yard, three-quarters, half-yard, quarter, nail!
Thou flea, thou nit, thou winter-cricket thou!
Brav'd in mine own house with a skein of thread?
Away, thou rag, thou quantity, thou remnant.

Shakespeare's insults are not always delivered in lengthy harangues, however. They often come in brief flashes of invective that may be overlooked in performance. To mention but a few: When Orlando and Jaques enter together in *As You Like It,* it is apparent that they have not taken to each other. Their exchange is a delightful instance of what might be called the sophisticated slight:

*Jaques:* I thank you for your company, but, good faith, I had as lief have been myself alone.
*Orlando:* And so had I; but yet, for fashion sake, I thank you too for your society.
*Jaques:* God buy you, let's meet as little as we can.
*Orlando:* I do desire we may be better strangers.

In a rare moment of levity in *Julius Caesar,* Casca, one of the conspirators, tells of hearing a speech by Cicero. "He spoke in Greek," Casca reports, and goes on, coining a phrase that has entered the language: "those that understood him smil'd at one another and shook their heads; but, for mine own part, it was Greek to me." While Desdemona waits anxiously for the safe arrival of Othello, Iago distracts her with entertaining banter about, among other things, the duplicity of women who "rise to play, and go to bed to work." Such delicious moments too often go unnoted in the swift passage of the dialogue, and theatergoers alert to them will better savor the full measure of Shakespeare's wit.

## Double Meanings, Puns, and Malaprops

A reading of the plays cannot capture the full flavor of their wit, nor can any analysis, such as that essayed here, hope to convey the comic effect of a live performance. Missing from the pages of a text are the stage antics of accomplished comedians, their sight gags and body language, the pratfalls, double takes, and pie-in-the-face surprises that must be seen to "set the [theater] on a roar." On the other hand, Shakespeare was a master of word play. The wit of his lines may often pass too quickly for an unprepared modern audience to catch, particularly when they refer to contemporary customs and events familiar to Elizabethan playgoers. It is in fact the reader of the plays who has the advantage here, blessed with the leisure to pause over a passage, consult footnotes, and savor the humor of it. Wordplay is such a pervasive element of Shakespeare's art that no commentary can hope to exhaust it, so we must resort to isolated instances of its comic effect to heighten a theatergoer's awareness of the humor in his crowded lines.

Hamlet is adept at repartee. He greets his fellow scholars, Rosencrantz and Guildenstern, with genuine pleasure, and they mark their reunion with the kind of clever, somewhat off-color banter that sophisticated college students delight in. Their first exchange dwells briefly on the traditional image of Fortune as a woman:

*Hamlet:* Good lads, how do you both?
*Rosencrantz:* As the indifferent children of the earth.
*Guildenstern:* Happy, in that we are not over-happy, on Fortune's
    cap we are not the very button.
*Hamlet:* Nor the soles of her shoe?

*Rosencrantz:* Neither, my lord.

*Hamlet:* Then you live about her waist, or in the middle of her favors?

*Guildenstern:* Faith, her privates we.

*Hamlet:* In the secret parts of Fortune? O, most true, she is a strumpet.

Later, as he awaits the start of the play, he toys erotically with Ophelia:

*Hamlet:* Lady shall I lie in your lap?

*Ophelia:* No, my lord.

*Hamlet:* I mean my head upon your lap?

*Ophelia:* Ay, my lord.

*Hamlet:* Do you think I meant country matters?

*Ophelia:* I think nothing, my lord.

*Hamlet:* That's a fair thought to lie between maids' legs.

After he kills Polonius, Hamlet is brought before the king, who asks where he has put the body. The prince responds with some nonsense about worms eating kings; and Claudius, with mounting exasperation, demands an answer. Hamlet replies with sardonic wit that "if you find him not within this month, you shall nose him as you go up the stairs into the lobby," and " 'A will stay till you come."

On a lighter note, this play on the double meaning of words is ubiquitous in the comedies of Shakespeare. In *As You Like It,* Rosalind confesses her sudden infatuation for Orlando to her friend Celia, and the two exchange puns based on their long petticoats:

*Rosalind:* O how full of briars is this working-day world!

*Celia:* They are but burs, cousin, thrown upon thee in holiday foolery; if we walk not in the trodden paths, our very petticoats will catch them.

*Rosalind:* I could shake them off my coat, these burs are in my heart.

*Celia:* Hem them away.

*Rosalind:* I would try, if I could cry "hem" and have him.

*Love's Labor's Lost* abounds in this kind of verbal gymnastics, as the four men press their ardor on the ladies and they in turn deflect their advances with clever retorts. The wit of these exchanges, mostly one-liners, come so quickly and is at times so obscure that a modern audience will be challenged to keep up with it, which may explain why Kenneth Branagh, in his delightful film version of the play, deleted most of the dialogue in favor of 1930s popular ballads and Busby Berkeley production numbers. One of the more accessible passages plays on the romantic notion of the beloved's face as the moon. The men ask the ladies to remove their masks and join them in a dance:

> *Berowne:* Vouchsafe to show the sunshine of your face,
>     That we (like savages) may worship it.
> *Rosaline:* My face is but a moon, and clouded too.
> *King:* Blessed are clouds, to do as such clouds do!
>     Vouchsafe, bright moon, and these thy stars to shine
>     (Those clouds removed) upon our watery eyne.
> *Rosaline:* O vain petitioner! Beg a greater matter,
>     Thou now requests but moonshine in the water.
> *King:* Then in our measure do but vouchsafe one change.
>     Thou bid'st me beg; this begging is not strange.
> *Rosaline:* Play, music, then! Nay, you must do it soon.
>     &#183;   Not yet; no dance: thus change I like the moon.
> *King:* Will you not dance? How come you thus estranged?
> *Rosaline:* You took the moon at full, but now she's changed.
> *King:* Yet still she is the moon, and I the man.
>     The music plays, vouchsafe some motion to it.

And so on.

Another comic figure is the lover who reads into a lady's innocent remarks evidence that she returns his affection. In *Much Ado About Nothing,* Benedick, who has been engaged in a "merry war" of words with Beatrice, listens in on a staged conversation among his friends, who have arranged matters so that he overhears them. They lament the fact that Beatrice actually loves him but is unwilling to confess it for fear that he will ridicule her. He suddenly becomes convinced that he loves her in return. When she is sent out to invite him in to dinner, she does so with her customary cutting manner, but he hears her scorn differently now:

> Ha! "Against my will I am sent to bid you come to dinner"—there's a double meaning in that. "I took no more pains for those thanks than you took pains to thank me"—that's as much as to say, "Any pains that I take for you is as easy as thanks." . . . I will go get her picture.

And in *Twelfth Night*, the austere Malvolio is tricked into believing that his mistress, Olivia, loves him. He appears before her, smiling absurdly and garishly dressed, in accordance, he has been led to believe, with her wishes. She is appalled at the sight of him and quickly exits, leaving orders that "this fellow is to be look'd to." He is exultant:

> And when she went away now, "Let this fellow be look'd to"; "fellow"! not "Malvolio," nor after my degree but "fellow." Why everything adheres together, that no dram of scruple, no scruple of a scruple, no obstacle, no incredulous or unsafe circumstance—What can be said? Nothing that can come between me and the full prospect of my hopes.

A malaprop is an unintentional misuse of language. The word itself was unknown to Shakespeare, since it did not enter the language until the late eighteenth century, when Richard Sheridan's play *The Rivals* featured a character by that name who excelled in the practice. A comic effect is produced when characters attempt to use elaborate words and phrases and get them wrong, so as either to garble their meaning or to say the opposite of what they intend. In *Much Ado About Nothing*, for example, Dogberry, the ridiculous chief constable of Messina, instructs his night watch to "comprehend all vagrom men," to "be vigitant," and to perform their duties in silence, since "talk is most tolerable and not to be endur'd." Though not limited to policemen, the malaprop does seem to be an occupational affliction. Constable Dull, in *Love's Labor's Lost,* insists that "I myself reprehend [represent]" the Duke. And later he entrusts a prisoner to another's care, instructing him that "you must suffer him to take no delight and no penance [pleasance, or pleasure]." And in *Measure for Measure,* Constable Elbow reports proudly that he has arrested "two notorious benefactors." When asked if he doesn't mean rather "malefactors," he replies, "I know not well what they are; but precise villains they are, that I am sure of, and void of all profanation in the world that good Christians ought to have."

As a comic device the malaprop can be cruel, though perhaps no more so that other forms of humor, whose laughter, as mentioned, is always at someone's expense. But the malaprop is especially so when the words are put in the mouth of lower-class characters who attempt elaborate language to impress their betters and make a hash of it. In *The Merchant of Venice,* Shylock's servant, Launcelot Gobbo, is discontented with his master and seeks a position with Bassanio who, flush with a generous loan from Antonio, is enlisting a personal staff appropriate to a suitor for the hand of the wealthy Portia. Launcelot and his father approach Bassanio, and the elder speaks first, indicating that his son "hath a great infection, sir, as one would say, to serve" him. The practice runs in the family apparently, for Launcelot hastens to add that his father's "suit is impertinent to myself," and the elder confirms that his son's request "is the very defect of the matter."

The aforementioned Dogberry is equally absurd when he informs his superior, Leonato, the governor of Messina, that his watch has "comprehended two auspicious persons." Later, when he brings the "plaintiffs," as he calls them, before Leonato, he is virtually incoherent. In fawning deference he compliments the elderly governor as "a most thankful and reverend youth" and hopes that God will restore the apparently robust Leonato "to health." On his departure he butchers his farewell: "I humbly give you leave to depart; and if a merry meeting may be wish'd, God prohibit it!"

Others, no matter whom they address, also mangle the language. Mistress Quickly, in *The Merry Wives of Windsor,* describes

Mistress Page "as fartuous a civil modest wife" and vows to help all three suitors for the hand of Anne Page, "but speciously Master Fenton." In the same play Corporal Nym is said to be "a fellow frights English out of his wits." And Shakespeare delights in the linguistic distortions of foreigners like the hot-tempered Frenchman Dr. Caius, whom Mistress Quickly describes as a man who abuses "God's patience and the King's English," and the heavily accented Welsh parson, Hugh Evans, who anxiously anticipates a duel with Caius: "How melancholies I am! I will knog his urinals about his knave's costard when I have good opportunities for the ork. Pless my soul!"

# *Falstaff*

Falstaff is unquestionably Shakespeare's best-known comic figure. His appeal derives in part from his irreverence, his uninhibited ridicule of all the values of an ordered society. He scoffs at honor, tells outrageous lies, calls incessantly for "sack," abuses his public office, and, having robbed the king's exchequer, regrets only that the money has been returned: "O, I do not like that paying back. 'Tis a double labor." But he loves a jest, delights in witty wordplay, revels in insulting exchanges, loses himself in drink, dance, and song, woos the ladies with extravagant ardor, and commands both affection and allegiance from all who are privileged to share his company. Who could help but love such a man?

In truth there are two Falstaffs, the boisterous fat knight of *Henry IV, Parts 1 and 2,* and the humiliated suitor of *The Merry Wives of Windsor,* of whom more later. It is Prince Hal's entertaining companion who has become the most famous and beloved comic figure in the English, perhaps the world, theater. Woody Allen, Robin Williams, Bill Cosby, and John Cleese may rule on film, but no one can match Falstaff's appeal on the live stage. In personal appearance he is generously overweight, red-faced from indulgence in "sack," and old—pushing sixty by his own admission. He has energy that belies his years, however, undertaking long nights to commit robbery and leading troops in battle; and he is irresistibly merry, laughing, dancing, drinking, and singing at any hour of the day or night. He delights in clever verbal exchanges, contests of wit, though many of his satirical sallies are to be found in the form of long monologues, only brief extracts of which can be repeated here, giving but a glimpse of his appeal.

Falstaff is a thief, unashamedly so, and his chief concern throughout the plays is monetary gain. In one of his early episodes with Hal in *Part I,* he insists that when the prince becomes king, he should henceforth refer to thieves benignly as "Diana's foresters, gentlemen of the shade, minions of the moon." He borrows, steals, and woos for money; and he seems to spend it profligately, since he never has enough left to pay his debts. He scoffs at what men call "honor," contemplating the concept before the battle of Shrewsbury:

> What is honor? A word. What is that word honor? What is that honor? Air. A trim reckoning! Who hath it? He that died a' Wednesday. Doth he feel it? No. Doth he hear it? No. 'Tis insensible then? Yes, to the dead. But will 't not live with the living? No. Detraction will not suffer it. Therefore I'll none of it, honor is a mere scutcheon.

He seeks a good name for himself, however. Coming upon the body of Hotspur, whom Hal has just killed in battle, he brazenly insists to the prince that he himself has done the deed and hopes to be "either earl or duke" as a reward for his valor. In *Part 2* he turns a prisoner over to Prince John, Hal's younger brother, anticipating that the prince will give a "good report" of his loyalty at court.

Falstaff loves his "sack," a blending of sherries, calling for a cup of it at every turn, and he scorns those who abstain from drink. Encountering the temperate Prince John, he contemplates such abstemious men:

Good faith, this same young sober-blooded boy doth not love me, nor a man cannot make him laugh, but that's no marvel, he drinks no wine. There's never none of these demure boys come to any proof, for thin drink doth so over-cool their blood, and making many fish-meals, that they fall into a kind of male green-sickness, and when they marry, they get wenches.

In recruiting soldiers for the king's army, he accepts bribes to release well-to-do prospects from the press and fills his ranks with "slaves as ragged as Lazarus in painted cloth." He is a coward. On the night when he and his followers rob the king's exchequer, Hal and his friend Poins, disguised in buckram, a stiff canvas overall, easily run them off. And when challenged in battle by the warlike Scot Douglas, Falstaff falls to the ground, feigning death.

To balance these disreputable traits, he is an irresistibly appealing companion, lighting up the room when he enters his favorite haunt, the Boar's Head Tavern in Eastcheap. He is ever ready with a witty retort, laughing at jests even when the joke is on him, and is prepared at any moment to put on a "play extempore," in which the revelers mock well-known public figures in impromptu skits much like those seen today on *Saturday Night Live*. When he returns to the Boar's Head after being run off by Hal and Poins, the two ask him innocently how the robbery went. He launches into a lengthy account of his valor on the occasion, vigorously demonstrating his swordsmanship, and increasing the number of his victims with each new instance of his prowess. Hal and Poins listen with barely concealed delight, egging him on:

> *Prince:* Pray God you have not murd'red some of them.
> *Falstaff:* Nay, that's past praying for, I have pepper'd two of them. Two I am sure I have paid, two rogues in buckrom suits . . . here I lay, and thus I bore my point. Four rogues in buckrom let drive at me—
> *Prince:* What four? Thou saidst but two even now.

*Falstaff:* Four, Hal, I told thee four.

*Poins:* Ay, ay, he said four.

*Falstaff:* These four came all afront, and mainly thrust at me. I made no more ado but took all their seven points in my target, thus.

*Prince:* Seven? Why, there were but four even now.

*Falstaff:* In buckrom?

*Poins:* Ay, four in buckrom suits.

*Falstaff:* Seven, by these hilts, or I am a villain else.

*Prince:* (aside) Prithee let him alone, we shall have more anon.

*Falstaff:* Dost thou hear me, Hal?

*Prince:* Ay, and mark thee, Jack.

*Falstaff:* Do so, for it is worth the list'ning to. These nine in buckrom that I told thee of—

*Prince:* So, two more already.

*Falstaff:* Their points being broken—

*Prince:* Down fell their hose.

*Falstaff:* Began to give me ground; but I follow'd me close, came in, foot and hand, and with a thought seven of the eleven I paid.

*Prince:* O Monstrous! Eleven buckrom men grown out of two.

Some critics cite this exchange as an apt example of Falstaff's bombastic behavior. Others come to his defense, insisting that he knows full well what has happened, is very much aware of the trick that has been played on him, and is deliberately acting out the charade for the amusement of Hal. Whichever the case, it is no wonder that the prince prefers his company to the stodgy decorum of his father's court.

The Falstaff of *The Merry Wives of Windsor* is different in some respects, and many find him a disappointingly diminished figure. The venerable Harold Bloom condemns the character in *The Merry Wives* as "a nameless imposter masquerading as the great Sir John Falstaff" and the play itself as a "farce" and a "tiresome exercise" that "dwindles into shallowness."[7]  Socially conscious scholars of today regret that Falstaff seems to have lost his irreverent wit, his scoffing at "middle-class values" such as honor, honesty, sobriety, loyalty, concern for others, and respect for the law, and his satirical dismissal of the high and mighty of the land.

The story goes that Queen Elizabeth, having enjoyed a performance of one of the *Henry IV* plays, asked for one about "Falstaff in love," and we are told that Shakespeare worked tirelessly on the play for six weeks to fulfill her request. True or not, the play does not portray him "in love"; he is actually pursuing his old familiar goal—gain. His attempts to seduce the two wives, the Mistresses Page and Ford, are motivated by the fact that they control the purse strings of their husbands' wealth, and he intends to make them his "exchequers," as he puts it. In doing so, he endures hilarious humiliation at their hands. Mistress Ford lures him to her house with the promise of an assignation, and he appears full of ardent expectation: "Have I caught thee, my heavenly jewel? Why, now let me die, for I have lived long enough: this is the period of my ambition. O blessed hour!" According to plan, they are interrupted by Mistress Page, who bursts in on cue to announce that Ford himself, a notoriously jealous man, is approaching "with all the officers of Windsor" (in fact he is, but that was not part of their plot). The ladies persuade Falstaff that his only means of escape is to hide in a basket of dirty clothes, which they have carefully prepared beforehand. Two burly servants then carry the basket out and, as they have been instructed, dump Falstaff unceremoniously into the Thames. He is enticed to come a second time, and when Ford appears yet again, the ladies disguise the knight as a local woman, the Witch of Brainford. Ford does not penetrate the disguise, but since he dislikes the woman and has forbidden her to enter his house, he gives Falstaff a sound thrashing as he makes his escape.

7. Harold Bloom, *Shakespeare: The Invention of the Human* (New York: Riverhead Books, 1998), p. 315. Bloom dismisses the play in three pages.

The Falstaff of *The Merry Wives of Windsor* admittedly lacks the satirical bite of Prince Hal's companion, since his long speeches are for the most part complaints about his rough treatment; but he is his old outrageous self, supremely confident of his appeal with the ladies. The play is indeed a farce, but it has remained a popular favorite on the Shakespeare Festival circuit for years, from which we are reminded that it is a mistake to underestimate the appeal of the farcical.

Shakespeare's comic invention is so inexhaustible that we can only scratch the surface of it here. His plays, like all theater, are meant to provoke an audience response—his comedies to make us laugh, his tragedies to make us shudder, and his histories to move us to admiration or regret. Whatever their form or intent, they place characters before us who are afflicted with the same human flaws. King Leontes in *The Winter's Tale* and Posthumus in *Cymbeline* are as wracked with jealousy as is Othello. Bolingbroke and Richard III are as ambitious as Macbeth. Duke Orsino in *Twelfth Night* is as love-stricken as Romeo. Prospero's Miranda is as innocent as Juliet or Ophelia. Kate is as shrewish as Tamora in *Titus Andronicus.* Antonio in *The Merchant of Venice* is as foolishly generous as Timon of Athens. Cressida is as seductive as Cleopatra and Troilus as angry at her betrayal as Antony.

The comedies tell us, however that mankind need not always suffer the terrible consequences of its follies. The wicked may prevail for a time and passions may blind us, but so long as we retain a faith in love and look upon our all too fallible humanity with a lively sense of its absurdities, our failings need not always lead to tragic death and despair. We are, as Alexander Pope later put it, "the glory, jest, and riddle of the world." Thus Shakespeare saw us, and thus his comic muse portrays us, though perhaps as more of a "jest" than a "glory."

# THE CHORIC VOICE

❧

THE CAST OF SEVERAL PLAYS includes a choric figure, who is of particular interest to us because the character often voices a theme of the work. The figure appears in many guises, at times as an individual, at others as a group. It can be commoners remarking uneasily on unfolding events, a character intimately involved in the action, or another entirely outside it, who introduces the play and guides us through its sometimes involved plot. Whatever its form, we learn to trust the choric voice as a reliable interpreter of characters and events, a figure that articulates the thought underlying the play's words and actions. Centuries of scholars and critics have been of different minds about the meaning of Shakespeare's plays; for knowledgeable theatergoers, however, his choric voices remain the most reliable authority for his themes.

The chorus played a key role in ancient Greek drama. Indeed, the theater first evolved from a choir's hymns and anthems sung during religious ceremonies. At one point, it is said, a single figure stepped out of the ranks and engaged in a dialogue with the whole choir; and then in time another joined the first, providing occasion for an interchange among them. And the theater was born. The plays of the early Greek dramatist Aeschylus conformed to this pattern, and then his younger contemporary Sophocles added yet a third actor. As the number of individual characters on stage increased, the importance of the chorus correspondingly diminished, until in the plays of Euripides it had a much lesser role.

The Greek chorus was often a group of commoners, village elders or matrons of the community, who interacted with the main characters but stood outside the central action, observing and commenting on developments. They voiced the sentiments of any number of commonsense citizens who are witness to the tragic course of human lives, responding as might any member of the audience to unfolding events. In effect, they stood in the place of the audience, differing from them only in one important respect—they did not share the playgoers' familiarity with the outcome of the play. Hence their response was that of any group of ordinary people appraising events without knowledge of where they will lead.

The chorus of Sophocles' *Oedipus Rex* illustrates their role. Briefly, the Delphic oracle prophesies that the young Oedipus will kill his father and marry his mother. Shocked, Oedipus leaves home and on his travels kills an old man who challenges him on the road. He later encounters the Sphinx and solves her riddle, thus releasing the city of Thebes from the monster's siege. The citizens of Thebes hail him as a hero and insist that he become their king by marrying Jocasta, their newly widowed queen. Later in his reign, Oedipus learns that he had been adopted in infancy, and he becomes obsessed with the need to discover the identity of his true parents.

The Greek audience, familiar with the legend, was well aware that Oedipus had indeed killed his father and married his mother, as the oracle had predicted, and that uncovering the truth would eventually destroy him. The chorus, a group of Theban elders, has no such insight into the past or the future, however, and can only comment on the determination of Oedipus as would anyone experienced in human affairs. They can only look on with mounting dismay as the truth unfolds, and pray to their gods, whose inscrutable will shapes their destinies for reasons they cannot hope to fathom.

Shakespeare occasionally introduces similar figures into a play, common people commenting on great events, those such as the gardener in *Richard II* or the three citizens in *Richard III*, but they seldom interact with the principal characters in the manner of the

Greek chorus. Some of Shakespeare's choric figures, on the other hand, are closely involved in unfolding events, though they stand slightly aside from the main action, observing and commenting on developments as they occur. Enobarbus plays such a role in *Antony and Cleopatra,* as does Thersites in *Troilus and Cressida.* Still others have a more formal role, one in which they stand outside the dramatic action entirely, introduce the play or acts within it, as in *Henry V* and *Pericles,* and summarize thematically from time to time.

## Commoners as Chorus

Ordinary citizens in Shakespeare's plays often assume a choric role, responding to developments with acute insight. In a brief scene from *Richard III,* for example, three citizens react to the death of Edward IV and assess the prospects for his twelve-year-old heir, Edward V. "I fear 'twill prove a giddy world," says one, and another warns: "Woe to that land that's govern'd by a child." They are fatalistically prophetic as they prepare for the worst: "All may be well; but if God sort it so, / 'Tis more than we deserve, or I expect." Such figures often demonstrate a more realistic understanding of events than do those closer to the intrigues of the mighty. One citizen remarks, "O, full of danger is the Duke of Gloucester [Richard]," in contrast to a number of characters in the play who, though they are intimately associated with Richard, seem to be blissfully unaware of just how "full of danger" he is. His brother Clarence trusts him implicitly; Hastings, the Lord Chamberlain, is convinced that he has Richard's full confidence; and Buckingham, who guides him step by step to the throne, is surprised when his king turns against him. All three are blind to what seems obvious to the ordinary citizen, and all suffer the fatal consequences of their misplaced trust. Clarence is drowned in a barrel of wine, Hastings is executed because he fails to endorse Richard's claim to the crown, and Buckingham falls out of favor when he hesitates momentarily to agree that the princes must be killed.

The diligent gardener foretells the deposition of Richard II and sees clearly the failures that have led to his fall. The king was inattentive to his duties, he tells his assistant, a monarch so preoccupied with the outward trappings and pleasures of the royal court that he has neglected to check the growing power of ambitious nobles. Richard, he says, has failed to tend his garden. A careful king, he explains, like a careful gardener, will trim his bushes and "root away / Noisome weeds." "Superfluous branches," he goes on, "we lop away, that bearing boughs may live" and trees stand in dutiful order to bear fruit. A theme of the play is the folly of princes who are so enamored of the splendors of their reign that they grow distant from their subjects and are blind to the resentment that their profligacy and indifference can arouse among their powerful nobles.

Three gentlemen appear frequently in *Henry VIII* to foreshadow the king's divorce from Katharine, his queen, and to praise her successor, Anne Boleyn. Shakespeare takes pains to preserve Katharine's honor and at the same time extol the virtues of Elizabeth I's mother. Of the queen, one gentleman asks sympathetically, "is't not cruel / That she should feel the smart of" her dismissal, and another says of Anne: "Believe me, sir, she is the goodliest woman / That ever lay by man."

Such short scenes are often cut from modern productions as peripheral to the unfolding of the plot. This is a pity because Shakespeare knew what he was doing when he included them. The commoners can only observe great events from a distance, but they have an instinctive understanding that the dynastic struggles of the mighty may in the end subject them to the oppression of tyrants and the ravages of war—so they are ever watchful. Shakespeare endows them with a wisdom the chief characters often lack; and the contrast between their earthy good sense and the headstrong ignorance of their betters is striking. In *Henry V* it is the common soldiers Bates and Williams who voice a central theme of the play, the justice of the cause; and it is the sentinels on nightly watch in *Antony and Cleopatra* who detect the departure of "the god Hercules, whom Antony lov'd," foreshadowing his defeat on the following day.

## Characters as Chorus

Shakespeare occasionally places a secondary figure in a play, one who has an active role in events but stands somewhat apart from them, an involved but at the same time detached observer of the principal characters. Such figures are choric in nature, interpreting events from the point of view of a knowing insider, one who does not directly address the audience but influences their response to plot developments.

Enobarbus is a minor figure in *Antony and Cleopatra,* but he has the indispensable role of defining the critical relationships for us. He is a Roman, a close associate and aide to Antony, though at the same time his temperament seems well adapted to Cleopatra's exotic court. We first see Enobarbus in the company of her attendants, trading witticisms with them as they await the entrance of the queen; and on hearing of the death of Antony's wife Fulvia, he advises the emperor cynically that "when old robes are worn out, there are members to make new," an oblique way of saying that he is now free to marry Cleopatra.

Pre-pubescent boys enacted female roles on Shakespeare's stage, so his productions had none of the advantages of modern stage and screen in physically demonstrating amorous passion. We have become accustomed to long, hungry gazes between lovers and athletic clinches to the accompaniment of soaring strings, during which they groan and grope and sigh. It is difficult to convey a mature Cleopatra's sensual appeal when she is portrayed not by Elizabeth Taylor but by a skinny youth, no matter how artfully he is padded out. Shakespeare conveys the force of her attraction in memorable

lines of poetry, and it is Enobarbus, in a choric role, who describes
her hold on Antony. It is he who gives an account of their first meeting at Cydnus, where,

> . . . she did lie
> In her pavilion—cloth-of-gold tissue—
> O'er picturing that Venus where we see
> The fancy outwork nature.

At one point Antony praises her as a woman "whom every thing becomes, to chide, to laugh / To weep." Enobarbus later confirms the
impression in more specific terms, describing an occasion when he
saw her

> Hop forty paces through the public street,
> And having lost her breath; she spoke, and panted,
> That she did make defect perfection,
> And breathless, pow'r breathe forth.

Antony, he insists in famous lines, will never leave her, for

> Age cannot wither her, nor custom stale
> Her infinite variety. Other women cloy
> The appetites they feed, but she makes hungry
> Where most she satisfies.

And later, when Antony marries the rather colorless Octavia in an
attempt to heal a breach between him and her brother Caesar, Enobarbus expresses his conviction that he will in time desert her and
return "to his Egyptian dish again."

We grow to trust the judgment of Enobarbus when he comments on developments. Later in the play, when Caesar prepares to
launch an attack on Alexandria, Antony exults in a reconciliation
with Cleopatra and calls for a night of unrestrained revelry before
the impending battle, declaring with a burst of bravado that "the
next time I do fight, / I'll make death love me, for I will contend /
Even with his pestilent scythe." Enobarbus observes his extravagant

behavior with dismay and concludes wryly that "a diminution in
our captain's brain / Restores his heart." "When valour preys on
reason," he goes on, "it eats the sword it fights with." He is a dependable observer but also a distinct character in his own right,
sometimes appealing, sometimes less so. When he notes "the diminution in our captain's brain," he decides to "seek / Some way to
leave him." After deserting Antony, Enobarbus dies of remorse over
his defection: "O Antony, / Nobler than my revolt is infamous, /
Forgive me."

We have elsewhere examined the role of Thersites as the essential antihero in Shakespeare's *Troilus and Cressida,* but he also fills
the function of a chorus.[1] He is the chief instrument of satire in the
play, as he reduces the Greek heroes to a group of mindless thugs,
whose boasting of their martial prowess he ridicules, to their face or
in bitter asides, as so much ignorant bluster. Thersites is not the detached observer, however, who comments dispassionately on developments. He is a figure who is angrily cynical about what he sees,
and we are meant to perceive events through his eyes. As a choric
voice, he shapes our response to the Greek warriors, and a tone of
comic absurdity permeates the play. Once he has established that
tone, even events that escape the satiric bite of his derision appear
ludicrous to us—the progress of love in Troy, for example, or the
circumstances surrounding the single combat between Achilles
and Hector. Thersites encourages us to look upon both love and
war as bitterly farcical. Under his influence we are made to forget
how these themes are portrayed elsewhere, in the tender passion
of a Romeo and Juliet, for example, or the audacious vision of a
Henry V.

Shakespeare's fools play a similar role, often proving a fount of
wisdom in a play. Feste utters a theme of *Twelfth Night* when he encounters Sebastian, the twin brother of Viola, who is herself masquerading as the youthful page Cesario. Mistaking Sebastian for his

1. See p. 209.

sister, Feste is bewildered when the young man insists that he is totally ignorant of events to date. In a play filled with disguises, misconceptions, and mistaken identities, Feste remarks in exasperation
that "nothing that is so is so." Earlier in the action he suffers the
scorn of the puritanical Malvolio, who dismisses him as "a barren
rascal." Later he joins Sir Toby Belch in a scheme to humiliate the
haughty steward, and he confesses at the end that he did so in retaliation for that insult. He concludes lightheartedly that "the
whirligig of time brings in his revenges," which is again a comic
theme of the play.

King Lear's Fool, with his quips and riddles, attempts to bring
his master to his senses, voicing the thematic sentiments of an attentive audience were they able to counsel the old man themselves.
It was folly, he tells Lear, to divide his kingdom between his two
daughters, since in doing so he "gav'st them the rod, and put'st
down thine own breeches." The Fool articulates in stark monosylla-
bles a central theme of the play when he claims that the king should
be whipped like a presumptuous fool because "thou shouldst not
have been old till thou hadst been wise."

## Choruses as Chorus

On other occasions Shakespeare makes use of a figure completely detached from the dramatic action, one who appears before the curtain
rises on a play or an act within it but takes no part in events. This
chorus differs from its ancient Greek predecessor in another feature
as well: it is omniscient, a teller of tales who knows the beginning,
the middle, and the end of the history about to unfold before the audience and offers itself as a dependable guide through the action.
This figure will often state the theme of the play in a succinct
phrase at the very outset or at its closing. In the Prologue to *Romeo
and Juliet*, the Chorus tells us that this is to be a play about two
"star-cross'd lovers" who fall victim to "civil broils that fill civil

streets with blood," a tale of love sacrificed on the altar of ancient grudges. The Prologue to *Henry VIII* explains that the play will show how transitory worldly fame can be. Foreshadowing the king's divorce from Katharine and the fall of Cardinal Wolsey, he concludes that the audience "may here find truth" in the tale, predicting that they will "think you see them great . . . then, in a moment, see / How soon this mightiness meets misery." In *Henry V* we are told that the play will portray the theme of warfare in which "the war-like Harry, like himself, / Assume[s] the port of Mars." And, the Chorus continues, to fully appreciate its grand events the audience will have to "piece out our imperfections with your thoughts," imagining that the few soldiers exchanging blows on the stage are vast armies locked in mortal combat.

Again, in *Pericles* the Chorus concludes with a brief account of the play's theme, the fruits of vice and the rewards of virtue. The King of Antioch engages in an incestuous relationship with his beautiful daughter and receives "for his monstrous lust the due and just reward"—they are both struck by a lightning bolt. The "wicked Cleon and his wife," she having plotted the death of Pericles' daughter Marina, are consumed by fire in their palace. In contrast, Pericles, his wife, and his daughter, their "virtue preserv'd from full destruction's blast" are "led on by heaven, and crown'd with joy at last."[2]

Shakespeare employs a chorus most frequently when the time frame of the tale extends over many years. When the plot occupies a few hours, or days, or even weeks, as in the case of *Hamlet,* Shakespeare depends on a minor figure in the play to give an account of events leading up to the opening scene. In *As You Like It,* it is the wrestler Charles who recites the "old news" of Duke Frederick's court, the banishment of Duke Senior. In *Hamlet,* Horatio reviews the history of Denmark's troubles with Norway before the appear-

---

2. In *Pericles,* our guide is the fourteenth-century poet John Gower. Shakespeare acknowledges his debt to his predecessor, who first told the tale in his *Confessio Amantis.*

ance of the ghost; and *Cymbeline* opens on a conversation between two gentlemen who provide the background of the plot. In *The Tempest,* of course, it is Prospero himself who tells Miranda of his overthrow as Duke of Milan and their subsequent survival.

When the plot spans a number of years, however, or great distances, Shakespeare provides a chorus to guide the audience through developing events. In *Henry V* the panorama of warfare extends over a period of five years, so the Chorus carries us from London to Southampton, where the army is marshaling, then to Harfleur and Agincourt, and finally to Paris, where we witness the negotiations for a treaty of peace. The peripatetic Pericles roams the entire eastern Mediterranean world in a play that spans the life of his daughter Marina from birth to marriage, and we depend on the chorus to tell us where we are and when we are there. There is a gap of sixteen years between acts in *The Winter's Tale,* so Shakespeare felt the need of a chorus, Time, to reveal that we have spanned those years and moved from Sicily to Bohemia. What's more, we are told, we are about to meet "a shepherd's daughter" whom we last saw as an infant abandoned on a deserted beach, and will soon learn "what to her adheres."[3]

The ancient Greek chorus, then, was a group of elders or matrons of the city whose role was to appraise events from the perspective of ordinary citizens who reflect on the meaning of the troubles they witness. They express the theme of the play in terms of common wisdom: The gods are inscrutable and should be feared. It is folly to challenge their will. Life is short and plagued with suffering. Be content with your lot.

The chorus in the plays of Shakespeare, whether internal or external to the plot, a single voice or several, like its Greek model, ar-

---

3. On the other hand, Shakespeare omits a formal chorus in *Antony and Cleopatra.* He depends on Enobarbus to guide us through a play that spans ten years of history and moves back and forth across the Roman Empire from Alexandria to Rome, Sicily, Greece, and Syria.

ticulates a theme of the work, but it has other functions as well: it fills in the plot's time gaps, moves us from place to place, describes the setting of a scene, characterizes relationships, and asks the indulgence of the audience for the inadequacies of the stage. It is tempting to hear the author's voice in such choric passages, but it is surely presumptuous on such slim evidence to suggest that we can divine what William Shakespeare believed, thought, praised, or condemned. He gave us living figures whose words and actions illustrate some of the enduring themes of the human condition, but his appealing villains, sage fools, and sometimes irresolute heroes are so diverse that it is impossible to say which of them speaks for the playwright.

# EPILOGUE

SHAKESPEARE GIVES US the "infinite variety" of the human race, the cruel and the kind, the common and great, comic and tragic, mean and noble, wicked and virtuous. His figures are afflicted with desires and dilemmas common to us all, and his plays stage the pressing questions of our existence: Why does love lead so often to despair and death? How may we avoid a descent into madness? Are the gods we worship malevolent or benign? What separates a king from a commoner? Are the rewards of high office worth the sacrifice of private happiness? Must death always be answered with death, an eye for an eye, a tooth for a tooth? Must goodness languish while evil prevails? Can virtue triumph, or is vice our natural legacy? Are there causes that justify wars, or are they all so much senseless expense of blood? Are we at the mercy of forces beyond our understanding, or can we chart our own destiny? Must human follies end in disaster, or can we be redeemed? Is mankind the glory of the world, or its jest?

Shakespeare stages all these questions—and he answers none of them. It warrants repeating, here at the close, that he does not judge the figures he places before us. He tells us only that we are a complex mixture of base desires and noble sentiments, paradoxical in our restlessness and our yearning for rest, contradictory in our driving ambition and need for quiet sanctuary, an eternal puzzle plagued by the painful divide between our dreams and harsh reality. So there are no answers in Shakespeare's plays, and in that respect he holds a mirror up to our nature, for answers are as elusive in life as they are in illusion. He says, quite simply, that this is the way we are. And his refusal to judge is a source of his endless appeal.

# Index

*Boldface numbers indicate where the entry is featured in the text.*

## A NOTE ON THE AUTHOR

Robert Thomas Fallon is emeritus professor of English at La Salle University in Philadelphia. Born in New York City, he studied at the United States Military Academy at West Point, Canisius College, and Columbia University, where he received a Ph.D. in English. For many years he has written and lectured on Shakespeare to a variety of audiences, including those at the Stratford (Ontario) Shakespeare Festival. His *A Theatergoer's Guide to Shakespeare* drew wide praise. He has also written extensively on the life and work of John Milton, and has served as president of the Milton Society of America. Mr. Fallon lives in Lumberville, Pennsylvania.

$2 Fine For Removing
the Bar Code Label

DANVILLE PUBLIC LIBRARY
DANVILLE, INDIANA

112870

WITHDRAWN